W9-CSU-783

Crazy Mosaic

Crazy Mosaic

Tracy Graivier Bell

with contributions by

Sarah Kelly

For my husband, Jay, my children, Lee and Pierce, my parents, Pauline and Len, and my siblings, Lisa and Carl, and Miles and Kathy.
Your unquestioning love and support is my rock, and you are the foundation of the mosaic that is me.

Tracy Graivier Bell

Published in the United States by
Laurel Glen Publishing,
An imprint of the Advantage Publishers Group
5880 Oberlin Drive,
San Diego, CA 92121-4794
www.advantagebooksonline.com

All notations of errors or omissions should be addressed to Laurel Glen Publishing, editorial department, at the above address. All other correspondence (author inquiries, permissions and rights) concerning the content of this book should be addressed to Quintet Publishing Limited, 6 Blundell Street, London N7 9BH.

Library of Congress Cataloging-in-Publication Data
Graivier Bell, Tracy
Crazy Mosaic/ Tracy Graivier Bell
p.cm.
Includes index.
ISBN 1-57145-655-4
1. Mosaic work. I. Title.

A QUINTET BOOK
This book was designed and produced by
Quintet Publishing Limited
6 Blundell Street
London N7 9BH

Senior Project Editor: Laura Price
Designers: Sharanjit Dhol, James Lawrence
Photographers: Jeremy Thomas, Robert Goodman, Neal Farris
Illustrators: Nicola Gregory, Jennie Dooge

Creative Director: Richard Dewing
Publisher: Oliver Salzmann

Typeset in Great Britain by
Central Southern Typesetters, Eastbourne
Manufactured in Hong Kong by Regent Pte Ltd.
Printed in China by Leefung-Asco Printers Ltd.

North American Edition:
Publisher: Allan Orso
Managing Editor: JoAnn Padgett
Project Editor: Elizabeth McNulty

1 2 3 4 5 00 01 02 03 04

PUBLISHER'S NOTE

When completing mosaic projects exercise care when using tools and materials.
Always follow the safety instructions given in this book, and always read the manufacturer's instructions on packages and labels.
To avoid inhaling the dust when sanding or sawing MDF a protective mask should be worn.

All statements, information, and advice given in this book regarding methods and techniques are believed to be true and accurate.
The author, copyright holders, and the publisher cannot accept any legal liability for errors or omissions.

Contents

Introduction

Folk mosaic is the metamorphosis of classical mosaic into a puzzle of nostalgic fragments. A folk mosaic work can be spontaneous; it can be simply appealing in form, color, and texture; or it can be carefully planned and executed to evoke sentimental memories. The folk mosaic artist bases his craft on instinctive feelings of design, proportion, color, symmetry, style, and balance rather than the formal constraints of traditional art theory.

Above: A detail from a mosaic screen by Mary K. Guth, created in 1994.

Folk mosaic has a legion of names: broken tile mosaic, pique assiette, bits and pieces, memoryware, funky mosaic, fragment work, fantasy mosaic. An accepted appellation is elusive. Yet working artists seem unfazed by the lack of categorization and, therefore, acknowledgment that their art form has received. In the true artistic spirit, they are preoccupied by the creative process and not by public acceptance. For the purposes of this book, and in the hope of establishing a heading under which some public understanding will develop, we will use the name "folk mosaic".

In the following pages, you will learn the secrets of how to create small and large folk mosaics. Broken dishes, tiles, glass, and memorabilia can be used to create fabulous gift and décor items as well as permanent works of art for your home or garden. Easy-to-follow step-by-step instructions with beautiful illustrations offer a wide variety of projects for varying skill levels. Some projects even can be adapted for children to do along with adult supervision.

Origin and History

The earliest known example of mosaic, or mosaic-like technique, is the embedded terra cotta cones found in the exterior walls and columns of buildings discovered in ancient Mesopotamia—now part of Iraq. Dating from about 3000 B.C., the black, white, and red colored cones were laid in geometric patterns and were functional (shielding the building bricks from the elements and adding strength to the structure) as well as decorative additions to the architecture. Apparently the technique was unsatisfactory in some way, as mosaics were not created again for more than 2000 years.

In the town of Gordium, near Ankara, Turkey, floors decorated with pebbles depicting rudimentary figures have been dated to the eighth century before the Christian Era (B.C.E.). Through time, the taste for floor decoration expanded and developed until the Greeks perfected the pebble mosaic technique in the late classical period. The best-preserved examples of this work are found in Olinthos and Pella, in the Macedonian region of northern Greece. In Olinthos the mosaic floors made in the fifth century B.C.E. show strong contrast between the dark pebbles used for background and the light pebbles used to create intricate patterns and detailed figures. The pebbles were mostly uniform in size, and very small black stones were used to outline detailed areas. By the fourth century B.C.E., artisans in Pella were successful in achieving even more realistic results in their floor mosaics by implementing several sophisticated techniques. First they painted some of their pebbles to create a broader color palette, especially adding greens and reds. Second, they began using terra cotta strips or lead wire to outline their scenes. And third, they used smaller pebbles so that they could be placed more closely together.

At the beginning of the third century, in the Hellenistic period, geometrically cut tesserae began to replace pebbles as the medium for mosaics. Tesserae are pieces of inorganic materials cut into roughly uniform size, thickness, and shape. The tesserae could be fitted more closely together than the pebbles, which reduced the visibility of the mortar and made the finished mosaics look more realistic. Stone tesserae were most common, but small amounts of glass tesserae began to be utilized as well.

The Romans, from the second century B.C.E. to the third century after the Christian Era (A.C.E.), are credited with the transformation of mosaic into a functional art form with practical applications. Although they still produced intricate mosaic floors in central locations, they also constructed simple monochromatic mosaic floors that could be installed expediently in less important areas like baths and courtyards. Functionality became the focus of the work. The Romans are also credited with moving mosaics to the wall. Prior to this

Above: Part of a mosaic guitar celebrating the impact of Presley's music, by Mary K. Guth.
Right: Linda Beaumont's modern shrine of three-dimensional mosaic tesserae.

period, mosaics were only found on the floor. They also began the trend of creating sacred and religious images in their mosaics instead of the traditional hunting, feasting, and fighting scenes.

During the Byzantine period, from the fifth to fifteenth centuries, mosaic making flourished. The mosaics from this period depicted Biblical scenes and were used to cover virtually every inch of the interior walls, ceilings, and domes of churches and cathedrals. The figures in these works were enlarged to match the scale of the architecture, and the use of glass tesserae became increasingly popular. Gold and silver tesserae were made by sandwiching bits of metal between layers of glass. The technique of tilting these metallic tesserae to catch the light resulted in the depiction of brilliant halos, glittering garments, and heavenly light around the natural stone tesserae used in the faces and hands.

In the fifteenth century, the Byzantine period ended and, with it, the rich atmosphere in which mosaic art had blossomed. The Italian Renaissance artists of the fifteenth and sixteenth centuries rejected the use of gold, which had become a key element in Byzantine mosaics. They were much more interested in pictorial realism, and mosaics essentially became imitations of painting. St. Mark's Basilica in Venice, the dome of St. Peter's in Rome, and many other churches and cathedrals were set with tesserae by artisans who filled in the "cartoons" drawn by renowned artists of the period such as Raphael, Titian, Veronese, and d'Arpino. Although technically sound, the work of the craftsmen lacked the artists' touch, and their mosaics could not compare to those of Byzantium.

Origins and History

Modern Mosaics

Folk Mosaic has evolved from the traditional mosaic of the ancient, Byzantine, and Renaissance periods into the unrestrained, more spontaneous mosaic of modern times. From the late 1800s through the mid 1900s, important strides in the art of mosaic were made by tenacious laypeople and professionals around the world, each with different motivations and results.

Above: A mosaic dragon lizard from Antonio Gaudi's Guell Parc in Barcelona.

Gaudi, the Founding Father

The Catalan architect, Antonio Gaudí, (1852–1926) led the Spanish art nouveau movement. He designed many structures in Barcelona and surrounding areas, and he took the innovative step of using broken tiles to cover virtually every exterior surface of his buildings. His early works, like the *Casa Vicens, Guell Estate*, and *Guell Palace* clearly show a Moorish influence, which is a mixture of Muslim and Christian design indigenous to Spain. Entire structures completed in the early 1900s like *Casa Batllo* and *Casa Mila* were designed in Gaudi's entirely original architectural style characterized by sensual free-form curves encrusted with fanciful, brightly colored mosaics. Gaudi's most renowned works are the towering spires on the *Sagrada Familia* Church (Church of the Holy Family) and the undulating benches and rooftop chimneys in Barcelona's *Guell Park.*

American Memory Jugs

American women in the early twentieth century began the tradition of adhering the simple souvenirs of everyday life onto discarded vessels slathered with putty. Once covered with costume jewelry, buttons, figurines, keys, and thimbles, these "memory jugs," as they were aptly called, were gilded or bronzed. They eventually oxidized, leaving a rich patina atop an alluring potpourri of domestic life. Diligent rounds of flea markets and antique stores will occasionally yield an authentic piece, the creator's anonymity preserved forever beneath its bumpy surface, but its charm still intact.

Isadore, the Scrounger

In France, the practice of using personal relics as part of decorative mosaic was extended beyond the jugs and urns utilized by the Americans and used on dressers, vanities, picture frames, tables, and armoires. The French used the expression "Pique Assiette" to describe their angle on the art form. Although not directly translatable into English, the expression describes someone who is a "scrounger" or a "sponger," as in stealing food from other people's plates. The term is fitting, as the Pique Assiette artist is a perpetual scavenger, gathering and then transforming conventional articles into enduring treasures. It was Raymond Edouard Isadore (1900–1964), a blue-collar working man, who was mockingly called the intentionally derogatory name Picassiette for hoarding bits of broken glass, porcelain, and dishes from the fields and local dumps near his home in Chartres, France. With the products of his scrounging, and over a period of twenty-four years, he proceeded to cover every visible surface of his entire home, his courtyard, and his gardens. His home is now a national treasure in France.

Watts Towers and the New Generation

Simon Rodia (1879–1965) was an Italian immigrant who built a series of lacy towers out of concrete and steel over 100 feet tall in his Los Angeles backyard. He had no formal training in engineering, architecture, or the arts, but he spent thirty-three years on the structures, which are completely covered in fragments of glass, tiles, seashells, and other found objects. The towers were almost disassembled until city engineers found them structurally sound, and the Watts Towers, as they are known today, have been deemed a cultural landmark.

History and Politics in Mosaic

In the 1930s and 1940s, the Mexican government commissioned many painted murals that depicted historical and political themes. The durability of ceramic and stone tesserae made mosaic the logical choice over paint when the

government decided to install murals on buildings' exteriors. Diego Rivera, Francisco Eppens, Xavier Guerro, and Juan O'Gorman all created enormous mosaics in the 1950's, which decorate the facades of public buildings in Mexico. O'Gorman was the most prolific mosaicist, and his best-known work is on the exterior walls of the library of the National Autonomous University of Mexico.

Tarot Figures in the Nineties

Niki de Saint Phalle is a household name in France, where she has been a recognized artist since the mid 1950's. Saint Phalle is best known for her exuberant, corpulent, and voluminous sculptures of women, dubbed "Nanas" or "Mom Art." The focus of Saint Phalle's work from 1979 to 1993 was "The Tarot Garden," a six-acre installation in Capalbio, Italy, about sixty miles north of Rome in the Tuscan countryside. Her long-time interest in tarot cards, which are used to predict the future, culminated with the creation of twenty-two sculptures of the tarot card figures ranging from life-size to building size. All of the undulating structures in her garden are covered with vivid mosaics of broken ceramics, tiles, glass, and mirrors.

Modern mosaic is an evolving art, an art form in constant transition. As freedom of expression has blossomed, the disregard shown to some of the modern mosaicists has been replaced with fascination and respect. Gaudí's work has been described as absurd and eccentric. Other Folk Mosaic has been called outlandish, ingenious, vital, evocative, playful, and refreshing. Today's artists concur, and although they have individual reasons for pursuing this particular form of artistic expression, there are some consistently recurring motivations: concern for the environment, an interest in recycling, rejection of the Industrial Revolution, the aggressive and therapeutic act of smashing dishes and tiles, passion, a desire to be surrounded by beauty, nature, and elemental simplicity.

This book is intended to be a celebration of the vast range of human creativity. A place to revel in the art of assemblage and to let the fragments of other people's lives conjure up long forgotten memories of one's own.

Left: Fabulous art nouveau mosaic roof at the Guell Parc.
Right: Mosaic wall and doorway by Linda Beaumont brings the majesty and beauty of the work indoors.

Tools and Workplace

The Workplace

The workplace can be as basic as your laundry room, basement, garage, or garden. The ideal situation is to be able to leave your tools and materials midproject without cleaning up so you can return and immediately begin working again. Whatever your situation, a well-organized work area with good lighting and ventilation can make the process of mosaic making more enjoyable than you could have imagined.

- Natural light is the best light source, so try to work near a window.
- Do all your exacting design work in the best lit areas.
- If using spray paints, always wear goggles and a protective mask and work in a well-ventilated area.
- Separate your tesserae by color and store them in glass jars, transparent bags, and clear plastic containers.
- Use a drawing board to map out your final designs
- An easily accessible water supply is very useful.
- Pour bags of powdered grout into plastic bins or empty coffee cans with plastic covers. Label the containers with the color.
- Allocate a clean, warm, dry area to leave your finished pieces to dry.
- Keep your safety gloves and goggles in arm's reach.
- Shallow foil pans, baking dishes, and cardboard boxes make ideal trays for laying out the tesserae you are working with. Surround your mosaic project with the full trays so your shards are within arm's reach.
- If working in a kitchen, bedroom or living area, cover floors and furniture with sheets or drop cloths to catch any shards and splinters. 
- Any repetitious task can cause muscular aches or even repetitive strain injury (RSI). Take regular breaks and make sure that your workplace, particularly your chair and work surface, is comfortable.
- When sitting down to work, small shards of glass and china can become lodged in your clothes. Take great care when brushing yourself off.
- Always sweep your work area after breaking dishes, tiles, and glass. Tiny splinters can be very dangerous to you, your family, and pets. A "shopvac" or other small industrial vacuum cleaner makes cleanup a breeze.
- Install a pegboard on a wall for hanging your tools. The tools will stay clean and will always be accessible when you need them.

Basic Tools and Equipment

Unlike many other crafts, mosaic work can be as straightforward as you like. Many mosaicists use the minimum number of tools, relying on mosaic nippers for shaping the tesserae and gloved hands for grouting. If you prefer, you can invest in all the tools available to help you in your mosaic craft.

MOSAIC NIPPERS OR TILE NIPPERS

Mosaic nippers are the single most important tools for making mosaics. With them you can clip dishes, china, ceramic tile, and glass into tesserae; create specific shapes like flower petals or leaves; or nibble away at an existing fragment to make it fit into a mosaic in progress. For many mosaicists the mosaic nippers are the only tool they use in their work.

The spring action of the handles and a comfortable fit in your hand are the most important features to look for when buying mosaic nippers. An investment in a pair of good quality nippers is worthwhile, but it is not necessary to purchase a pair with replaceable tungsten carbide jaws or compound leverage. Your local hardware or tile supply store may refer to mosaic nippers as tile nippers.

GLASS NIPPERS

The concept of the glass nippers is the same as mosaic nippers or tile nippers, but the jaws are made of sharpened carbide wheels that can be rotated when dull.

1. Craft knife
2. Spirit level
3. Paintbrushes
4. Tile nippers with scorer wheel
5. Smoother
6. Ruler
7. Tape measurer
8. Whetstone
9. Spatula
10. Mosaic nippers
11. Scissors
12. Screwdrivers
13. Hammer
14. Dustpan and brush
15. Bucket

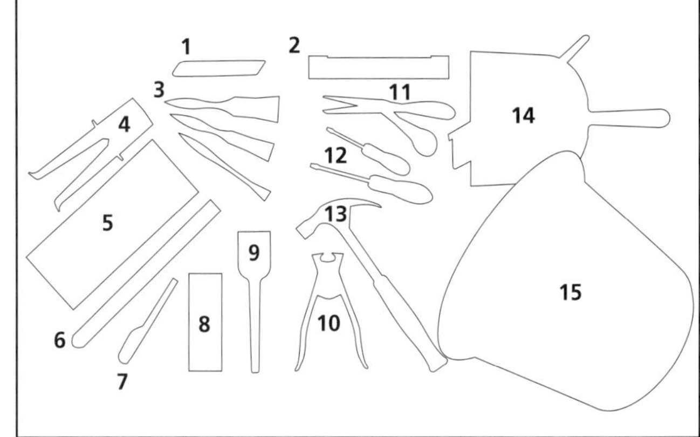

The spring action of the handles allows for quick and precise clipping. Glass nippers can be used on china and dishes, but they do not have enough leverage to successfully nip ceramic tiles. Be aware that repeated use on anything other than glass will dull the wheels and shorten the life span of the glass nippers.

TILE CUTTERS AND RUNNING PLIERS

Tile cutters are an all-in-one tool similar to a glass scorer and running pliers. The tungsten carbide wheel is used to etch a score line on the glazed surface of the tile. Then the tile is squeezed between the breaking jaws to snap it. This tool is only necessary for cutting ceramic tiles into straight-sided pieces. Once stained glass has been scored, tile cutters or running pliers are used to snap the glass along the score lines into the pre-etched shapes. The jaws of the running pliers have a notch cut out of one side which is placed directly over the score line and pressure applied to break the glass. Running pliers are available in a variety of sizes, and an inexpensive pair will serve you as well as an expensive one.

GLASS SCORER

All glass scorers have a small metal wheel at the end that is used to etch the surface of the glass. A good quality scorer has a receptacle for oil to keep the scoring wheel gliding smoothly, which is the key to achieving successful results when working with stained glass.

T SQUARE

A ruler with a "T" mounted at one end, the T Square is the straightedge used while making score lines on stained glass or ceramic tiles. An everyday ruler can be used, but the T Square is easier to work with and provides more accuracy.

HAMMER

Used to break ceramics into irregular shapes. Place tiles in a thick plastic or heavy paper bag before smashing to avoid injury from flying pieces.

WORK GLOVES AND PROTECTIVE EYEWEAR

Broken dishes, china, ceramic tiles, and glass have sharp edges that can be very dangerous to skin and eyes. Always protect yourself when breaking, nipping, cutting, and smashing by wearing work gloves and safety goggles or glasses.

other equipment

The other items you will need are generally already in your home or can be purchased inexpensively at any neighborhood store.

- Disposable container and stir stick for preparing grout.
- Dull knife, spatula, or rubber potter's kidney for spreading grout.
- Sponge and rag for removing grout.
- Newspaper or scrap paper for covering work surfaces.
- Rubber gloves to protect your hands.
- Pencil and crayon for marking out your design.
- Scissors, masking tape, white glue (PVA), and a paintbrush for preparing and finishing your pieces.
- Small plastic glue spreader to apply PVA to tesserae or mosaic base.

1. Dry rag for buffing
2. Scraper
3. Scraper
4. Smoother
5. Sponge
6. Grout
7. Rubber

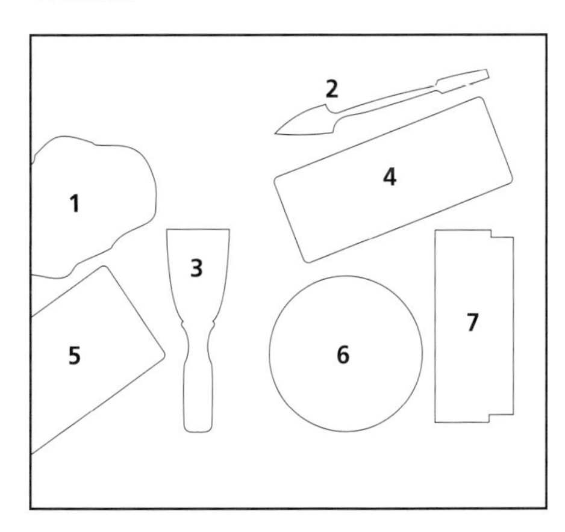

The Substructure of the Project

> **tip**
>
> One of the greatest joys of Folk Mosaic is the lack of restrictions and expense associated with it. The rank beginner can get started with little or no investment.
>
> - Any substructure can be used, as long as it is not flexible.
> - Any materials and surfaces can be used together, and no special preparation, like sanding or priming, is required.
> - The only tool needed for breaking dishes or tiles is a hammer, although a mosaic nipper makes this process much simpler and more precise.
> - Adhesives and grout are inexpensive and widely available.

Each project needs a base or supporting form, like a frame, a box, a steppingstone, a tabletop, or a vase, to which you will apply your mosaic project. Look for a shape that you like. The color or pattern of the form is irrelevant because you will be covering it with fragments and grout. The substructure can be made from most rigid material, as long as it is prepared properly and the correct adhesive is used.

WOOD AND WOOD SUBSTITUTES

Exterior grade or marine plywood is the only suitable wood to use for building a mosaic project base. It is warp resistant but still needs to be prepared by thoroughly sealing it with a mixture of white glue and water (one part glue to four parts water) or by coating it with a commercial waterproofing sealer available at any local hardware store. If you purchase a prefabricated wood base like a box or picture frame and the wood is untreated, waterproof it in the same fashion.

For interior use only, medium-density fiberboard is an excellent alternative to wood, as it is less expensive and also less prone to warping. Cement board, also known as "hardybacker" is made of a thin layer of concrete surrounded on both sides by plastic mesh and completely covered in cement. It is a waterproof board used in construction under countertops, showers and other wet areas, and it is therefore the best choice for substructures of exterior-sited mosaic projects, such as garden pieces.

CEMENT, TERRA COTTA, AND FIRED CLAY

Prefabricated steppingstones, doorstops, birdbaths, wall sconces, and flowerpots made of cement, terra cotta, or fired clay are ideal bases for mosaics. These materials are weatherproof and need no preparation before sticking the tesserae to them except for unglazed terra cotta which can be sealed with diluted PVA to prevent it absorbing moisture from the tile adhesive and therefore potentially weakening the bond.

GLASS

Light fixtures, lamps, vases, bottles, mirrors, tabletops—indeed almost anything else made of glass—can be used as the substructure of a mosaic.

PLASTIC

Hard, rigid plastic forms can be used as mosaic bases as long as there is no flexibility whatsoever in the plastic. If there is any pliancy at all, the grout will crack and pop off the base form.

CARDBOARD

The only suitable cardboard bases are those that are made of heavy stock, are not flexible, and are small enough to bear the weight of a mosaic. Always waterproof a cardboard base as you would a wooden one before use. Cardboard is certainly not an ideal base, but it can be used as a last resort.

Dishes, Memorabilia, Tiles, and Glass

Tesserae are pieces of inorganic materials such as glass, stone, or marble cut into roughly uniform size, thickness, and shape and used to make a mosaic. The word tesserae is of Greek derivation and means "four-sided" or "cube." The definition of the word has been broadened and is now used to describe any pieces of material used in a mosaic, whatever their shape, size, or origin.

In contemporary mosaic making, anything goes in terms of what you can use as tesserae. The projects in this book are made of dishes, china, memorabilia, ceramic tiles, stained glass, mirror, and pebbles. Feel free to experiment with materials commonly used by the ancient Greeks like granite, stone, marble, and slate. The subtle earth tones of these elements can be used to produce striking effects. Smalti (the chunks of colorful handmade glass used in the Byzantine Era and made by firing molten glass with metallic oxides) continue to be manufactured in Italy and, although expensive, are still widely available today. A modern version of smalti is vitreous glass. These small, colorful machine-made tiles are smooth on one side and grooved on the other for adhesion. Vitreous glass tiles are thin and easy to cut or break, and they can be purchased individually or on paper-backed sheets. Broken mirror is another material to try out. Whether you use a few random pieces or make an entire mosaic from mirror shards, the effect will be dazzling.

DISHES AND CHINA

Very colorful and highly patterned dishes and china may be unappealing whole, but can be fabulous broken up into tesserae. Tell your family and friends that you are interested in recycling their broken treasures. Make the rounds of local garage sales and flea markets for great retroware before buying at antique shops or department stores. At retail establishments, chipped or damaged dishes and china are often heavily discounted or even thrown away. You may be surprised at how many people are willing to contribute to your collection! When you have a wide selection, you can choose pieces that curve in sympathy with the shape of your substructure—or not, depending on the effect you want to achieve.

MEMORABILIA

Assorted found objects such as buttons, keys, shells, bottle caps, and beads make wonderful tesserae. Dig through your drawers and scour grandma's attic before purchasing anything. The average home is full of goodies to break up.

Thrift shops, consignment stores, and resale shops are good sources for costume jewelry, trinkets, and figurines of people and animals.

CERAMIC TILES

Widely available and inexpensive, household ceramic tiles are available in an endless range of colors, textures, and sizes. Ceramic tiles are easy to break using a tile cutter or hammer, and a variety of effects can be achieved depending on the tesserae you create. Many tile suppliers and hardware stores give away discontinued sample boards and breakage. You can also make your own ceramic tiles at the now common paint-your-own-pottery shops, or you may have leftovers from a recent renovation right at your fingertips.

STAINED GLASS

Translucent and opaque stained glass is easily transformed into regular or random shapes and can be used alone or combined with tesserae made of other materials. Stained glass is manufactured in thin sheets and sold by the piece at specialty glass shops and arts and crafts stores. Prices vary depending on a wide set of variables including color, quality, and whether the glass is handmade or mass-produced. Artists who work in traditional leaded stained glass and art schools that teach the technique often sell their scraps by weight or may even give them away.

GLASS MARBLES OR GEMS

These brightly colored stones are made of glass and have a flat side for easy adhesion. They are available with a glossy or frosted finish in every imaginable color. Whole marbles can be used but are more difficult to secure to your project. Each gem will vary slightly in size and shape, and they are available in mesh bags or by the piece at arts and crafts stores, specialty glass stores, and candle stores.

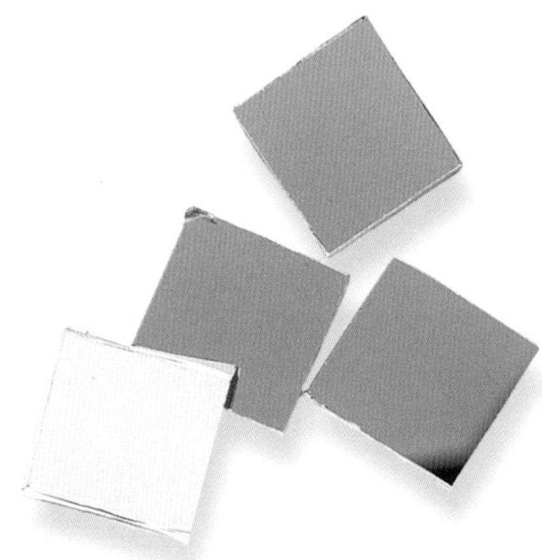

MIRROR

Pieces of mirror can be used to add sparkling highlights to specific areas of your mosaic, combined with stained glass, or used on its own to make a really stunning design. Save the shards from mirror accidents at home or buy whole mirrors or mirror tiles from glass or DIY shops. Some glass shops may let you have offcuts for free.

Mirror can be broken with the tile nippers, a glass cutter, or a hammer. Some mirror, especially mirror tiles, may have a reinforced plastic backing that needs to be peeled off before you can cut it effectively. Break the mirror in half with the tile nippers and then carefully peel off the plastic backing before nipping into shape.

PEBBLES

The best pebbles to use in mosaic are small, smooth, round, and of a uniform color. Black and white work well

together because of their strong contrast, but you could experiment with different combinations such as brown and white, black and gray, or more subtle combinations depending on the colors you have access to.

Mass collecting from beaches is generally regarded as environmentally unfriendly and may even be illegal if the beach is part of a conservation area, so you may have to search for pebbles elsewhere. As a last resort some home decoration stores may sell bags of them as decorative accessories or you could try garden centers. The advantage of this is that the pebbles will be ready-washed and sorted by color.

children

All of the projects in this book are suitable for children with adult participation and supervision. An adult should do the breaking, cutting, and clipping of the materials, but children will thoroughly enjoy applying the tesserae onto any substructure. The creative process begins with experimentation, so allow children the freedom to design and implement their own mosaics. The tactile aspect of mosaic is superb for hand–eye coordination and the development of fine motor skills.

GLASS SMALL TESSERAE
PATTERNED GLASS TESSERAE
GLASS SHARDS
GLASS LARGE TESSERAE
BUTTONS
SHELLS
BROKEN CERAMIC
PLAIN TESSERAE

Adhesives

Different types of adhesive are used to make mosaics, and several kinds might be used on one mosaic project. The factors to consider are whether the mosaic will be situated indoors or outside, and what the tesserae and the substructure of the project are made from. All of these adhesives should be available in your local hardware store.

CERAMIC TILE ADHESIVE

Also known as mastic, ceramic tile adhesive is latex-based and appropriate for mosaic pieces used indoors. It is odor-free, has the consistency of cake frosting or peanut butter, and is completely dry 48 hours after use.

CEMENT-BASED MORTAR

Also called "thinset," cement-based mortar comes in powder form and is mixed with water to achieve an oatmeal-like consistency. It is used for mosaic projects that will be sited outdoors. This adhesive is either spread directly onto the project base or onto the back of each tesserae in the same fashion as the ceramic tile adhesive. A small amount of PVA can be added to the mixed mortar to strengthen the bond.

CLEAR SILICONE OR ANOTHER CLEAR QUICK-DRYING ADHESIVE

These adhesives are viscous and used for bonding glass tesserae to any mosaic project base except metal. Because they

tip

Never attempt to speed up the drying process of your adhesive by artificial means, for example, by leaving your mosaic near a heater. To provide a really firm bond, especially when using ceramic tile or cement-based adhesives, it is vital that it dries out in its own time.

Below: A selection of mortars and household glues that can be used in mosaic work. Always read the manufacturer's instructions on application and use. Check that the glues are suitable for the materials you intend to bond.

Tile Adhesive
Ceramic tile adhesive is used by spreading a thin layer onto the project base and pressing the tesserae into it or buttering the back of each tesserae and pressing them onto the substructure.

PVA
When using PVA to stick tesserae to ceramics or a vertical surface, it is best to apply a layer to the base and allow it time to get tacky before buttering and applying tesserae. This will stop the pieces from slipping.

dry clear, light will be able to radiate through transparent stained glass if used on a sheer base. When working with these adhesives, squirt a small bubble onto the project substructure and use the tip of the applicator tube to spread it into a thin layer. Press pieces of glass into the wet adhesive. Be sure to cover the area completely so that the grout does not seep under the glass during the grouting process. These types of adhesive dry very quickly so you can only work on a small area at a time.

EPOXY RESIN, HOUSEHOLD CEMENT, OR ANOTHER STRONG BONDING ADHESIVE

Epoxy resin is composed of one part resin and one part hardener that must be mixed together immediately prior to use. It dries very quickly and gives off strong toxic fumes, so it must be used in a well-ventilated area. Epoxy resin is the correct adhesive choice when working with metal base forms; however, household cements and other strong bonding adhesives are less expensive, less malodorous, and completely satisfactory for adhering figurines and other memorabilia to your mosaics.

WHITE GLUE, NONWATER SOLUBLE POLYVINYL ACETATE (PVA)

A good basic adhesive for attaching tesserae to wooden or highly varnished surfaces, such as glazed vases and bowls, before grouting. PVA, or white glue, dries clear and is used for both bonding and sealing (when mixed with water). Use the PVA that is intended for household use rather than the childrens' version, which is not as strong.

PVA can stick ceramic and glass to ceramic and wood. Don't use it to stick mirror as it can dull the mirror's shiny backing over time.

tip

- If you are using ceramic tile adhesive or cement-based mortar and you want to remove fragments while these adhesives are still wet, simply slide the shards off of the substructure and wash them clean with soapy water. Be sure the fragments are completely dry before reusing them.
- If you want to remove shards from any type of adhesive that has already dried, pry them off the project form with a screwdriver or another blunt tool. Scrape off any dry adhesive left on the substructure or on the shards before replacing fragments.
- Use a damp sponge to wipe excess ceramic tile adhesive or cement-based mortar off the surface of tesserae while these adhesives are still wet.
- Excess dry adhesive of any kind can be removed from the surface of tesserae with a razor blade or dull knife.

Grout

Grout is the material used to fill the cracks and crevices between the tesserae. It not only adds physical strength to the mosaic but also adds definition to it, completing the mosaic visually. The grout is applied after the adhesive used to attach the tesserae is completely dry. Grout comes packaged in powdered form and is available in a wide variety of colors. The color you choose can either contrast or blend with your mosaic, depending on the overall look you want to achieve. Water is added to the grout powder to turn it into an oatmeal-like paste. White grout can be tinted by mixing it with a mixture of water and acrylic paint or by adding colored powders available from tile stockists. These should be added to the powdered grout before mixing with water. However, reproducing a color could prove difficult, which could pose a problem if you ever need to match a color for repair. Be sure to seal porous tesserae and raw wood before grouting or they will absorb the grout color.

UNSANDED GROUT (WALL GROUT)

This has a smooth finish when dry but has a tendency to crack if used in joints larger than ½ inch. It can also be rather difficult and time consuming to clean from a mosaic.

SANDED GROUT (FLOOR GROUT)

Sanded grout has a sandy texture when dry and can be used to fill in larger joints than unsanded grout. Sanded grout is easy to clean off of tesserae by simply rubbing with a dry cloth before it is completely dry.

SILICONE SEALANTS

Some grouts have silicone included to add strength and flexibility. Silicone is also available in liquid form, which can be added to the grout powder along with the water. These silicone-based products are far more costly than basic floor and wall grout.

GROUT SEALER

Grout is extremely durable and water resistant when completely dry. However, if your mosaic will make its home outdoors, it is a good idea to weatherproof it with two coats of any commercial grout sealer. This product is available in any local hardware or tile store and can be applied to the mosaic after the grout has air cured for at least forty-eight hours.

tip

- When using colored grout, remember it will dry lighter than it appears when it is wet, except, strangely, for grays made using black powders which can sometimes dry considerably darker than they look when applied.
- Use masking tape over scrap paper or newspaper to protect delicate porcelain flowers or figurines while grouting. The grout will not damage the item, but it can be difficult to clean from intricate cracks and crevices.
- An old toothbrush can be a useful tool for brushing away dried grout from nooks and crannies.

Above: There is a vast difference between a pale, a neutral, and a dark grout on identical tesserae, although all have their own effects and bring qualities to the piece.

Basic Techniques

Breaking and shaping

Once you have collected some dishes, tiles, memorabilia, and glass, they need to be broken up into tesserae. For some types of materials you can put on your safety glasses and gloves, grab your hammer, and find a place to smash everything—a fabulous way to reduce tension and stress! Other materials require more care and attention during the breaking process in order to preserve details.

CUTTING GLASS

Making geometric tesserae instead of randomly shaped fragments out of stained glass is not a difficult technique to master, but be prepared for some unclean breaks even when you become proficient at the technique. The scraps never go to waste because you can always use them in another mosaic project. If you are making squares or rectangles, adjust the glass a quarter turn, and score it again with perpendicular etched lines.

1. Score a piece of stained glass into even strips using a glass scorer to etch it and using a T Square as a straight-edged guide.

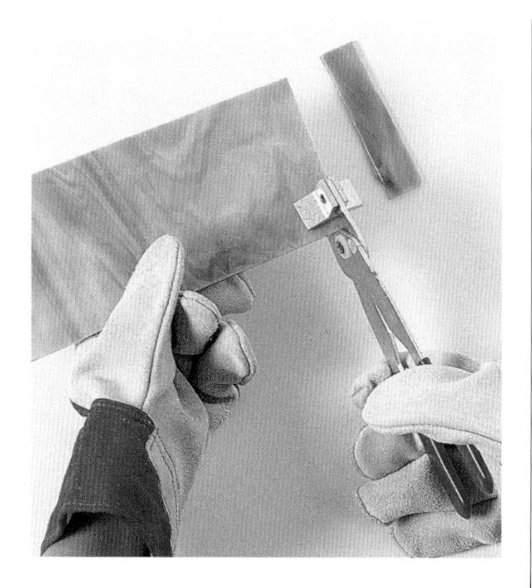

2. While wearing safety goggles and work gloves, snap the glass into strips by placing the notched jaw of the running pliers directly over one score line at a time and applying gentle pressure.

3. Then pick up each strip and use the running pliers to snap it into the pre-etched squares or rectangles. You can use the same scoring and snapping technique to make triangles by adjusting the angle of the stained glass after the initial strips are scored. Score the stained glass twice more, first on one diagonal and then on the other, before snapping.

tip

When choosing stained glass to score and snap, pick smooth-surfaced glass. Highly textured glass is easy to clip with mosaic nippers but can prove difficult to score consistently.

NIBBLING GLASS SHAPES

Preparing specific or unusual shaped pieces from glass is best achieved with nippers. The nippers will allow enough control to shape curves for petals and circles. The curves will not be perfect, but the rugged edges will add to the essence of the mosaic.

tip

Sort all usable fragments by color or pattern. Store them in glass jars, transparent plastic bags, and clear containers for easy access. Sweep up and throw away any tiny splinters or shards that could be dangerous or are too small to use.

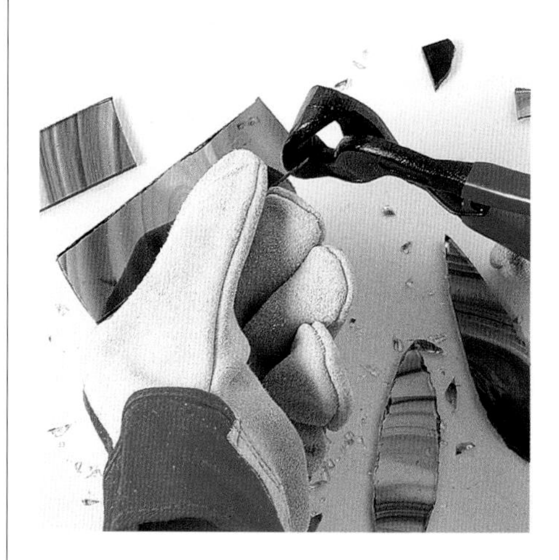

To cut shapes such as petals, hold the glass in your left hand and nibble the shape into the glass, working around the piece in a clockwise direction. The smaller and more delicate the cuts you make, the smoother the outline of the finished shape.

CUTTING TILES

Tiles are ideal for geometric shapes, especially for an unpatterned background to a central motif. Consider the pattern on the tiles, if there is one, when cutting your strips.

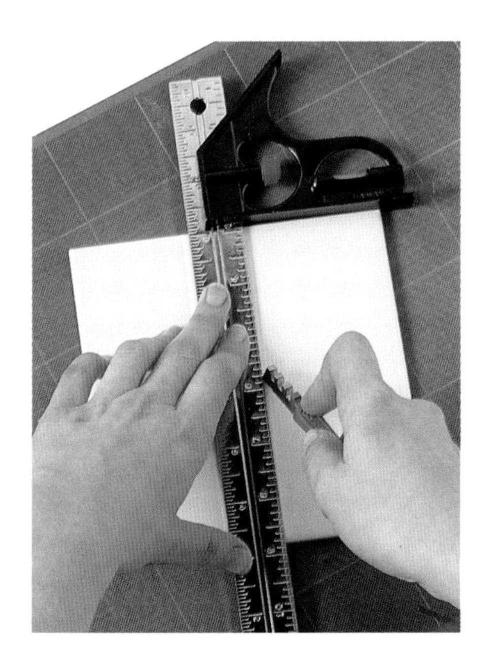

1. Use the tungsten carbide wheel of a tile cutter to etch a score line on the glazed surface of a tile. A T Square should be used to provide stability and a straight edge.

2. Center the jaws of the tile cutter and apply even pressure to snap the tile in two along the score line. Consider the dimensions of the tessera you want and snap the width accordingly.

3. Uneven or sudden pressure, or a lightly or unevenly scored line, may cause the tile to snap unevenly. You may have to score several times along the same line to ensure a clean break.

tip

If you need to cut a large quantity of ceramic tiles, you may want to have them cut for you professionally on a wet-saw. Professional tile layers and tile supply stores will own or have access to this large piece of equipment and are generally willing to cut tiles to your specifications for a minimal fee.

4. Snip the strips into squares with the nippers or, if the tile strip is too wide, repeat the scoring and breaking process to reduce ceramic tiles into geometric tesserae.

SMASHING

Ceramic tiles and some dishes, like those made of thick pottery or earthenware, can be successfully broken using a hammer.

Put the ceramic tiles or dishes into a thick plastic or heavy paper bag and smash them through the bag. If your bag is see-through, you can judge your broken pieces as you smash them. If your bag is opaque, check inside the bag frequently to see how you are doing. The broken pieces should be a variety of sizes ranging from ¼ inch to 2 inches in diameter. Don't be overly concerned with shape, as you can always rebreak or trim fragments later. Be sure to wear safety goggles and heavy work gloves to protect yourself from flying shards.

CLIPPING

To achieve the most successful results from china, memorabilia, and glass, clip them into random shapes with a mosaic nipper rather than smashing these delicate objects with a hammer. A nipper allows you much more control, creates less waste, and reduces the risk of leaving behind dangerous glass splinters. Always wear protective eyewear and work gloves when nipping to protect yourself from flying shards. This is not an exact science, and the only way to learn is to experiment. Some of your attempts may go awry, but what may seem like a disaster could turn out to be a gem.

Don't despair if you break a specific piece, such as a flower, by mistake while you are cutting it out. The good thing about mosaic is that these broken pieces can still be used by reassembling them during the sticking process.

Hold the nippers in one hand and place only the tips of the jaws on the piece to be broken. Squeeze the nipper handles; the pressure will cause the break. It is very important that only about ⅛ inch of the nipper jaws extend onto the piece you are breaking. If you try to use the entire jaws, then you will have to exert an enormous amount of pressure to make a successful fracture. Not only will you be frustrated, but your hands will hurt! While you are cutting, it helps to exert an equal counter-pressure with your other hand on the piece you are breaking. This makes for a cleaner and more accurate break.

Above: Clip your handle until you achieve the finished piece you require.

Begin by clipping a dish or piece of stained glass into large pieces, and then reduce each large piece into tesserae by nibbling away until the desired size is reached. When working with memorabilia, make initial nips around the flowers, handles, knobs, or figurines you are trying to remove. Then clip away the excess bits a little at a time until you are satisfied with the remaining portion.

WARNING

Always protect yourself by wearing work gloves and goggles when working with potentially sharp materials and implementing techniques that could send splinters flying.

CLIPPING OFF HANDLES

Nippers are the best tool to use for removing handles intact from cups and jugs.

tip

Always have more handles than you will need. It is not unusual for the handles to snap or shatter as you clip around them. Practice, however, really does help.

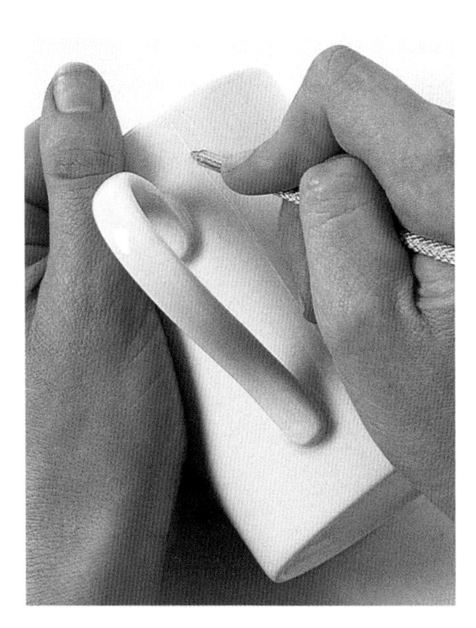

1. Score along the length of the cup, either side of the handle.

2. Nibble down the right-hand score line, removing large chunks of the cup away from the handle.

3. Nibble down the left-hand score line to free the handle, then clean up the edges.

NIBBLING CIRCLES

Geometric straight-edged tesserae can be shaped into circles and ovals by nibbling around the edges.

1. Hold your piece of tile or glass in your left hand and begin to nibble around the piece in a clockwise direction.

2. Continue nibbling until you have completed the circle. You can then tidy the edges by nibbling away any small uneven pieces.

tip

PLATE CLIPPING

When clipping a plate or bowl, nip out the ridge on the underside. Either discard these thick rounded pieces or save them to use when making a heavily textured mosaic.

CLIPPING A MEDALLION

A reconstructed recognizable image can make a stunning central mosaic motif. You can use whole plates or clip out smaller medallions from parts of plates or larger tiles and memorabilia. The result is a clearly fragmented whole image.

1. Clip a medallion out of a piece of china with mosaic nippers. When removing the lip of a plate, start by nibbling around from the outside.

2. When you have cut out the medallion completely, tidy the edges then break the medallion into several pieces with a hammer or mosaic nippers.

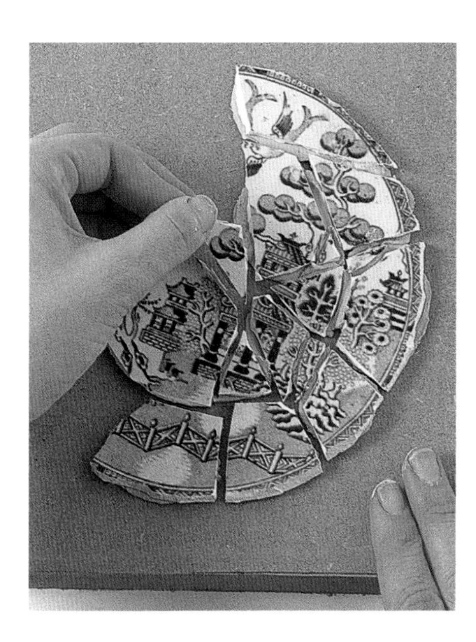

3. Place it back together in your mosaic, leaving small joint spaces to be filled with grout. This technique can be very visually effective.

Designs, Colors, and Inspiration

A lot of the designs and colors you use in your mosaics will probably be governed by the pieces you have collected. Sometimes the form of the things you are using as tesserae, such as cup handles or glass gems, will dictate quite naturally the way the mosaic comes together and flows. A broken decorative mug or plate incorporated as a main theme or feature in a mosaic can be echoed by choosing other tesserae to complement it in color and texture. For example, a fine china mug used in a mirror surround can be complemented by using delicate tesserae also cut from pieces of china in similar colors or colors that work in harmony with it. This relies on your own instincts for color and what looks pleasing to you. The delicate effect will be lost if you surround your broken cup pieces with chunky crudely cut tesserae in bright colors, although these can be used in another project to produce a different but equally stunning effect.

Color combinations can be either harmonious or contrasting, depending on the effect you want. The effect given by using blue china with lilacs and greens will be totally different from mixing it with oranges and terracottas, for example. Try laying out different colored tesserae on a tray or tabletop before you start. The way certain colors interact together may lead you to try color combinations you hadn't even considered before!

As for the designs themselves, you can take pattern ideas from fabrics and decorations around your home or use the patterns on the ceramics or china you are using as a starting point. Books on favorite artists or styles are a fertile ground for inspiration and the designs will take on a whole new look when you use them as a starting point for mosaic. Things you notice around you every day can also be used as an inspiration—a window box full of flowers, a flock of birds, the patterns of tree branches against the sky. The lovely qualities of the individual tesserae can make even the simplest design, like a checkerboard of squares for example, look amazingly rich and wonderful when done in mosaic.

Putting the Puzzle Together

Think of your mosaic as a puzzle. Each fragment should fit comfortably into the space left by the surrounding tesserae, while subtly mimicking their form. If you need to trim a fragment to make it fit, don't hesitate to use your mosaic nippers. The spaces between the tesserae are called "joints," and they will be filled with grout after the adhesive is completely dry. The joints should be no more than ⅛ inch to ¼ inch wide both for practical purposes (the grout will have a tendency to crack in wider joint spaces) and for aesthetic purposes.

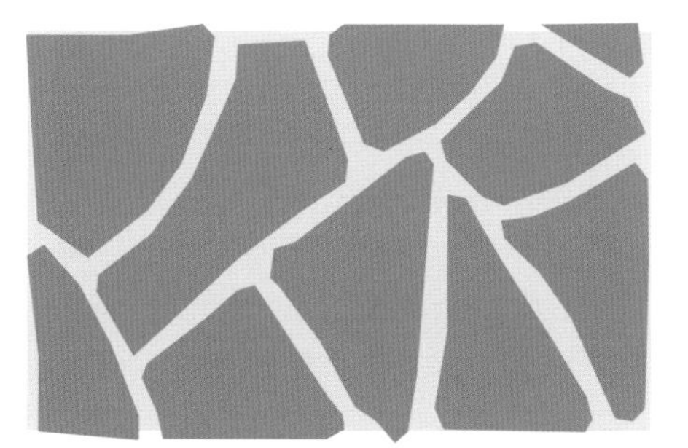

Correct Placement

Incorrect Placement

Where you begin laying your tesserae depends on each mosaic project. There is no right or wrong place to begin, and each project will differ. If you are working on a vase without a specific pattern, you may begin at the top and work down or at the bottom and work around. If you are working on a large installation, such as a countertop, you may begin at one side and work across or in the middle and work outward. Explicit instructions as to where to begin laying the tesserae are given for each project in this book. When you design your own mosaic projects, use some logic, and trust your instincts.

CENTRAL MOTIFS

If you are working on a project with a pattern or central motif, begin by working on the detailed areas and then complete the project by laying the background tesserae.

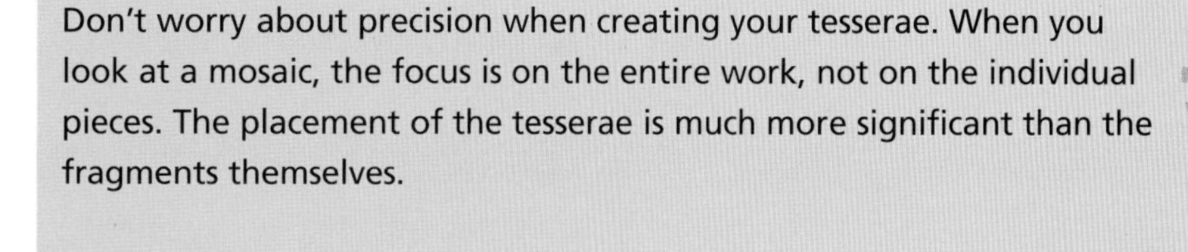

tip

Don't worry about precision when creating your tesserae. When you look at a mosaic, the focus is on the entire work, not on the individual pieces. The placement of the tesserae is much more significant than the fragments themselves.

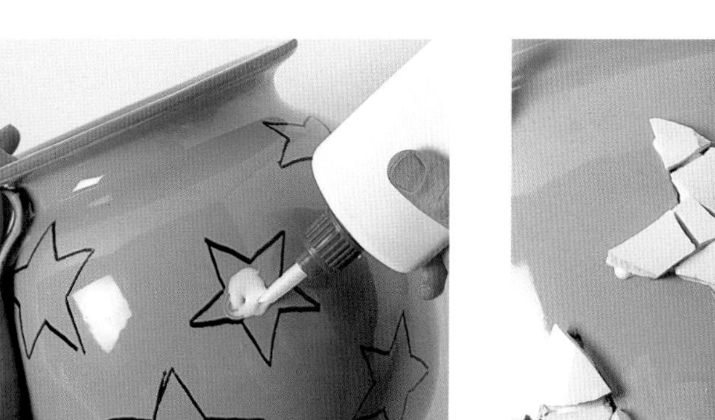

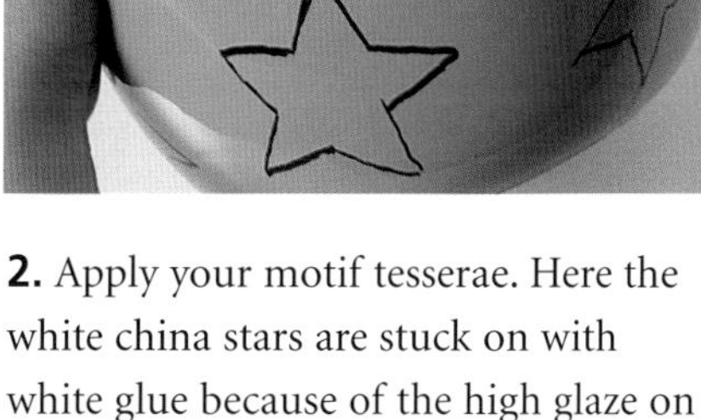

1. Draw the raised or central motif onto the substructure. A nonpermanent marker is easily rubbed off for outlines, although a permanent marker is best if you are covering the whole substructure.

2. Apply your motif tesserae. Here the white china stars are stuck on with white glue because of the high glaze on the substructure.

3. A background can be applied when the central images are set, or the motifs can be grouted without background tesserae for a relief effect.

Grouting

Grouting can appear to be a messy and time-consuming task with none of the delights of creation found within the mosaic process itself. However grouting is the vital finishing touch that will transform your mosaic from a collection of individual tesserae into a whole and complete surface. The matte qualities of the grout seem to enhance the shine and sparkle of the tesserae, and if the grout is colored, it can add a whole new dimension to the design. You can either purchase pre-colored grout or color your grout using grout colorant or powder paint.

Mixing grout is easy as long as you follow these simple steps. Before you start any part of the process, lay down plenty of newspaper or scrap paper over your work surface and put on rubber gloves.

1. Place powdered grout in a disposable container and make a well in the center.

2. Add water in proportional amounts according to the package directions.

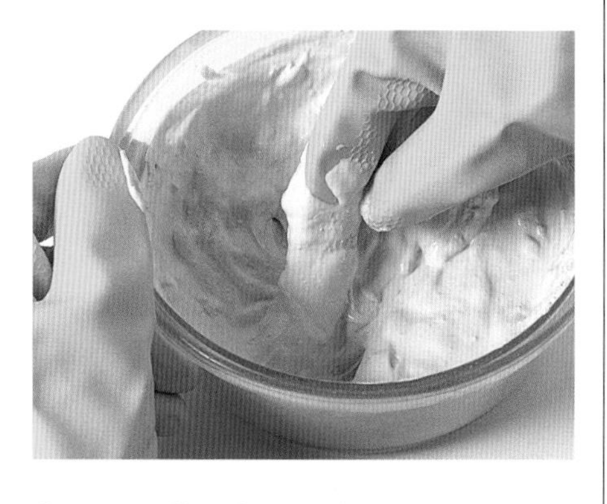

3. Mix well with gloved hands or a stir stick until the grout is the consistency of oatmeal. If the grout is too dry, add water drop by drop until it is the desired texture.

4. If the grout is too wet or soupy, either add more grout powder or allow the mixture to stand for ten to fifteen minutes to dry to the desired consistency.

tip

Rinse your hands in vinegar to neutralize the alkalinity of the grout and to restore the pH level in your skin. Then wash with soap and water and apply skin cream generously.

COLORING GROUT

Mixing grout with pigment or paint to the required color can make all the difference to your mosaic piece. Coloring is easy, but selecting colors that work well together takes a little practice.

1. Prepare your grout as above but mix some of your chosen color into the powdered grout before adding water.

2. Prepare your grout as above but mix some of your chosen color into the powdered grout before adding water.

tip

Save a small amount of powdered grout in a plastic bag in case you ever need to make a repair. Label the bag with a description of the mosaic it was used on. This is particularly useful if you have achieved the color you want before adding water. This way you will not have to mix and match to repair with the correct color grout.

tip

It is always possible that some pieces of mosaic may fall off during the grouting process. This is especially common with pieces at the edges of the mosaic, as they are not fully supported by surrounding pieces. Ideally you should thoroughly clean the space of grout and restick the piece, regrouting that area when the glue has dried. This is an excellent reason for keeping some of your special-colored unmixed with water. It may be possible to carefully patch the grout over the piece directly after resticking, although this is not strictly recommended, especially if more than one or two adjacent pieces have come away. Never ever attempt to restick the piece using grout only.

3. Add water in proportional amounts according to the package directions.

4. Begin to mix the water into the grout, pulling the powder in from the edges a little at a time for an evenly mixed result.

5. Mix well with gloved hands or a stir stick until the grout is the consistency of oatmeal.

6. If the grout's color is too pale, add a little more color until you have the shade you want. Remember: Grout will dry lighter than its wet color.

tip

If you are unhappy with your grout color after the grouting process is complete, tint it with acrylic paint. Brush the paint on the entire mosaic, and wipe the wet paint off the tesserae.

tip

Sometimes, more than just a slightly dampened sponge is needed to remove excess grout, especially if you are using unsanded grout. Fill a bucket or container with water to rinse and remoisten your sponge. NEVER throw this water down the sink when you have finished—this will quickly block it. Dispose of it elsewhere, such as an unused part of the garden, bearing in mind that if your grout was highly colored, the water could leave behind a colored residue when it evaporates.

GROUTING YOUR WORK

Grout is not toxic, but because it contains cement, it will dry out your hands, so you may want to wear rubber gloves during this process. Take care when rubbing grout into your mosaic with your fingers, sharp-edged tesserae can cause painful cuts.

WARNING

The grout clean-up process must be completed in a timely fashion or the grout will dry on the tesserae. Dry grout can only be removed with a diluted solution of hydrochloric acid and water, which is a process that you want to avoid at all costs.

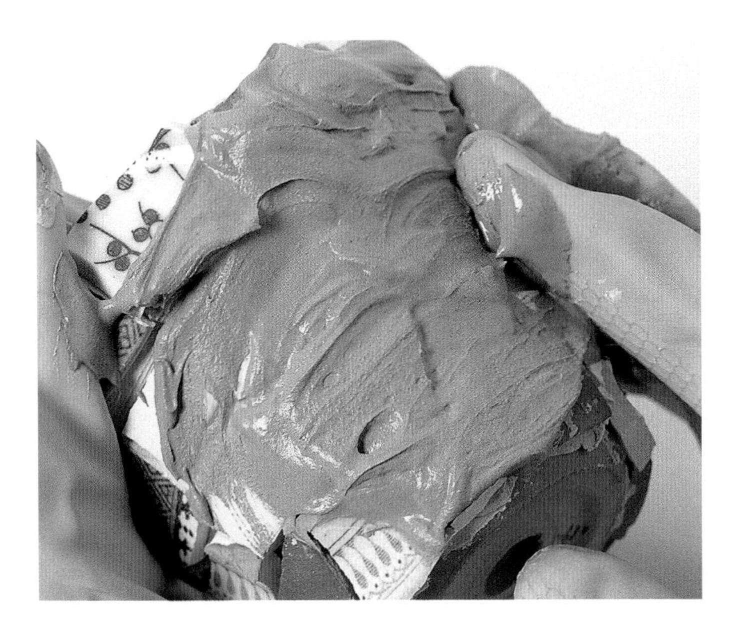

1. Spread the prepared grout onto the mosaic as if you are making a mud pie or icing a cake with your hands. Be sure to fill in all the joints and push the grout between every nook and cranny. A spatula or grout float can be used, but your fingers are really the best tools.

2. Continue to grout up over the rim of the piece, unless you intend to use the substructure color as a contrast to the tesserae. Grouting the rim gives extra hold and protection to the uppermost tesserae, and helps to prevent them being knocked out of place.

3. Immediately wipe the excess grout from the tesserae with a barely damp sponge or your fingertips. Remove as much grout as possible without disturbing the joints. You cannot help but leave a thin layer of grout on the tesserae.

4. Allow the mosaic to stand for approximately fifteen minutes until you see the grout remaining on the tesserae turn to a chalky haze. Vigorously buff the haze with a dry rag or paper towel. If you use a wet rag, you will streak the still damp grout and have to wait for it to turn chalky again. The grout joints will appear dry at this point although they will not be truly dry for approximately twenty-four hours.

Projects

Mask Plate

TOOLS & MATERIALS

- Smooth, fairly flat plate, with a gentle curve and no ridge on the back
- Washable felt pen
- A selection of ceramics and china in bright colors
- Tile nippers
- Ceramic tile adhesive or PVA
- Small plastic glue spreader
- Protective eyewear and gloves
- Sanded grout (ocher or color of your choice)
- Newspaper or scrap paper
- Rubber gloves
- Disposable container
- Stir stick
- Sponge
- Dry rag

Created by
Sarah Kelly

The back of a smooth plate makes a perfect base for a mosaic face, using ethnic masks as an inspiration. Use bright, chunky ceramics, mixing patterns and colors to create a vivid and lively design.

1 Draw the design of the face onto the back of the plate with the felt pen. This design is based on an Indian sun face—you can copy this one, adapt it, or design your own. Try to contain the face and the bands of color within the natural sections and divisions of the plate. If you make a mistake, wipe it off with a damp rag and start again.

2 Wearing the protective goggles and gloves, cut some patterned china into roughly triangular petal shapes to go round the outer rim. Arrange them around the plate before you stick them down to make sure they fit evenly. Trim them down or cut out others if necessary. Apply a layer of adhesive to the rim of the plate, then butter each "petal." If you are using PVA, wait for it to become slightly tacky before applying tesserae. Stick each piece into place.

3 Fill in the spaces between the petals with a plain bright color. You can trim shapes to fit exactly, or use

randomly cut, smaller tesserae to fill the gaps. Apply the glue in the same way as before. Working inward, cut some thin rectangular tesserae from a contrasting plain color and glue them in a ring inside your outer band. This should mark the beginning of a different "section" of the plate's construction. Continuing to move inward, glue another, wider ring of patterned tesserae next to the previous one, completely surrounding the central area you will use for the face.

4 Start the face by doing the features, as they are the most important part. Cut out a few thin rectangular tesserae in black and stick them down to form eyebrows, arching them slightly. Try to cut the tesserae as finely as you can. Use the same technique in brown to form almond shapes for the eyes. When you are gluing these in place, try to make sure you leave a big enough gap between the eyes and the brows to be able to fill them quite easily with the background skin color. Nibble out two small circles in black and trim off the top edge. Fit these inside the eyes, trimming where necessary. Use tiny fragments of white to fill in the rest of the eyes.

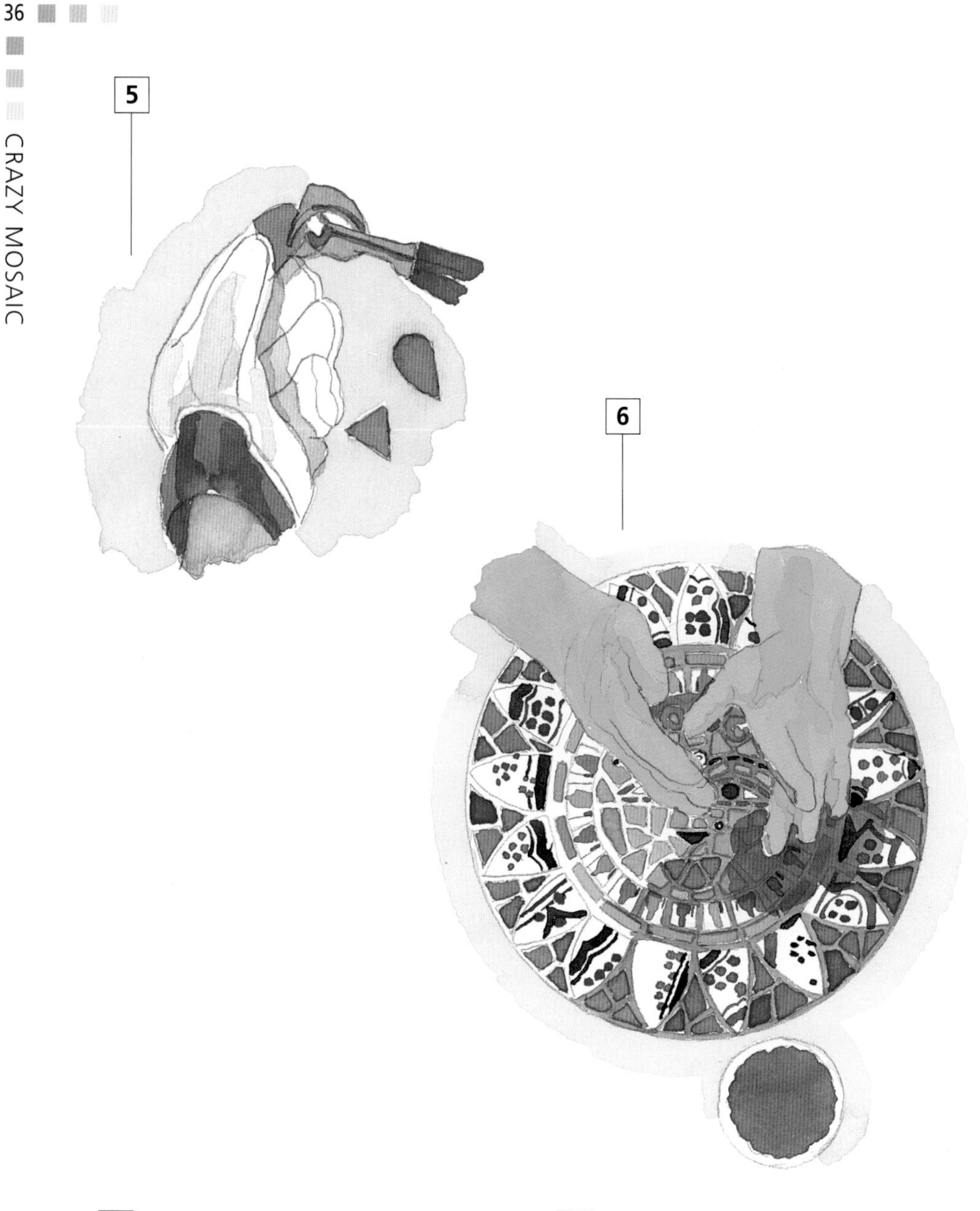

1.

2.

3.

5 Make a mouth by cutting three triangles, giving the top edges of the outside ones a slight curve with the nippers and making the central one a smaller, more equilateral triangle. Glue it into place near the bottom of the face (leaving a bit of space to suggest a chin), then cut a roughly semicircular piece in black or brown and place it between the eyes and mouth to make a nose.

Next, add any decoration you want to put on the rest of the face. On the one shown here, different flowers have been cut out to make forehead adornments and a tiny one has been used as a piece of jewelry for the nose. Finally, mosaic the rest of the face using a plain, light color, trimming the tesserae to fit into the gaps that are left. Leave to dry naturally for forty-eight hours.

6 Put on rubber gloves and mix up some ocher-colored grout (or another color that harmonizes with the colors of your mosaic), following the instructions on pages 30-32. Apply it to the surface of your mosaic using your gloved hands, making sure the grout goes into every crevice. Rub it into the edges of the mosaic on the outer rim of the plate as well, to create a smooth, neat finish. Immediately remove the excess grout with a dampened sponge, smoothing over as much as you can any areas where the depths of the tesserae vary. Wait for fifteen to twenty minutes before polishing with a dry rag.

Inspiration from the figure

1. Mary K. Guth *Female I*. Broken plate has been used to create the face and background area.
2. Mary K. Guth *Female II*. Glass, images, and stone create this classic glamor icon.
3. Cleo Mussi, *Yo, Brother Sun*. Another figure commissioned by the Public Arts Commissioning Agency for the Queen Elizabeth Hospital in Birmingham, England.
4. Cleo Mussi, *Mexican Wave*. This figure stands about 1 meter tall and draws upon Latin American themes and colors.
5. Philip Danzig, *General Grant*, 1973. This mural forms part of a series at the General Grant National Memorial, in New York City. Danzig joined forces with the Chilean sculptor and community artist, Pedro Silva, for these pieces.
6. Cleo Mussi, *Mother Earth*. This figure was commissioned by the Public Arts Commissioning Agency for the Queen Elizabeth Hospital in Birmingham, England.

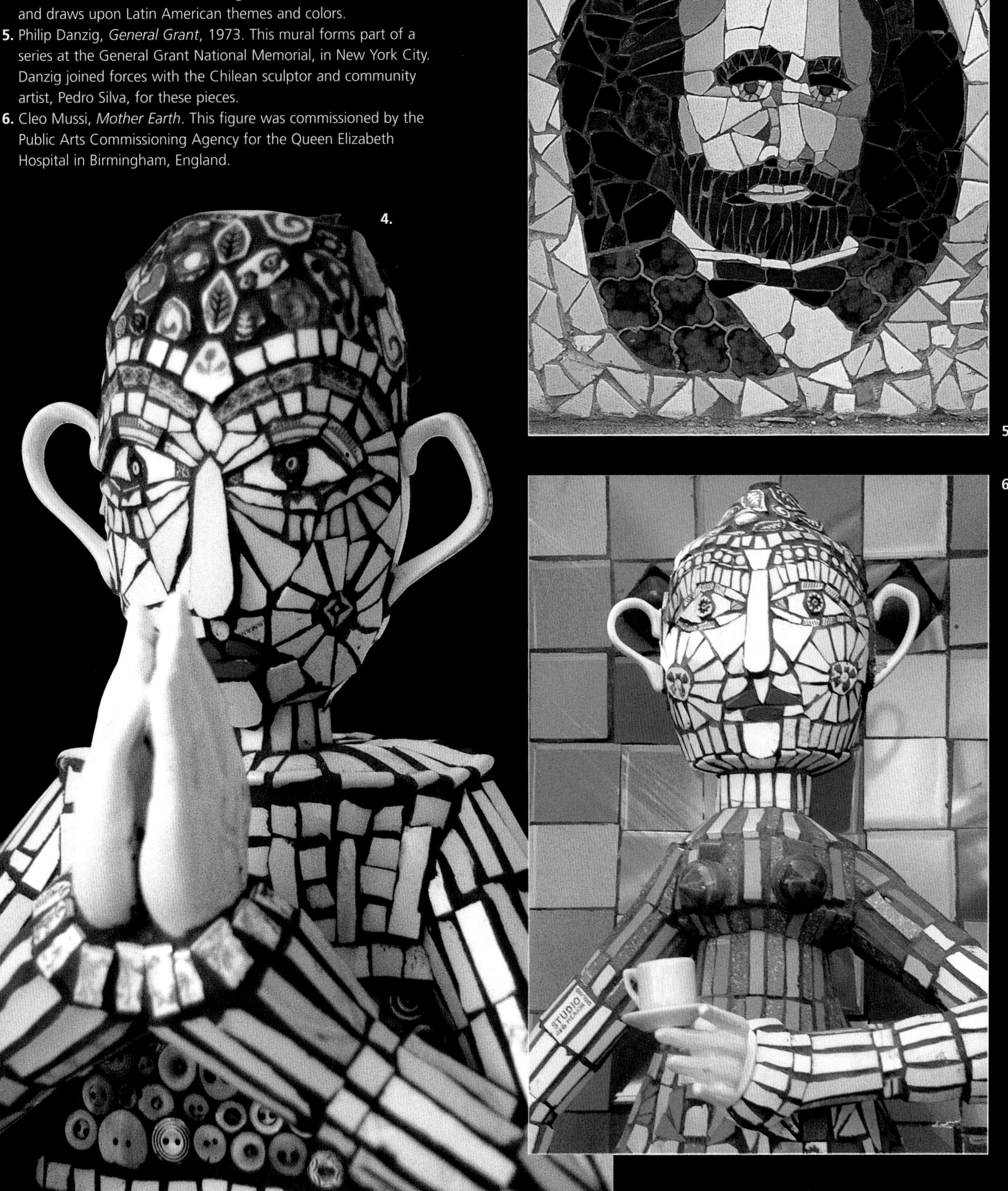

4.

5.

6.

Ceiling Light Cover

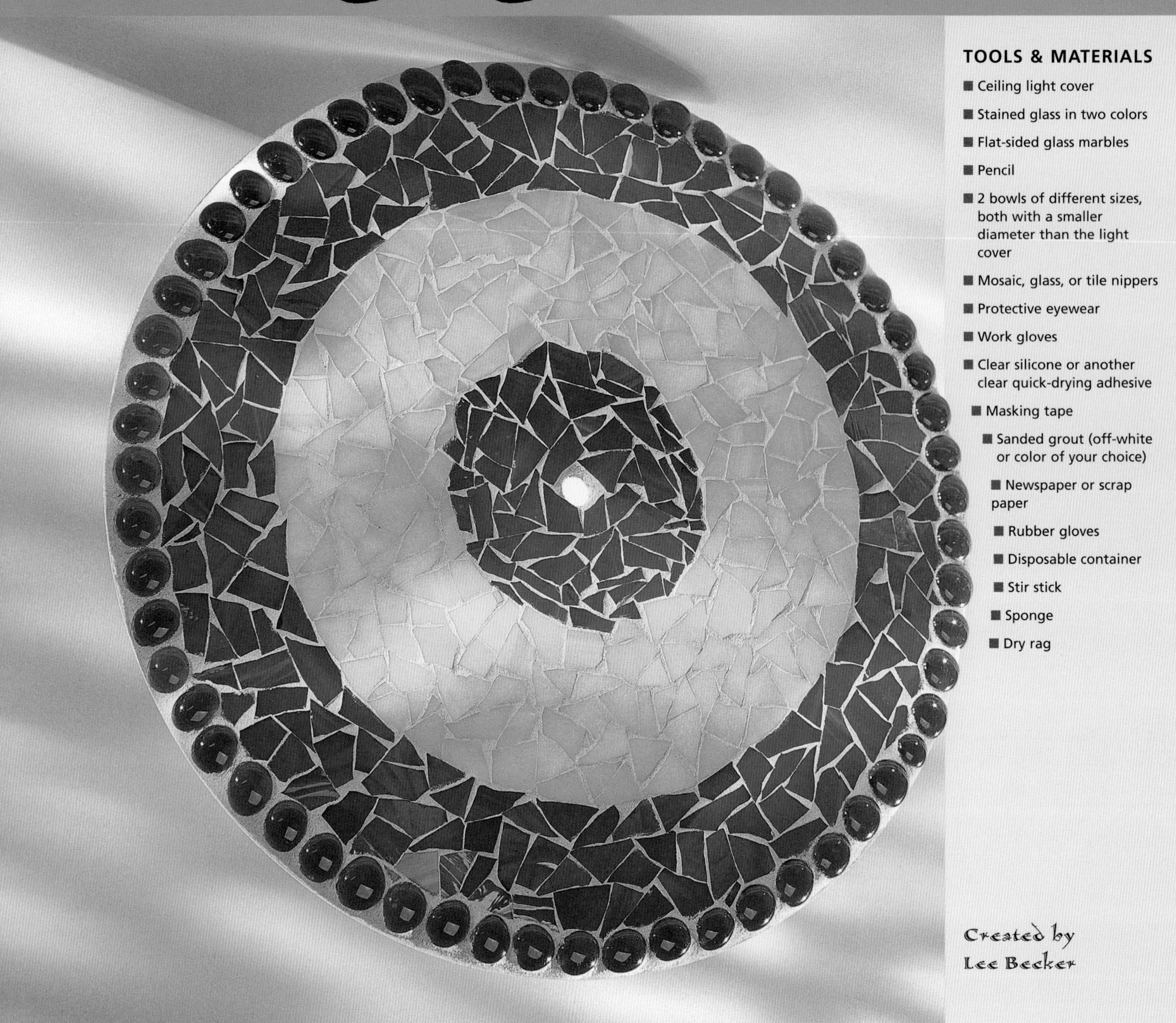

TOOLS & MATERIALS

- Ceiling light cover
- Stained glass in two colors
- Flat-sided glass marbles
- Pencil
- 2 bowls of different sizes, both with a smaller diameter than the light cover
- Mosaic, glass, or tile nippers
- Protective eyewear
- Work gloves
- Clear silicone or another clear quick-drying adhesive
- Masking tape
- Sanded grout (off-white or color of your choice)
- Newspaper or scrap paper
- Rubber gloves
- Disposable container
- Stir stick
- Sponge
- Dry rag

Created by
Lee Becker

Transform a plain ceiling light cover into the focal point of a room with broken glass. A ring of flat-sided glass marbles around the edge adds texture to the otherwise smooth surface. Whether you choose transparent or opaque glass, the overall effect will be dazzling!

COLOR VARIATIONS

a Use shades of white and off white, using very pale creams, pale silvery grays, and clear gems backed with silver leaf. Cover with off-white or white grout.

b Try red and orange with cream color grout.

c Replace the dark blue with an olive green and the yellow with a rose pink. Use pale gray grout.

d Try pale blues and lilacs with pale blue or cream grout.

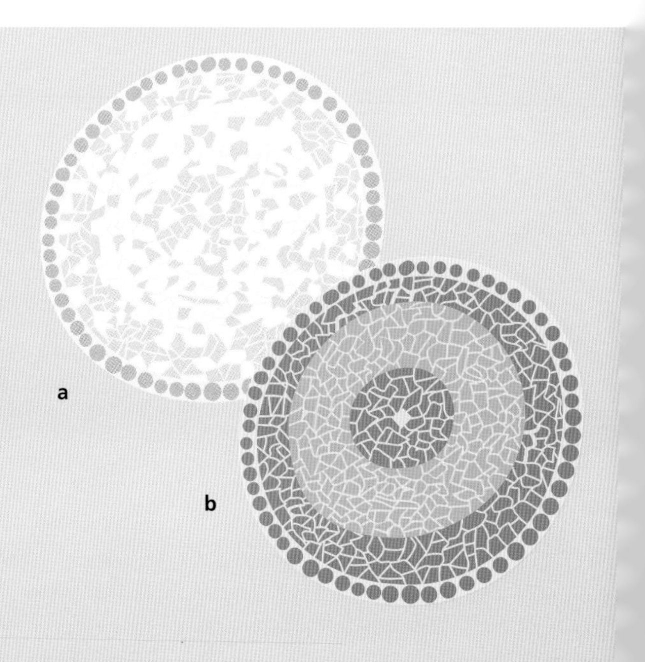

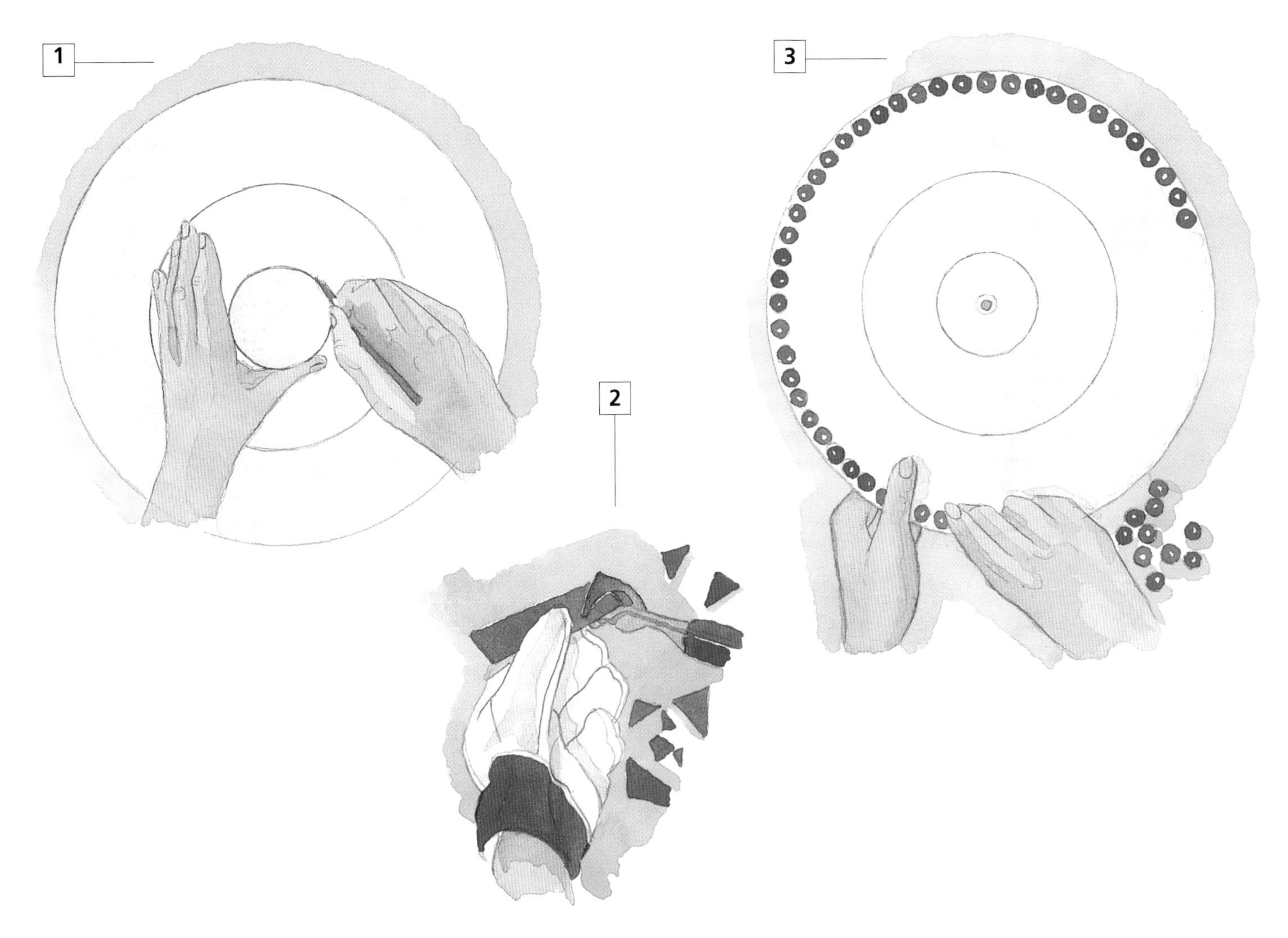

1 Find a ceiling light cover made of clear or white glass. They are easy to locate at any local hardware or lighting store, or you may already have one in your home. Lay the larger bowl on the center of the cover, and use a pencil to draw a line around it. Repeat the process with the smaller bowl. These lines will serve as the borders for the rings of colored glass.

2 Use your nippers to clip the glass into small irregular shapes. Although you may be tempted to use a hammer, using a nipper creates much less waste and reduces the risk of leaving behind dangerous glass splinters. Always wear protective eyewear and work gloves when nipping, breaking, or smashing to protect yourself from flying shards.

3 Glue the flat-sided marbles onto the light cover to create a ring of colored gems around the outside edge with clear adhesive. These marbles are weighty, so you may need to secure them with masking tape while allowing them to dry securely. You can continue working on the mosaic if you are careful not to disturb the marbles.

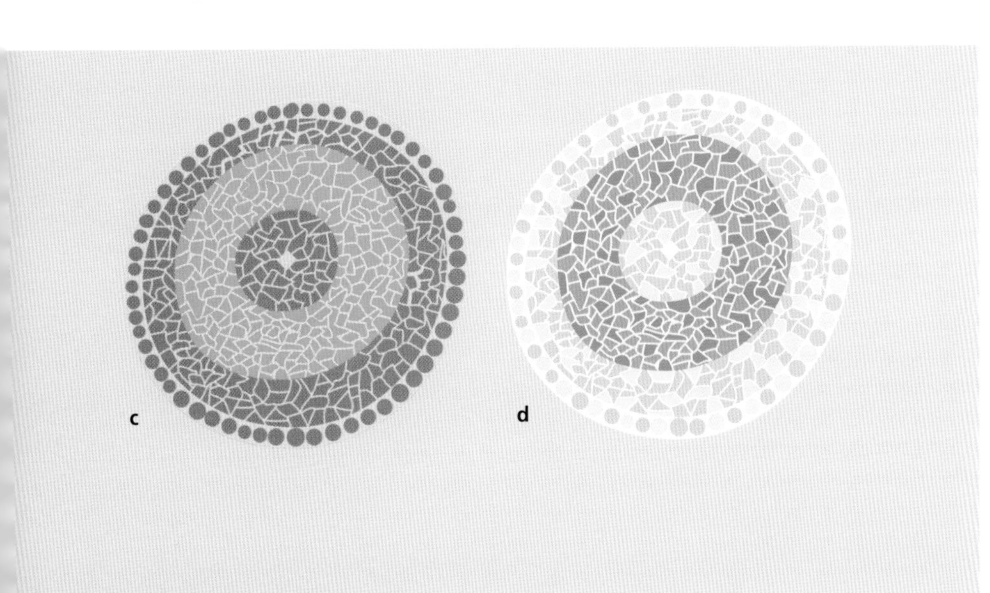

tip

- Ceiling light covers are available round or square and in several sizes. Some are concave, others are flat. All work equally well.
- Stained glass in yellows, golds, ambers, and dark reds will give off warm light when the fixture is illuminated.
- Use flat-sided glass marbles between each ring of color, instead of just one row of marbles around the outside rim of the light.

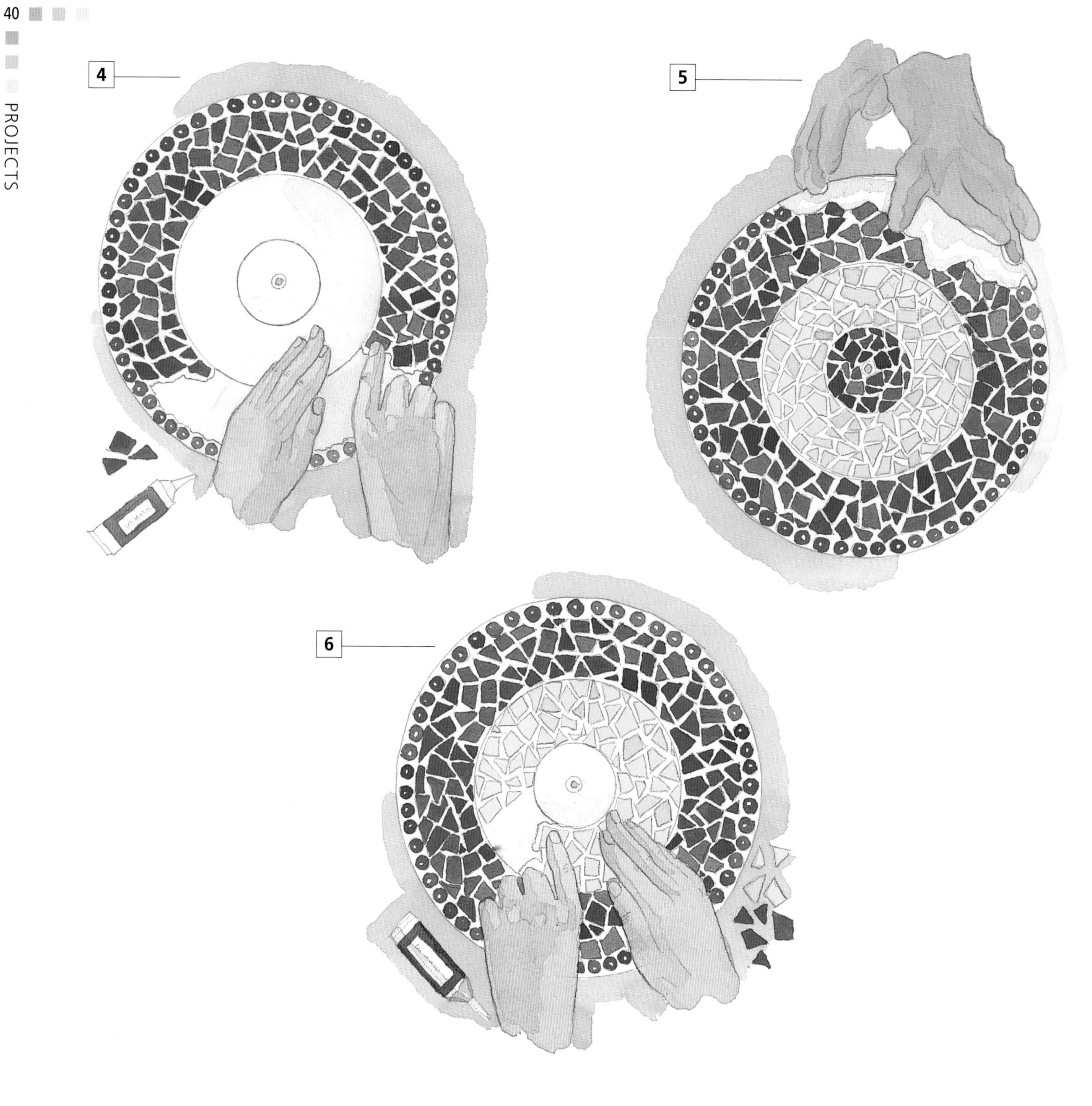

4 Begin with the largest ring of the light cover (adjacent to the marbles) by squirting a bubble of clear adhesive onto this section. Use the tip of the applicator tube to spread the adhesive into a thin layer. Only cover a small area at a time because the adhesive dries very quickly. Place the broken glass on the wet adhesive. The grout will creep between the smallest of spaces, so don't hesitate to place the shards tightly together. Work around the light cover in the outside ring until you reach the pencil line border.

5 Repeat this process in the middle ring with your second color of broken glass. Repeat again for the third and smallest ring with the first color of glass shards. Allow the project to dry undisturbed for twenty-four hours before removing the masking tape and beginning the grouting process.

6 While wearing rubber gloves, spread the prepared grout onto the ceiling light cover. Fill every space between the glass pieces and the marbles. Be sure to clean out the center hole where the light cover will be attached to the ceiling. Wipe the excess grout from the glass and then allow the grout to dry for about twenty minutes. Buff off the remaining chalky haze with a clean dry rag.

Bathroom Accessories

TOOLS & MATERIALS

- Tissue box
- Soap dish
- Cup
- Assorted dishes
- Mosaic or tile nippers
- Protective eyewear
- Work gloves
- Ceramic tile adhesive
- Dull knife or spatula
- Sanded grout (blue or color of your choice)
- Newspaper or scrap paper
- Rubber gloves
- Disposable container
- Stir stick
- Sponge
- Dry rag
- Grout sealer
- Paintbrush

Created by
Tracy Graivier Bell

tip

- Create a focal point in a simple monochromatic bathroom by using highly patterned and colorful tesserae on the bathroom accessories.
- Use primary colors for a child's bathroom.
- Mix browns, golds, and blacks for an elegant tortoiseshell effect.
- Use broken glass in assorted colors instead of broken dishes to mosaic this set. A great way to use up your leftover scraps.

Add the finishing touch to your bathroom by making your own mosaic tissue box, soap dish, and toothbrush holder or cup to complement your décor. This set is made of broken blue-and-white patterned china randomly mixed with textured white china to create a useful and elegant accessory set.

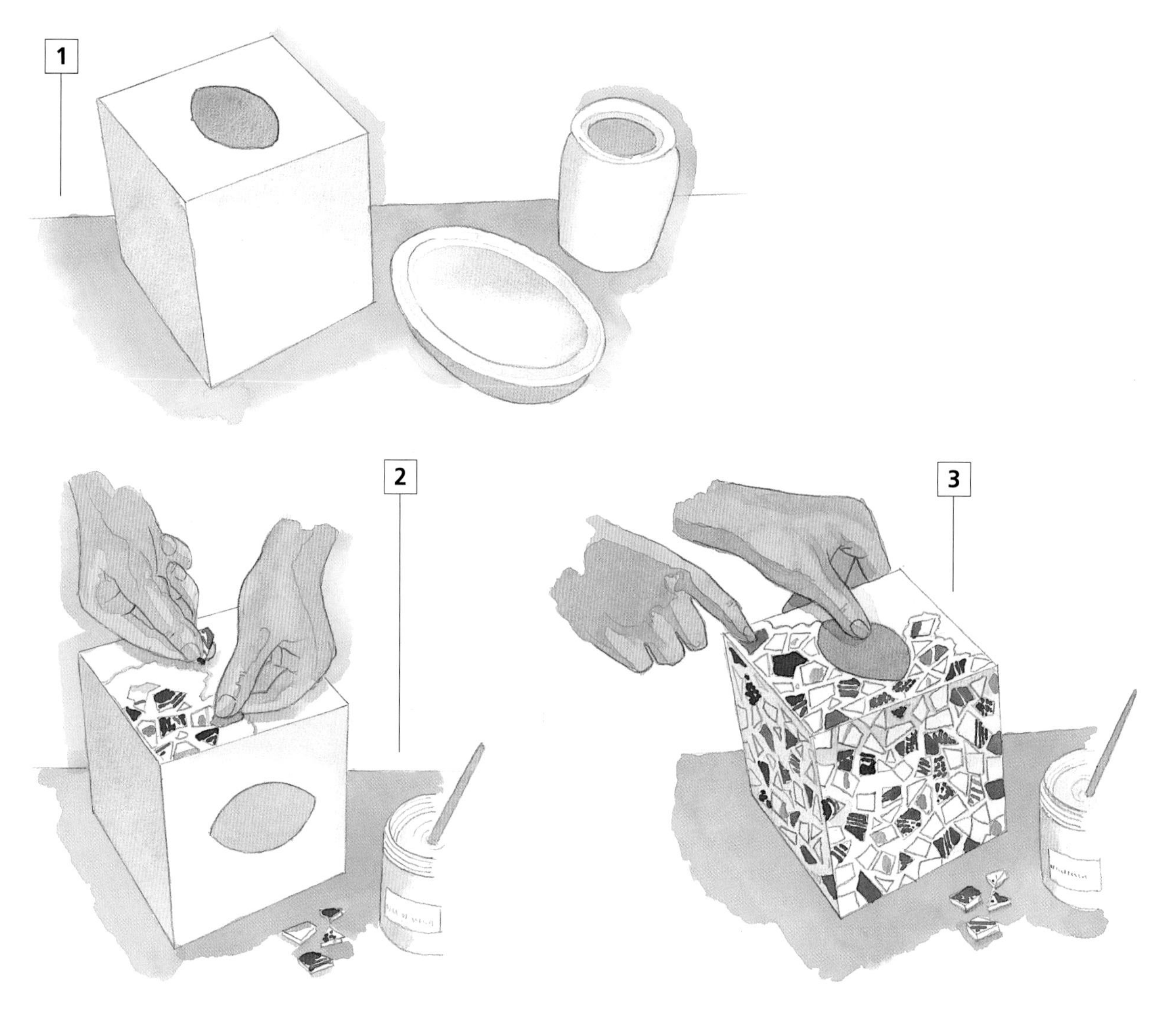

1 Buy a tissue box, soap dish, and cup at a home furnishings or department store. Choose shapes that are aesthetically pleasing, relatively smooth, and made of ceramic or non-flexible hard plastic. Take into consideration that the inside of the cup and other small areas of the accessories may be visible when the projects are complete, so find base forms that blend with the colors of your mosaic. Use the nippers to clip the china into small irregular shapes. Always wear protective eyewear and work gloves when nipping, breaking, or smashing to protect yourself from shards and splinters.

2 Lay the tissue box on its side, and using a dull knife or spatula, spread a thin layer of ceramic tile adhesive onto a small section. Place the china fragments closely together on the adhesive, randomly mixing the patterns and solids. Continue adding to the mosaic until the side of the tissue box is completely covered with fragments up to, but not over, the edges. Remember that each fragment should fit comfortably into the space left by the surrounding pieces, so trim shards with your nippers where necessary. Turn the box on to the next side, and repeat the process on the uppermost side. Repeat again for sides three and four. Be careful not to disturb the pieces you have already placed when turning the tissue box from side to side.

COLOR VARIATIONS

a Use pink and white tesserae with a pink grout.
b Try turquoise and sea green with greenish blue grout.
c Make splashes of lilac, mauve, and golden yellow, offset by blue grout.
d Use peaches, creams, and pale oranges and a cream or peachy coloured grout.

a

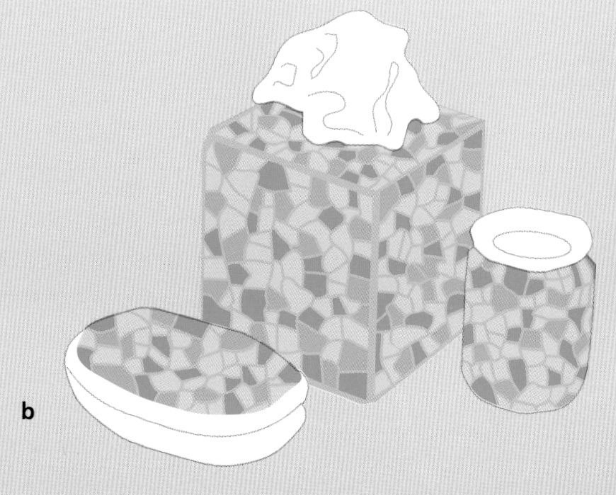
b

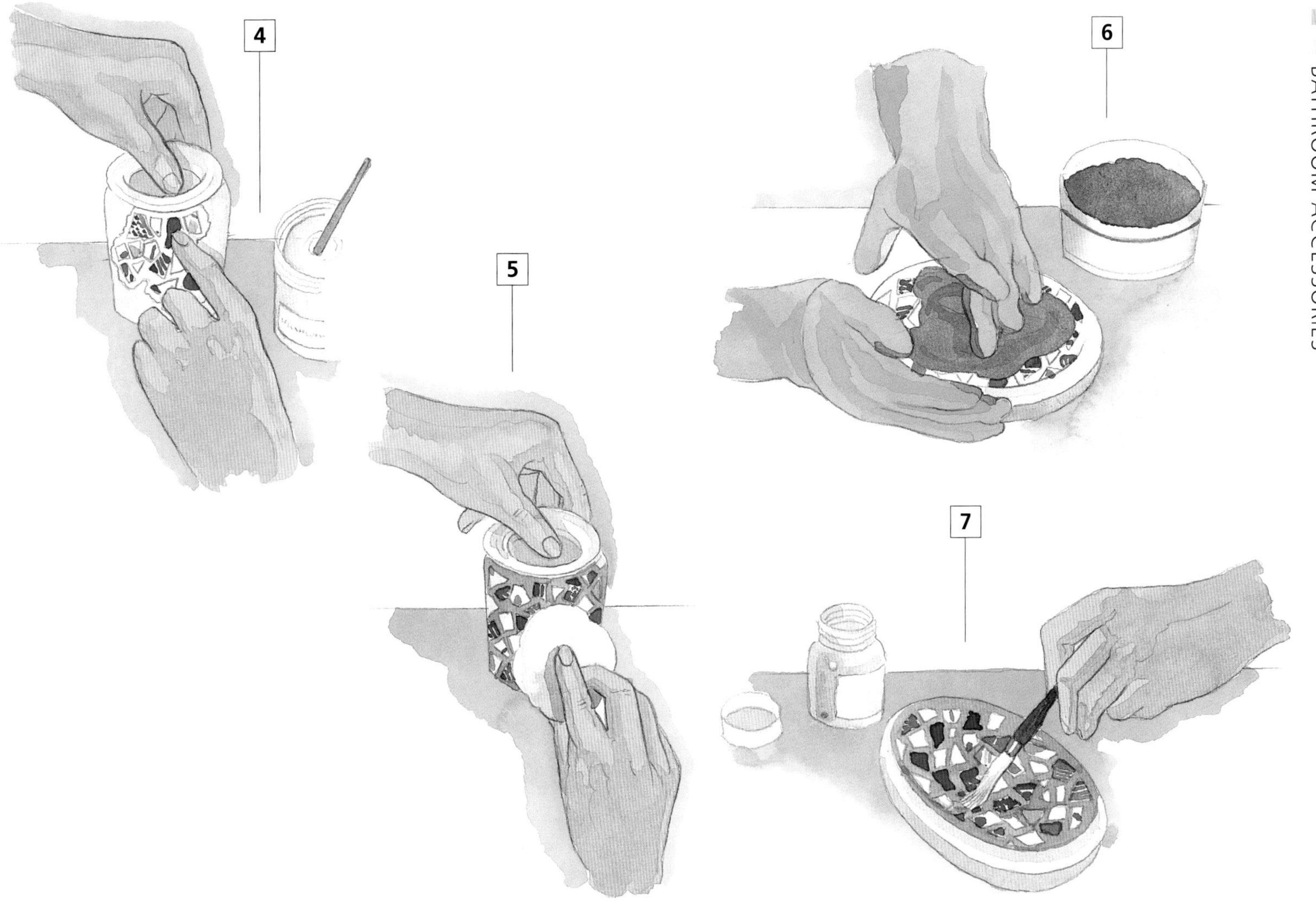

3 When all four sides are covered with shards, carefully stand the tissue box upright. Spread the top with ceramic tile adhesive and cover it with china fragments. When the fragments are all in place, allow the tissue box to air-dry for at least forty-eight hours before applying the grout.

4 While the tissue box is drying, begin working on the soap dish and cup. These pieces are much smaller, so you should be able to complete them rather quickly. Allow to dry for forty-eight hours.

5 Prepare and carefully apply the grout while wearing rubber gloves. The full procedure is given on page 30-32. Be sure to fill every space between the fragments. As the grout begins to set, vigorously wipe the excess from the fragments and then allow the grout to dry for about twenty minutes. Wipe off the remaining chalky haze with a clean dry rag.

6 Apply grout to soap dish and remove as before.

7 In order to make the soap dish completely waterproof, allow it to air dry for forty-eight hours and then apply two coats of grout sealer, a product available in any hardware or tile supply store.

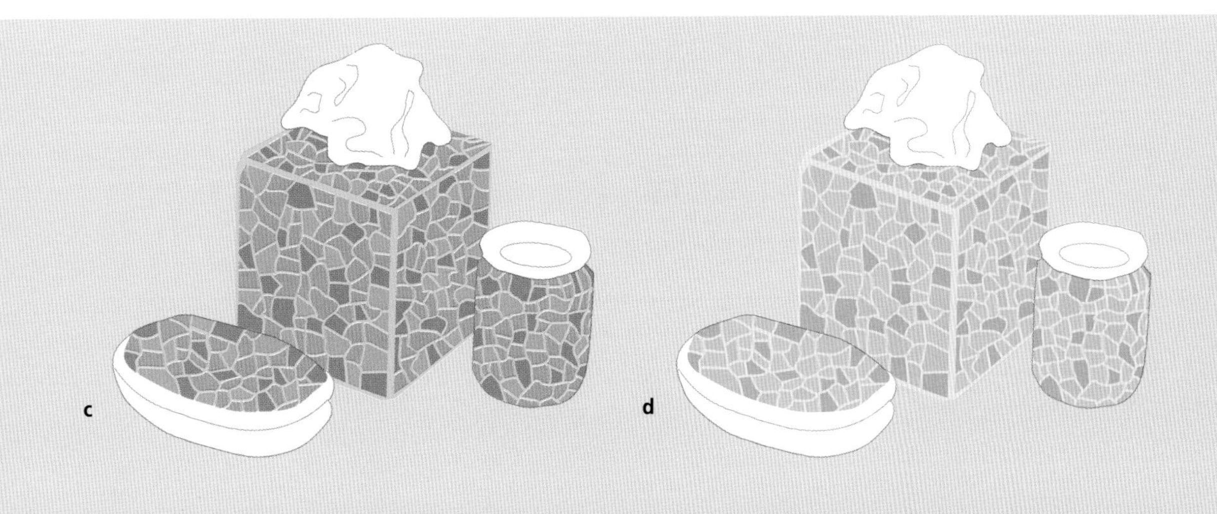

Steppingstone

TOOLS & MATERIALS

- Precast steppingstone
- Ceramic tiles in assorted colors
- Carbon paper
- Pencil
- Hammer
- Heavy paper bag
- Protective eyewear
- Work gloves
- Mosaic or tile nippers
- Cement-based mortar
- Disposable container
- Stir stick
- Dull knife or spatula
- Sanded grout (light gray or color of your choice)
- Newspaper or scrap paper
- Rubber gloves
- Disposable container
- Stir stick
- Sponge
- Dry rag
- Grout sealer
- Large paintbrush

Created by
Linda Zimmerman
and
Cindy Boldebuck

Create a whimsical garden path of steppingstones decorated with colorful insects or flowers. A single stone can add a fanciful touch to a small outdoor area. Buy a precast steppingstone at a local garden center or hardware store. You can choose a circular stone or a square stone, as the pattern will work on both. These mosaics are made of broken ceramic tiles and are extremely durable. Use the pattern templates provided on pages 125-127 or create your own!

tip

- Steppingstones are available in round, square and rectangular shapes. Experiment with each shape to determine your preference.
- Have each grandchild make a steppingstone to create a fanciful garden path for grandma and grandpa ... for a special occasion or for no reason at all!

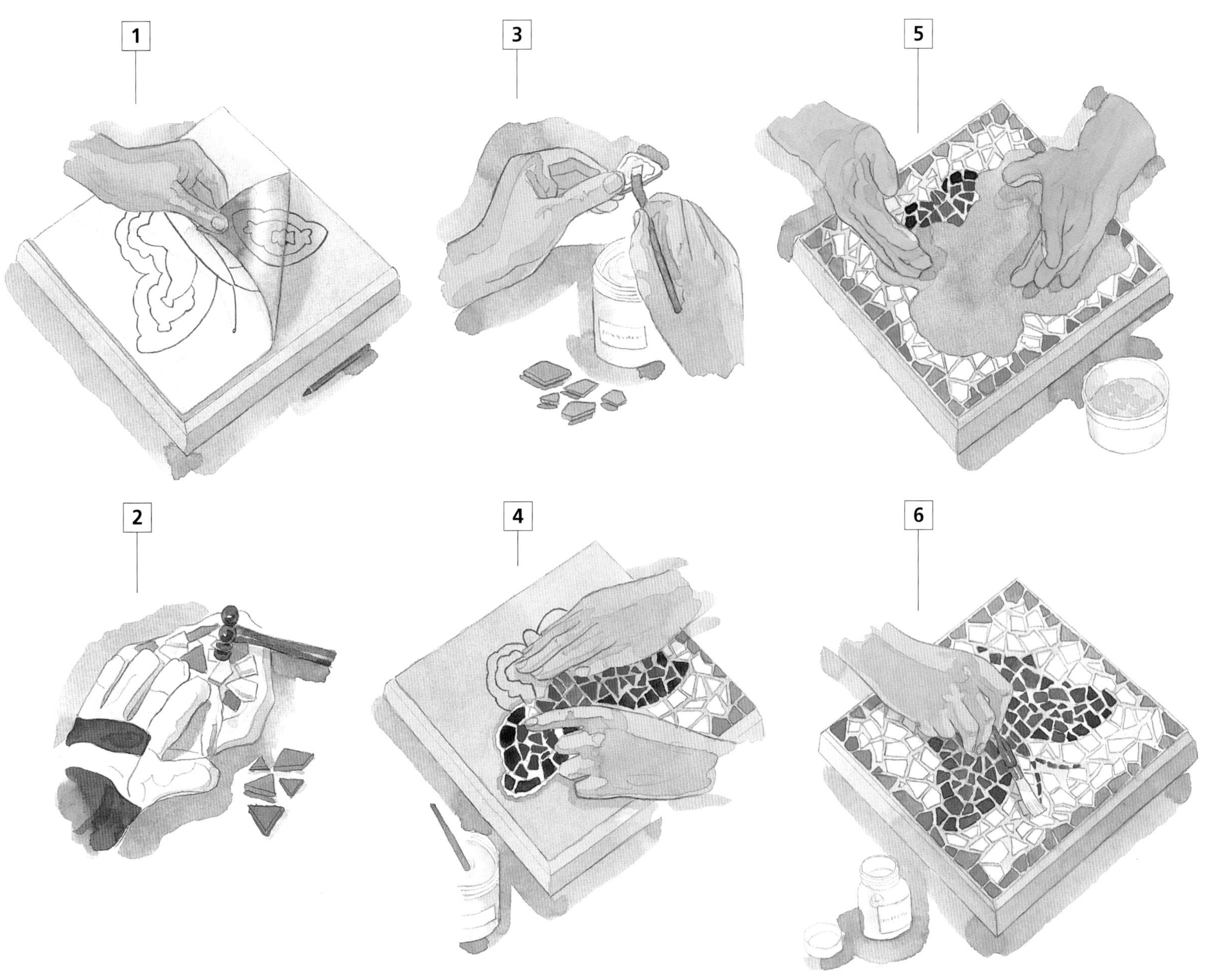

1 Enlarge the butterfly pattern on a photocopy machine, and trace the butterfly pattern onto the stone using carbon paper.

2 Put the ceramic tiles into a heavy paper or thick plastic bag and smash them with your hammer. Be sure to wear safety goggles and heavy work gloves to protect yourself from flying shards. Check the pieces frequently to see how you are doing. The broken pieces should be a variety of sizes ranging from ½ inch to 2 inches in diameter. You can always nibble the largers pieces into the shapes you need with your nippers.

3 Prepare the cement-based mortar in a disposable container according to the package directions. Using a dull knife or spatula, butter the back of the broken tiles with a thin layer of mortar approximately ⅛ inch thick. Press each buttered tile onto the steppingstone within the pattern.

4 Work section by section until the top of the stone is completely covered with broken tiles. Remember that each fragment should fit comfortably into the space left by the surrounding pieces, so trim shards with your nippers when necessary. Allow the steppingstone to dry for at least forty-eight hours before grouting.

5 Prepare and carefully apply the grout while wearing rubber gloves. Be sure to fill every space between the fragments. As the grout begins to set, wipe the excess from the fragments and then allow the grout to dry for about twenty minutes. Buff off the remaining chalky haze with a clean dry rag. Allow to air dry for another forty-eight hours before applying grout sealer.

6 In order to make the stone completely weatherproof, brush the surface with two coats of grout sealer, a product available in any hardware or tile supply store.

COLOR VARIATIONS

a Make the wings burnt orange, lilac, and yellow, with a brown body. Add a turquoise background with a purple border. Use light gray or terra cotta grout.

b Put red and white markings on black wings, a dark brown body, and cream colored background. Add a deep red border and use pale or dark grey grout.

c Make wings in shades of cornflower blue with a white border. Use a darker blue or cool gray for the body. Add a green background and white border with a pale gray or pink grout.

d Make the wings and body as above, but add a pink background with a lilac border. Apply pink or light gray grout.

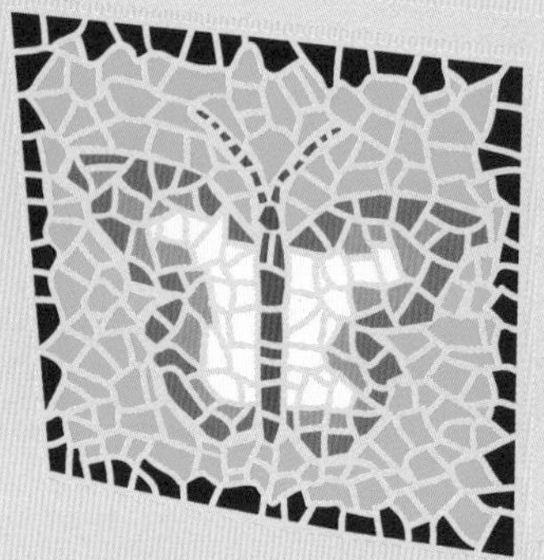

a

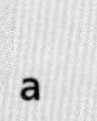

b

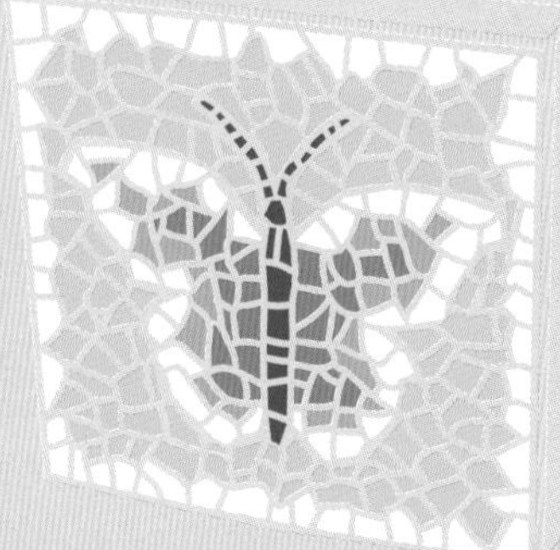

c

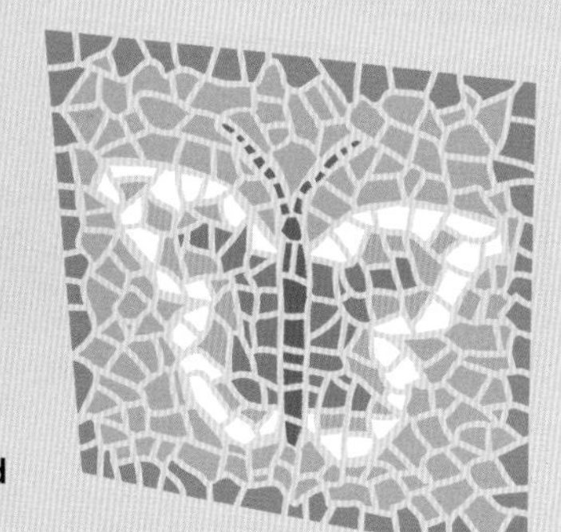

d

1. Sarah Kelly, *Tiger*. This colorful big cat looks stunning peering out of long grass.
2. Carlos Alves, *Save the Waters*. An ocean whirlpool creates a fun optical illusion on this New York City floor, and would make a striking design for pool- or pond-side stepping stones.
3. Sonia King, *Adam and Eve*. A garden theme with a difference.
4. Carlos Alves, *Save Our Oceans*. Another water design with primary colors for pool- or pond-side stepping stones.
5. Another natural theme from Sarah Kelly. Picture these huge daisies dotted across your garden.
6. The water theme continues with these bright dynamic fish from Cleo Mussi.

1.

2.

3.

Gallery of steppingstones

Gallery of stepping stones

4.

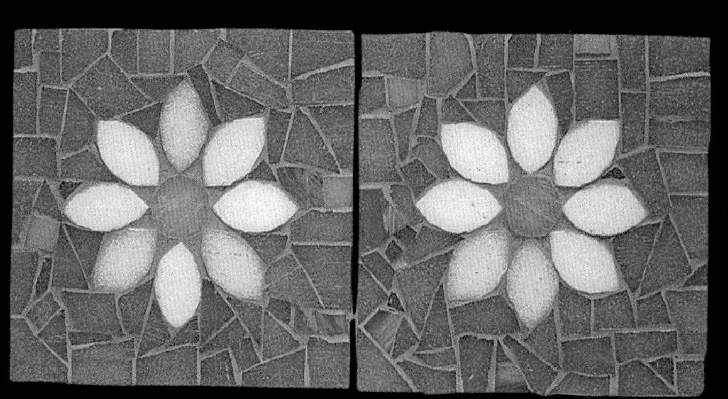

5.

6.

Rose Bangle

TOOLS & MATERIALS

- Plastic or wooden bangle
- Eight small rose medallions
- Fine pink and white china (thin cups and saucers are best)
- Tile nippers
- Household cement or another strong bonding adhesive
- Protective eyewear and gloves
- White grout (unsanded)
- Rubber gloves
- Newspaper or scrap paper
- Disposable container
- Stir stick
- Sponge
- Dry rag

Created by
Sarah Kelly

Transform a cheap plastic bangle into an original piece of jewelry using mosaic. Tiny rose medallions combined with a "ribbon" of pink and surrounded by delicate white tesserae create a look reminiscent of an antique nightgown.

BEFORE YOU START

Find a suitable bangle to use as a base. It needs to be at least 1 inch wide and quite flat with a smooth surface. Try to make sure that the color of the bangle will work with the colors of the mosaic, as the inside of it will still be visible. If not, you could always paint it with acrylic paint or glue a band of felt around the inside at the end.

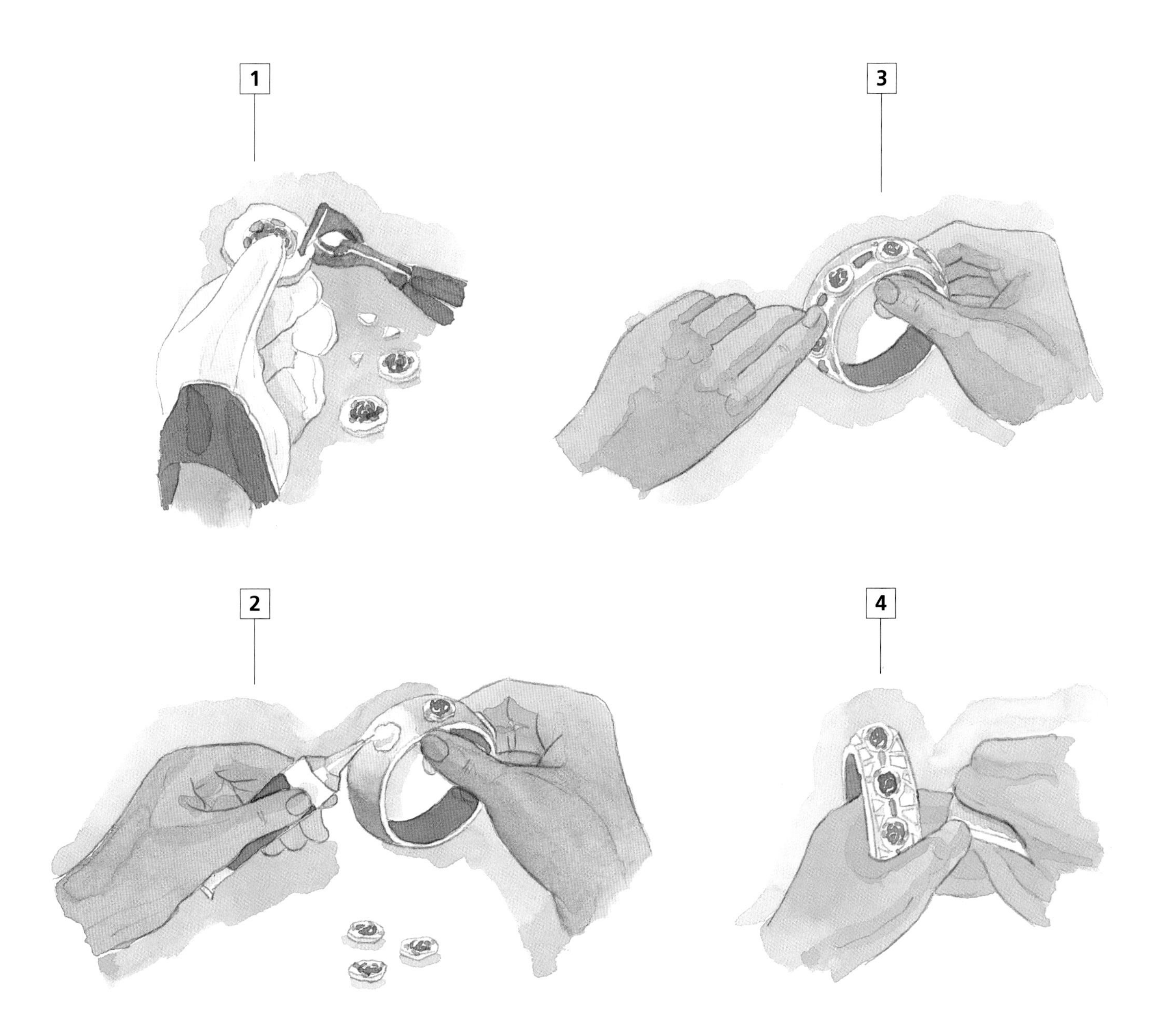

1 Put on the work gloves and protective eyewear. Cut out the rose medallions into circles, trimming them right down to the flower, then cut some very delicate white china into small tesserae. Include the naturally beveled edges of the cups or saucers—these are the best choice as the china needs to be quite thin—to use on the edges of your bangle.

2 Glue a rose medallion onto the bangle, placing it centrally within the width of the band. Turn the bangle around and glue another one directly opposite. Stick another at 90 degrees to the first one and then another opposite that one. Use the remaining four medallions in the spaces left, so that they are all evenly spaced.

3 Cut thin tesserae from the pink china to fit between the roses, so that it looks as if it is linking them together like a ribbon, and glue each one in place. Surround all of this with a mosaic of the white tesserae, using the beveled edges on the edges of the bangle—you don't want sharp points sticking into your arm! Try to get the mosaic as smooth as possible. You could also incorporate tiny rosebuds into this section, but make sure they don't detract from the main design. The area is so tiny that it would be easy to overwhelm the design and lose the charm of the bangle.

4 Leave the mosaic to dry for forty-eight hours, then put on the rubber gloves and prepare the grout. You will only need a small amount. Apply it carefully over the mosaic, smoothing any edges if necessary. Wait a few minutes before wiping the excess off with a damp sponge (make sure it's very clean so as not to dirty the white grout). After fifteen to twenty minutes, polish the bangle with a soft dry rag. Be sure to wipe off any grout on the inside surface of the bangle as well. Leave to dry thoroughly for another forty-eight hours, then paint or cover the inside of the bangle with felt, if you prefer.

Birdbath

TOOLS & MATERIALS

- 8-inch terra-cotta flowerpot
- Stainless steel mixing bowl
- Epoxy resin or another strong adhesive approved for exterior use
- Wax crayon
- Ceramic tiles in blues, greens, and reds
- 2 three-dimensional frog figurines (optional)
- Hammer
- Heavy paper bag
- Protective eyewear
- Work gloves
- Mosaic or tile nippers
- Cement-based mortar
- Dull knife or spatula
- Sanded grout (off-white or color of your choice)
- Newspaper or scrap paper
- Rubber gloves
- Disposable container
- Stir stick
- Sponge
- Dry rag
- Grout sealer
- Large paintbrush

Created by
Linda Oldham

Birds will flock to your garden to take a dip in this whimsical birdbath. If possible, find two small ceramic frogs to use in your birdbath. If you cannot locate any, your lily pads will look just fine without any amphibian friends perched atop them. The miniature frog figurines serve as ideal perches for your feathered friends to sunbathe upon, and when the blue-tiled birdbath is filled with water, the water lily and lily pads appear to be floating. If you do not want to make your own birdbath base form, feel free to use a precast cement birdbath available in most garden centers or hardware stores.

Try these theme ideas:

- Caterpillars and butterflies
- Fish and seaweed
- Stars, sun, and moon

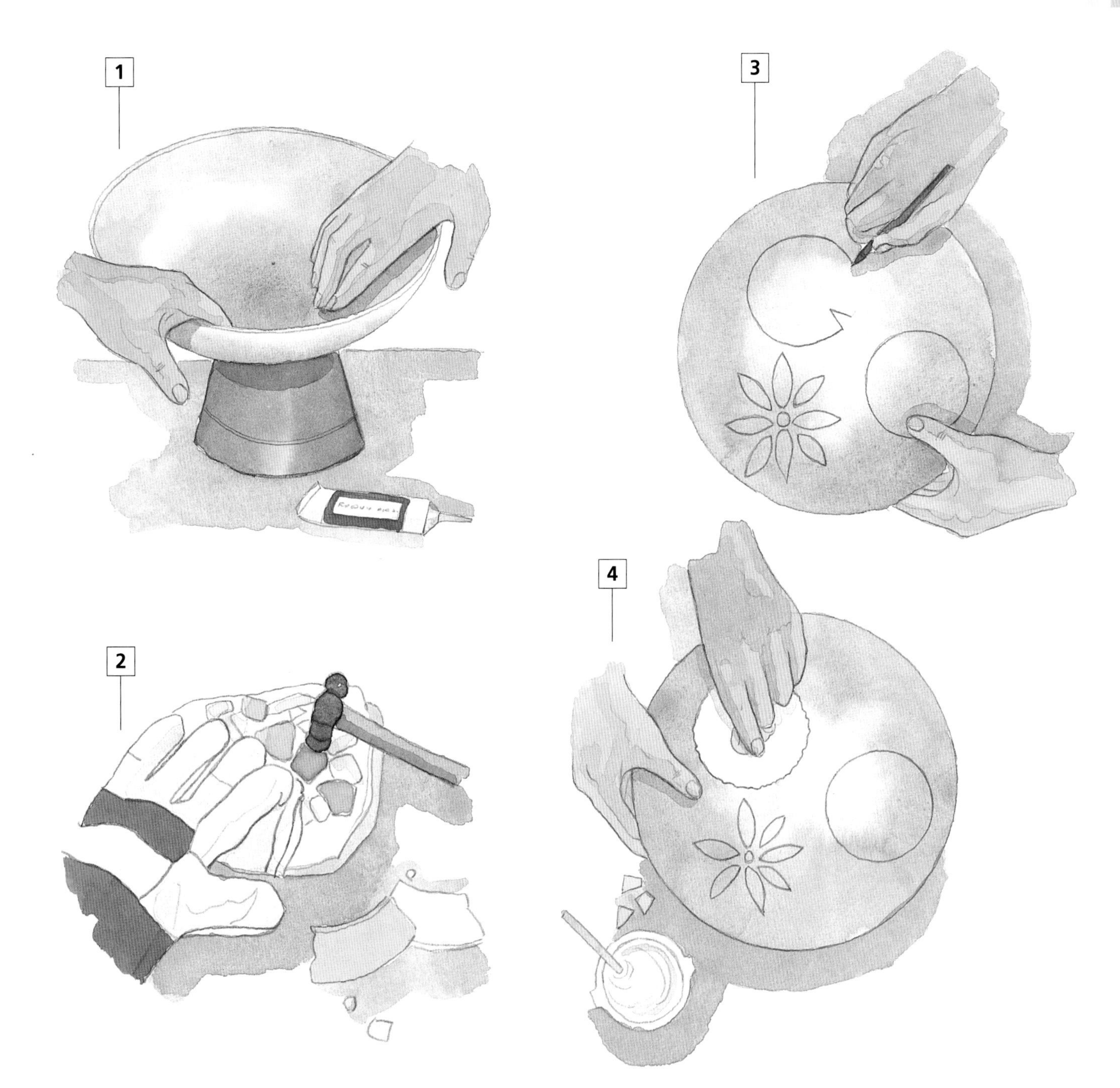

1 Buy a terra-cotta flowerpot, approximately 8 inches high, at a local garden center or hardware store to use as the pedestal portion of your birdbath. Then locate a stainless steel mixing bowl to use as the basin. (A wide shallow bowl is ideal, although any shape will do.) Turn the flowerpot upside down and squeeze a generous portion of epoxy resin or exterior grade bonding adhesive onto it. Center the bowl above the pot, and press it firmly into place. If the bowl feels secure, leave the birdbath form to dry for forty-eight hours before proceeding. If it feels wobbly, tape the two components together, then allow it to dry well.

2 Put the ceramic tiles into the heavy paper or thick plastic bag and smash them with your hammer. Be sure to wear safety goggles and heavy work gloves to protect yourself from flying shards. Check inside the bag frequently to see how you are doing. The broken pieces should be a variety of sizes ranging from ½ inch to 2 inches in diameter.

3 Use your wax crayon to draw two ovals for lily pads and one simple flower for a water lily in the basin of the birdbath. Don't concern yourself with too much detail. The rough shapes will serve as your basic pattern and guide.

4 Prepare the cement-based mortar according to the package directions. Using a dull knife or spatula, spread a thin layer of mortar approximately ½ inch thick in one of the ovals. Press a frog figurine (if you have one) into the center of the mortar, and then surround the frog with assorted colors of broken green tiles. Repeat with the second oval.

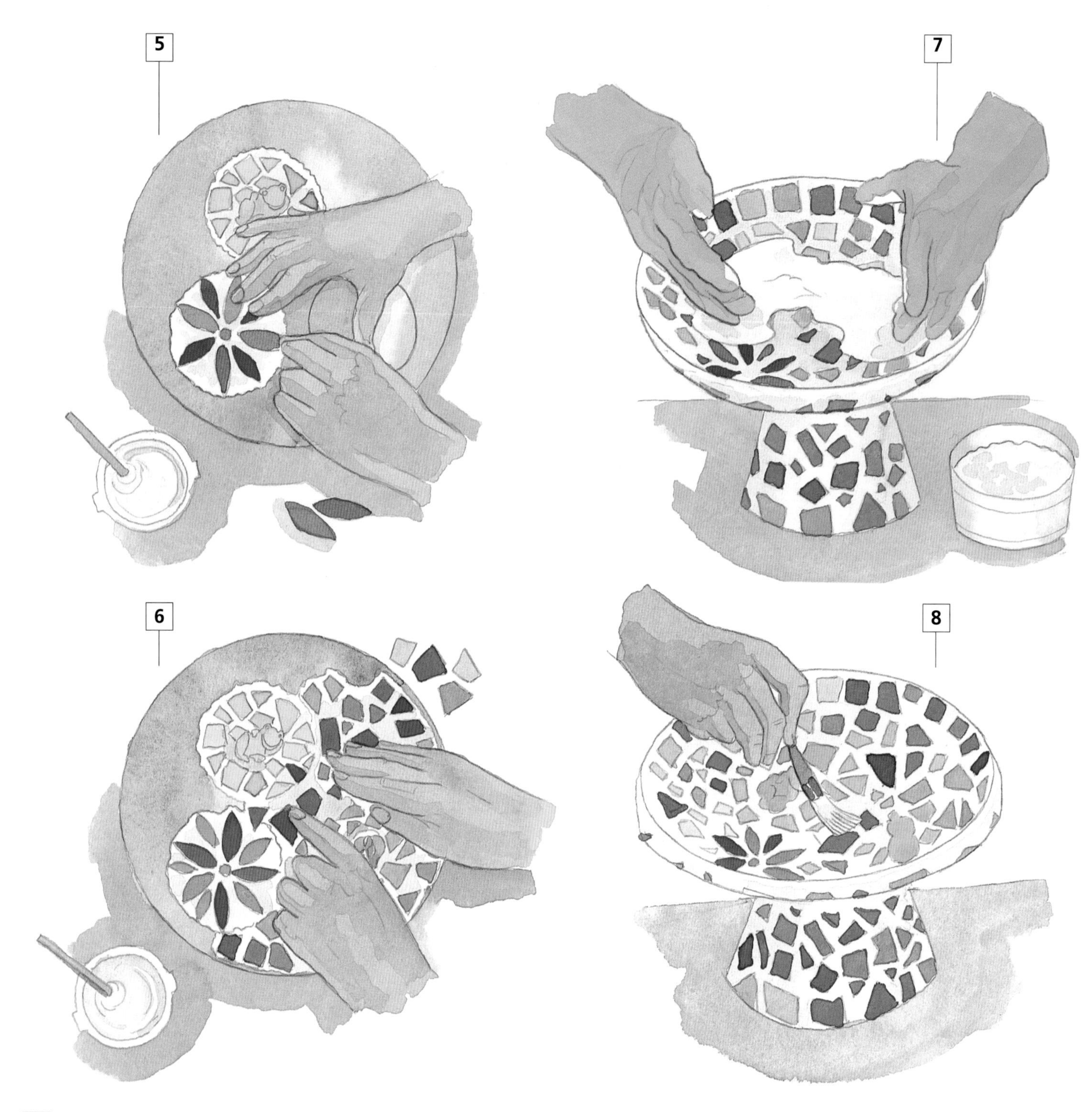

5 Next spread a thin layer of mortar onto the water lily shape. Use your nippers to clip away at pieces of broken red tiles to fit into the flower pattern. Press the pieces of red tile into the mortar.

6 Fill in the rest of the basin with fragments of blue tiles to look like water. Next mosaic the underside of the basin and then the pedestal portion with fragments of assorted blue tiles. Allow the birdbath to dry undisturbed for at least forty-eight hours before grouting.

7 Prepare and carefully apply the grout while wearing rubber gloves. The full procedure is given on pages 30-32. Be sure to fill every space between the fragments. As the grout begins to set, wipe the excess from the fragments and then allow the grout to dry for about twenty minutes. Vigorously buff off the remaining chalky haze with a clean dry rag. Allow to air dry for another forty-eight hours before applying grout sealer.

8 In order to make the birdbath completely weatherproof, brush the surface with two coats of grout sealer, a product available in any hardware or tile supply store.

Jar with Roses

TOOLS & MATERIALS

- Vase or pot
- 3 to 4 Porcelain flowers
- Assorted floral patterned china
- Stained glass (one color to coordinate with china)
- Mosaic or tile nippers
- T square
- Glass scorer
- Running pliers
- Protective eyewear
- Work gloves
- Household cement, epoxy resin, or other strong bonding adhesive
- Clear silicone or other clear quick-drying adhesive
- Ceramic tile adhesive
- Dull knife or spatula
- Masking tape
- Sanded grout (charcoal gray or color of your choice)
- Newspaper or scrap paper
- Rubber gloves
- Disposable container
- Stir stick
- Sponge
- Dry rag

Created by
Linda Oldham

tip

- Off-white grout, or another light color, will change this jar into a softer, more antique looking piece.
- Use small porcelain birds, butterflies, shells, or figurines instead of flowers.

Find a jar or pot to use as the base of your project. It can be made of glass, ceramic, or porcelain. If you choose a jar with a wide mouth, be sure you like what you see when you look inside! This nostalgic rose jar is reminiscent of grandma's house with the delicate floral china patterns and porcelain roses. This rim of this jar is trimmed with iridescent stained glass cut into small geometric rectangles. Scour your neighborhood garage sales, flea markets, and antique shops for china with floral patterns and porcelain flowers. A little goes a long way.

COLOR VARIATIONS

a Same pink roses, but white grout.
b As above, but very pale green grout.
c Try yellow roses and green leaves with white grout.
d As above, but pale yellow grout.

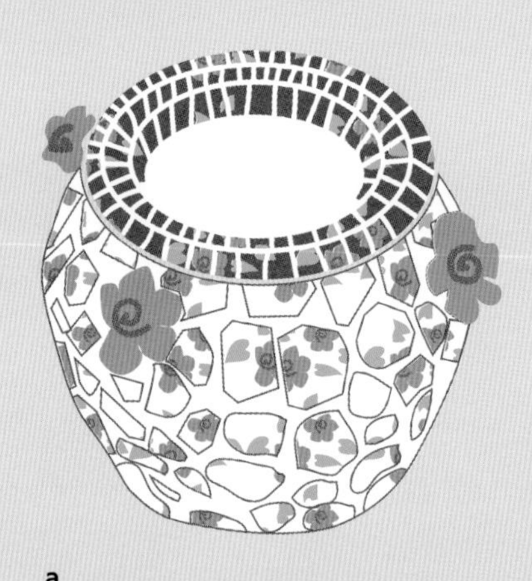

a

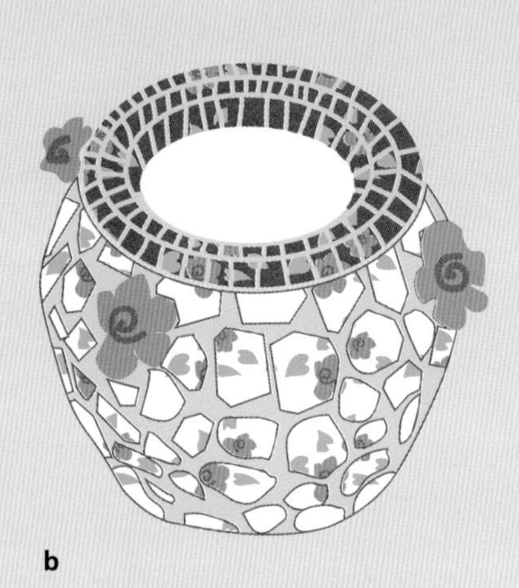

b

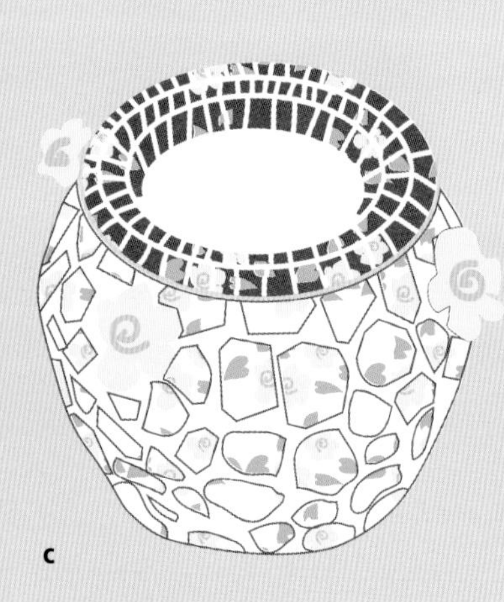

c

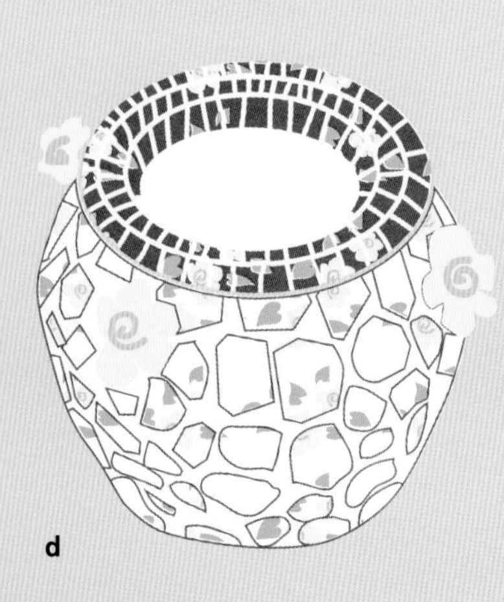

d

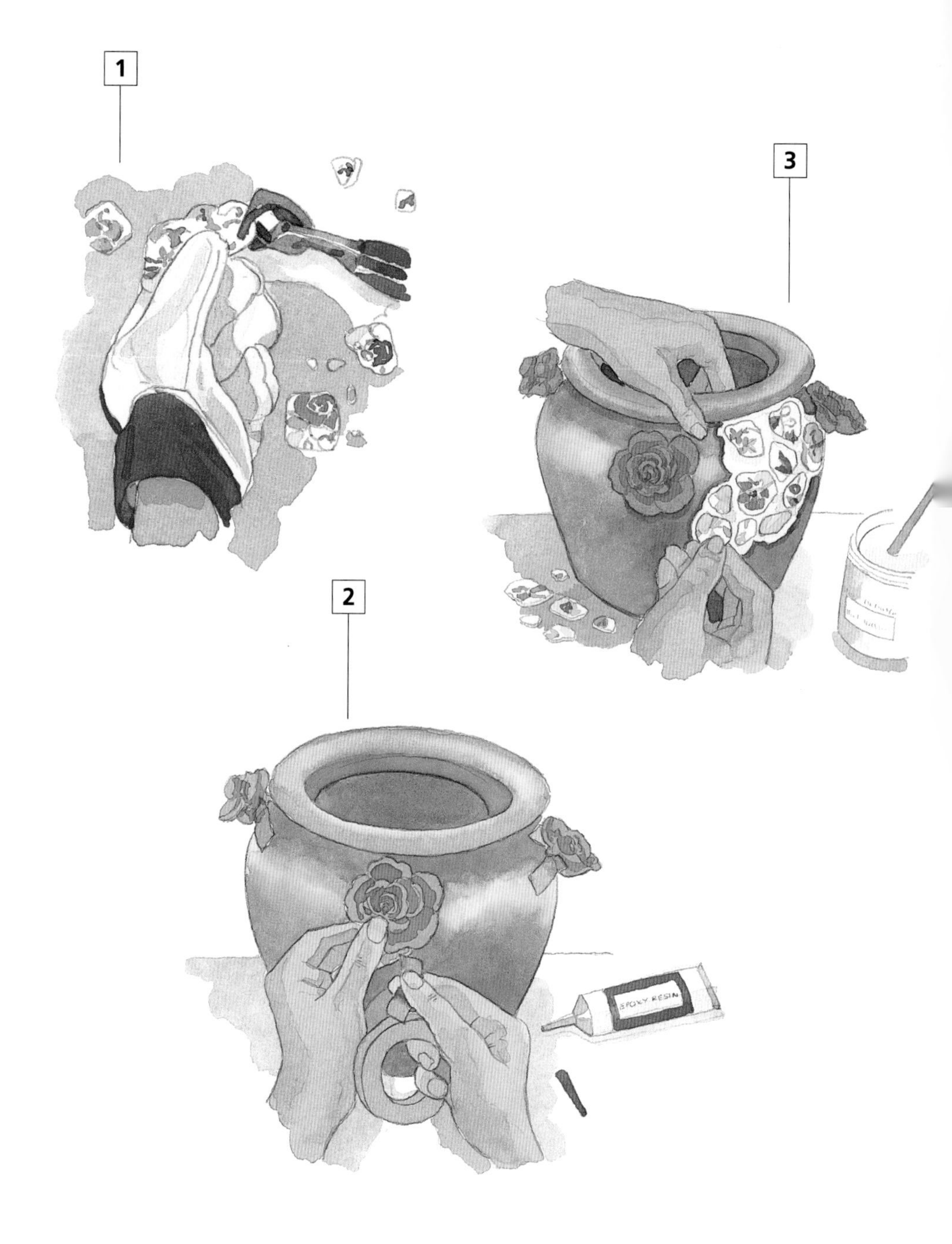

1 While wearing safety goggles and work gloves, clip your china into small pieces using the nippers. The porcelain flowers can be generally be dislodged intact if you are careful. Refer to page 000 for more detailed instructions on breaking and nipping, and always wear protective eyewear and work gloves to avoid injury from flying shards.

2 Using the T square as a guide, score the stained glass into strips approximately ¼ inch wide with the glass scorer. Snap the scored glass into strips with the running pliers. Clip each strip into small rectangles using your nippers.

3 Use the household cement, epoxy resin, or other strong bonding adhesive to adhere the porcelain flowers to the jar just beneath the rim. Tape each flower in place with masking tape and allow to air-dry for at least forty-eight hours.

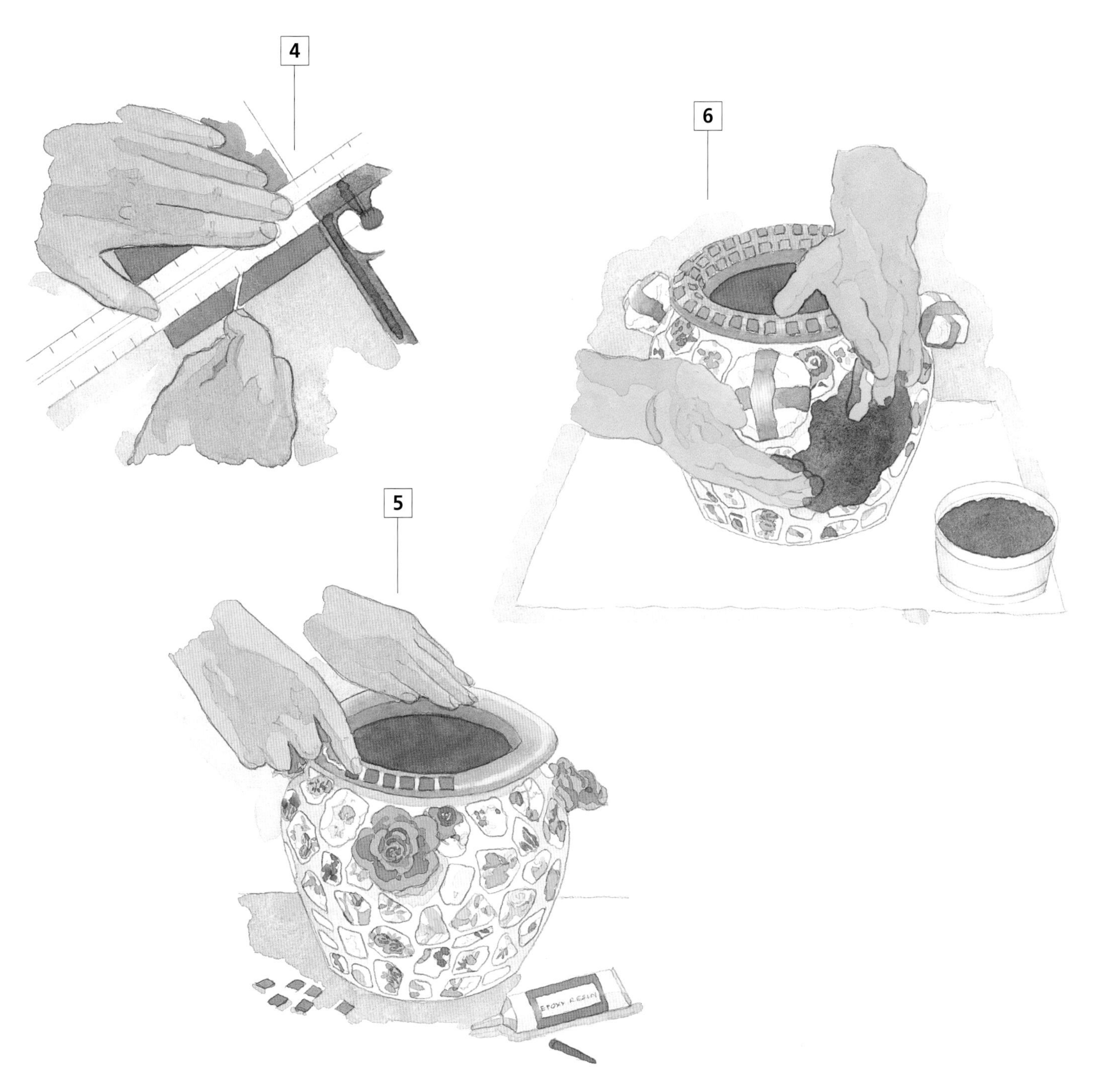

4 Using a dull knife or spatula, spread a thin layer of ceramic tile adhesive onto a small section of the jar. Press fragments of the broken floral china into the adhesive. Work section by section until the jar is completely covered with fragments. Remember that each fragment should fit comfortably into the space left by the surrounding pieces, so trim shards with your mosaic nippers when necessary. Be careful not to disturb the pieces you have already placed, as the ceramic tile adhesive will not be completely dry for forty-eight hours.

5 Affix the small stained glass rectangles to the rim of the jar with the clear silicone or another clear quick-drying adhesive. Feel free to use the same adhesive you used to attach the porcelain flowers to the pot. Squirt a bubble of adhesive onto the jar rim and use the tip of the applicator tube to spread it into a thin layer. Press pieces of glass into the wet adhesive. These types of adhesive dry very quickly, so only work on a small area at a time. Completely cover the rim, inside and out, and then allow the jar to dry undisturbed for forty-eight hours before grouting.

6 Use masking tape over scrap paper or newspaper to protect the porcelain flowers while grouting. The grout will not damage the flowers, but it can be difficult to clean from all the cracks and crevices. Place the floral jar on some old newspaper, and prepare your grout. While wearing rubber gloves, spread the grout onto the jar, covering it completely, as if you are icing a cake. Wipe off the excess grout and allow the jar to stand undisturbed for approximately twenty minutes. Buff the chalky haze with a dry cloth. Carefully remove the tape and paper from the porcelain flowers.

Key Box

TOOLS & MATERIALS

- Wooden box, approximately 10 inches x 12 inches with hinges on one side
- 1/4-inch round molding strips (optional)
- Miter box and saw (optional)
- Miniature cup hooks
- Cabinet magnet
- Hanging brackets or long screws
- White glue or waterproofing sealer
- Paintbrush
- Paint or wood stain
- Assorted dishes and tiles
- Mosaic or tile nippers
- Hammer
- Heavy paper bag
- Protective eyewear
- Work gloves
- Household cement, epoxy resin, or other strong bonding adhesive
- Ceramic tile adhesive
- Dull knife or spatula
- Sanded grout (blue or color of your choice)
- Newspaper or scrap paper
- Rubber gloves
- Disposable container
- Stir stick
- Sponge
- Dry rag

Created by
Tracy Graivier Bell

Inside this wooden box, which is hinged on one side, are a dozen miniature cup hooks for hanging all your keys. Find a wooden box to use as the key box base. You can purchase a ready-made box at most craft stores, or you can have one built out of plywood. You can attach hanging brackets on the back of the key box before you start the mosaic, or you can drive long screws right through the back of the box into the wall when the project is complete.

BEFORE YOU START

A box is an excellent choice for a mosaic project. The sides are flat, making it an easy surface on which to work. Find a box with a lid to use as the base of your project. It can be made of heavy cardboard, wood, or hard plastic. Most craft stores and gift shops carry a good selection of inexpensive, sturdy, decorative boxes in a variety of shapes and sizes. Be careful not to choose a very small box or you will need to break and nip your dishes into tiny pieces. A box made of bits and pieces of broken treasures is a wonderful place to store treasured possessions.

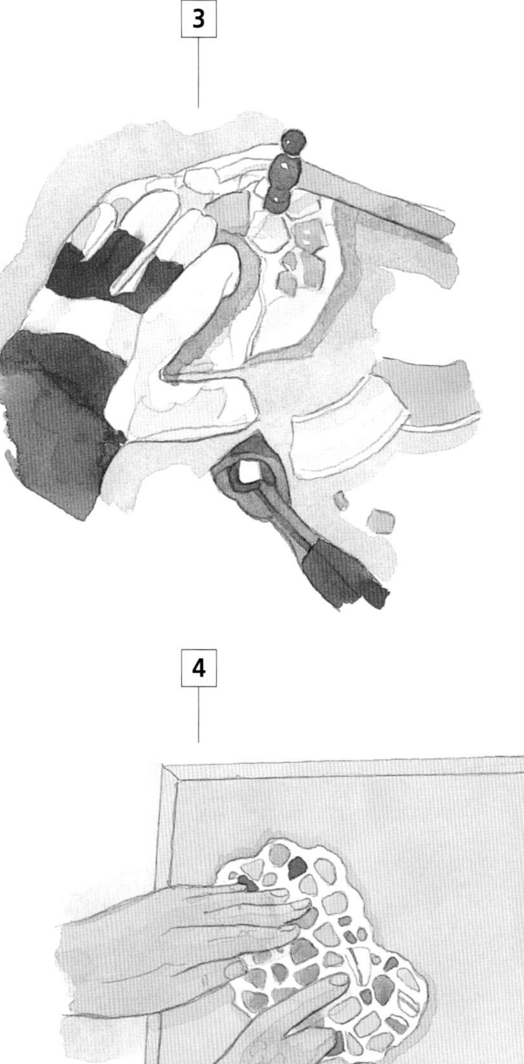

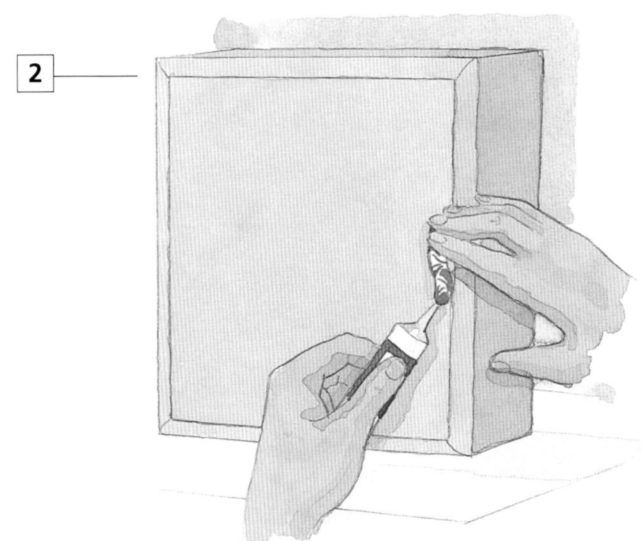

1 Although not required, ¼-inch round molding that has been cut in a miter box and glued onto the box top provides a durable frame and border for your mosaic. If the wood is raw, waterproof the box top by painting it with a mixture of white glue and water (one part glue to four parts water) or coating it with a commercial waterproofing sealer available at any hardware store.

tip

- Use old keys in the key box mosaic.
- Use old coins, nuts, and bolts, or even the face of an old watch.
- Try greens, yellows, and burnt oranges for the classic country kitchen feel.
- Black and white tesserae against gray grout make a bold statement in a contemporary hi-tech home.

2 Use the nippers to clip the dishes into small irregular shapes. Smash the tiles in a heavy paper or thick plastic bag with a hammer. Check the pieces frequently to see how you are doing. The broken pieces should range in size from ½ inch to 2 inches in diameter. Always wear protective eyewear and work gloves when nipping, breaking, or smashing to protect yourself from flying shards.

3 Find a handle for your key box that you can grasp easily. The lid of a teapot or the handle of a broken mug work well. Attach the handle to the key box door using household cement, epoxy resin, or another strong bonding adhesive. Allow this to dry well, as it needs to be strong enough to open and close the key box door on a daily basis.

4 Using a dull knife or spatula, spread a thin even layer of ceramic tile adhesive onto a small section of the key box door. Press the broken dishes and tiles into the adhesive. Work section by section until the door is completely covered with fragments. Remember that each fragment should fit comfortably into the space left by the surrounding pieces, so trim shards with your nippers when necessary. When the fragments are all in place, allow the mosaic to dry undisturbed for at least forty-eight hours before grouting.

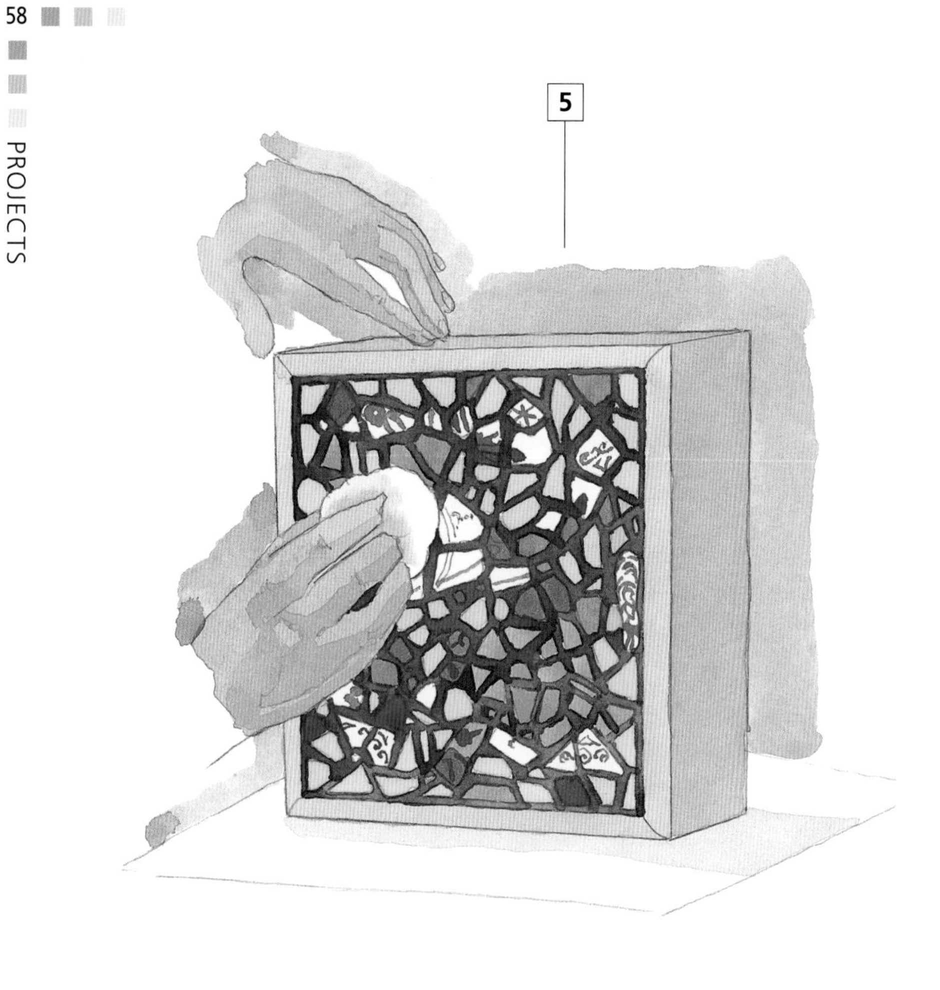

5 Prepare and carefully apply the grout while wearing rubber gloves. Be sure to fill every space between the fragments. As the grout begins to set, wipe the excess from the fragments and then allow the grout to dry for about twenty minutes. Vigorously buff the remaining chalky haze with a clean dry rag.

6 Tint the wood box with stain or watered-down acrylic paint (one part paint to two parts water), or use a clear varnish if you prefer natural wood. Screw the miniature cup hooks into the back of the interior of the box and the cabinet magnet onto the door. Then hang the key box on the wall.

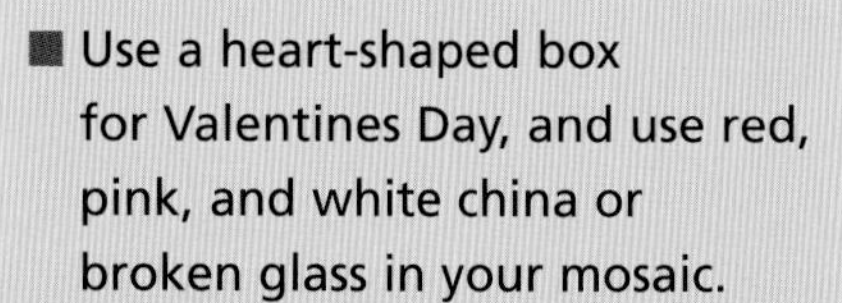

tip

- Boxes are great for mosaic because they come in so many shapes and sizes.
- Use a heart-shaped box for Valentines Day, and use red, pink, and white china or broken glass in your mosaic.
- Attach a teapot handle and spout on opposite sides of a round or oval box form to create a mosaic teapot box.

COLOR VARIATIONS

a Use shades of white and off white, incorporating many different textures and apply a very pale gray grout.
b Try blue, or blue and white with pale gray grout.
c Deep reds and russet browns will work well with dark terra cotta grout.
d Use blue and lilac with pink grout.

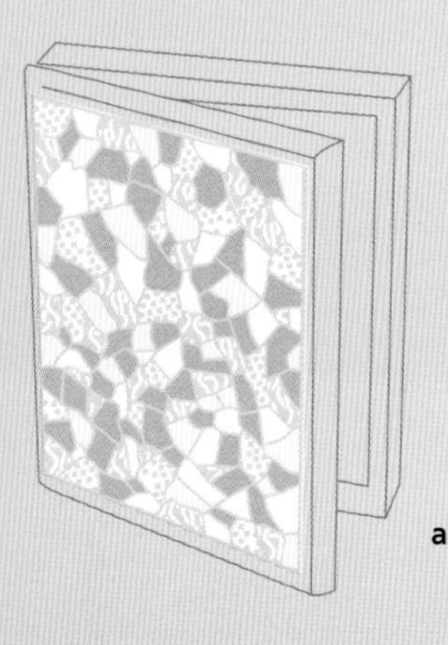
a

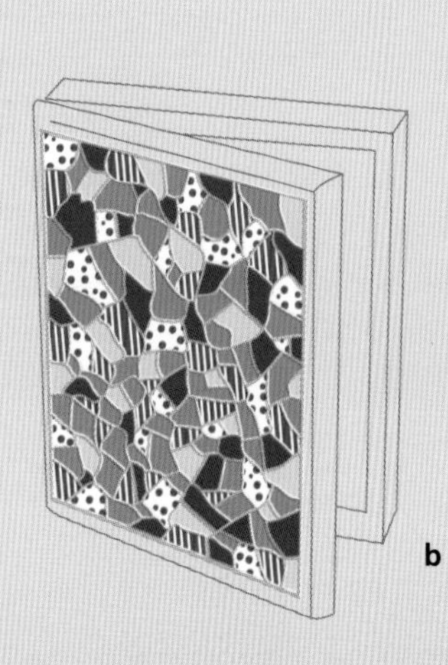
b

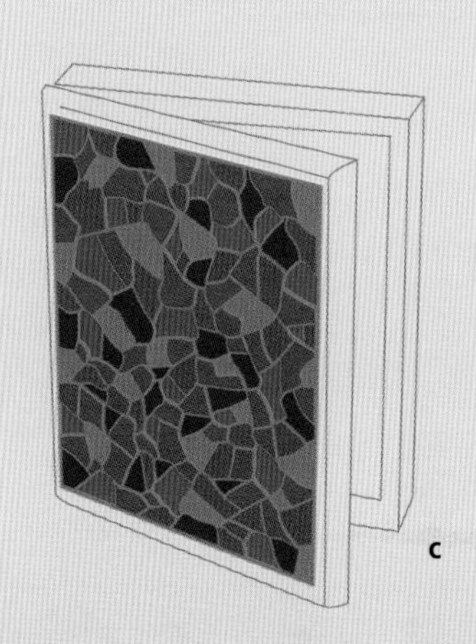
c

d

Gallery of boxes

1.

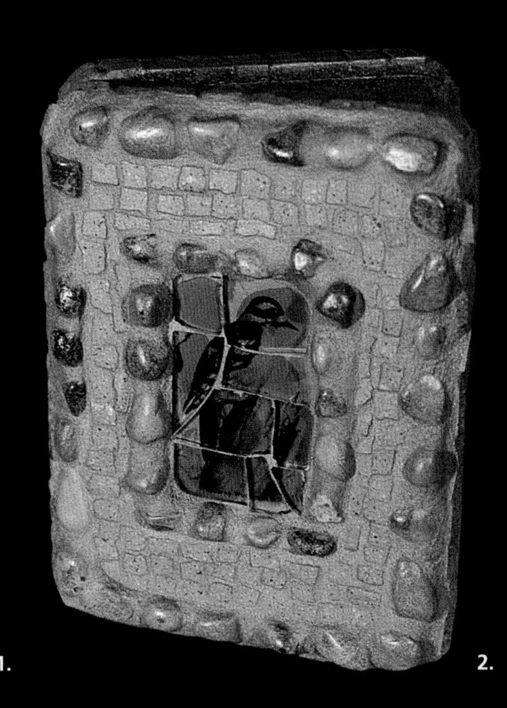

2.

3.

4.

1. Mary K. Guth, *Chance Box*. This stylish jester is created from plate shards, stone, and glass.
2. Mary K. Guth, *Bird II*. A similar theme to Number 3 but with a gentler natural feel, although the bird seems caged within the box.
3. A lighter style from the *Mosaicwares* designers, Rebecca Dennis and Paula Funt. The funky door handles include a boot and a bunch of grapes.
4. Mary K. Guth, *Chance Box*. The interior of the above image. A brightly colored invitation to take a gamble on the box.
5. Hap Sakwa. Gloriously colorful building blocks for the child within you.
6. Tracy Graivier Bell uses a three-dimensional item, toy clogs, and a cup-handle lid handle to give her box added visual appeal.

5.

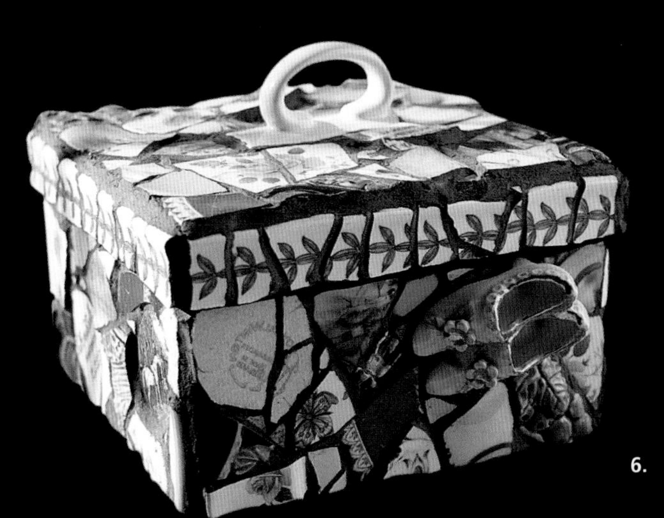

6.

Light Fixture

- Use reflective mirror glass for a retro disco-era look.
- Use pink, mauve, and blush-colored glass for a young girl's room.
- Use dark green glass to create the feel of a billiard parlor.

tip

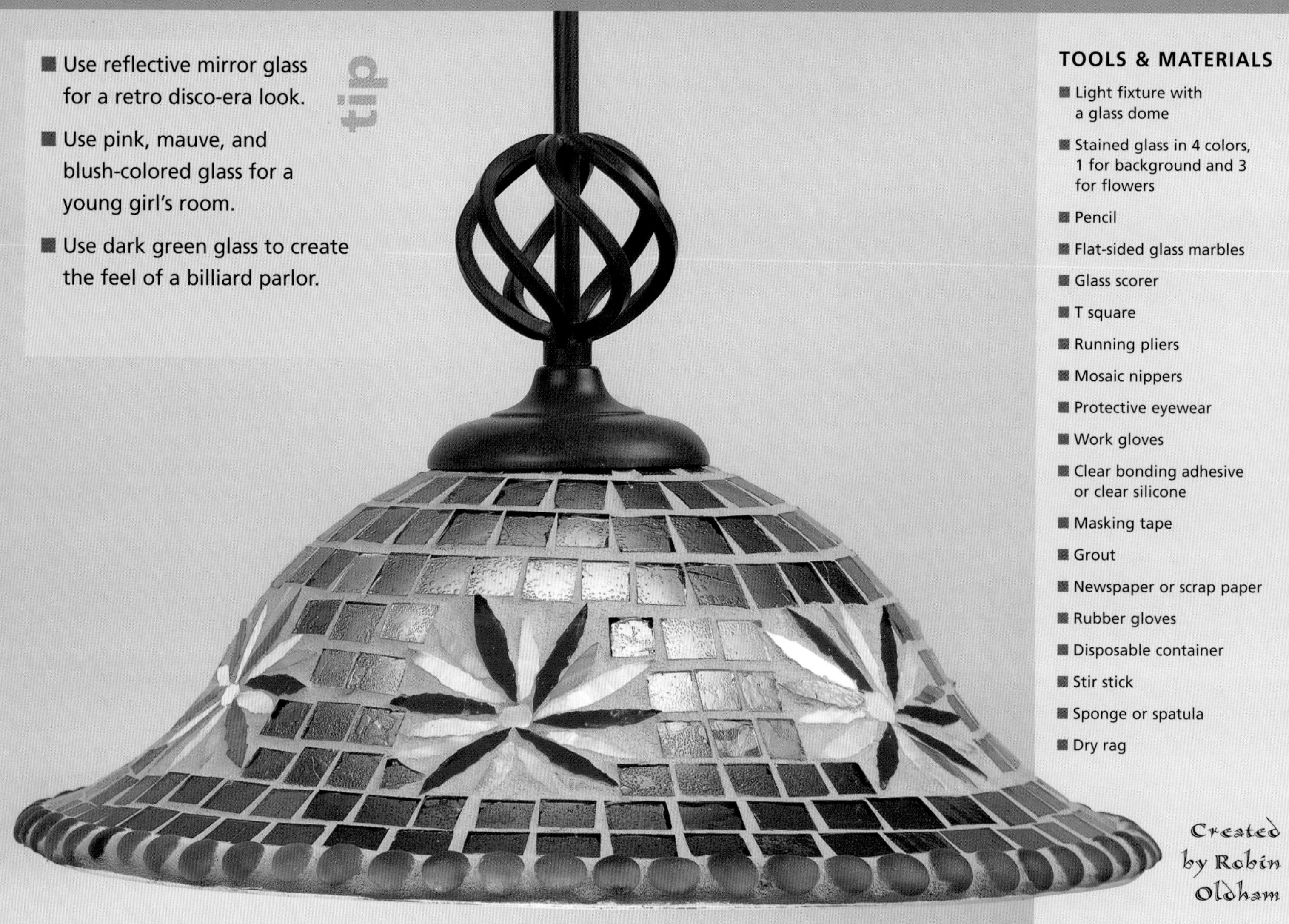

Created by Robin Oldham

TOOLS & MATERIALS

- Light fixture with a glass dome
- Stained glass in 4 colors, 1 for background and 3 for flowers
- Pencil
- Flat-sided glass marbles
- Glass scorer
- T square
- Running pliers
- Mosaic nippers
- Protective eyewear
- Work gloves
- Clear bonding adhesive or clear silicone
- Masking tape
- Grout
- Newspaper or scrap paper
- Rubber gloves
- Disposable container
- Stir stick
- Sponge or spatula
- Dry rag

A warm glow of light radiates through this elegant light fixture, which is constructed from translucent stained glass. The mixture of geometric square tesserae with free-form flower petals provides an interesting design contrast. The ring of flat-sided glass marbles around the bottom is a whimsical addition. This fixture should be hung low so that it can be seen from all viewpoints.

BEFORE YOU START

Find a light fixture with a clear or frosted glass dome. Remove the glass dome from the electrical fixture. Place the decorative metal washer that fits on the dome of the fixture in place, and use a pencil to draw a line around it. This line will serve as the guiding border to show you where to begin placing your glass tiles.

CUTTING YOUR TILES

Using the T Square as a straight edge, score the stained glass for the background into 1/2" (12 mm) squares with the glass scorer. Snap the pieces along the score lines with the running pliers. Nibble away at the other three colors of stained glass with your mosaic nippers to form petals and leaves. The size of your glass dome will determine how many flowers will fit on the fixture. Always wear protective eyewear and work gloves while scoring, breaking, and nipping glass to avoid injury from tiny glass shards.

COLORWAYS

a Classic reds and greens for a formal look
b Funky orange and purple, ideal for the kids
c Summery seaside yellows and blues
d Oranges and reds reminiscent of the Fall

a

b

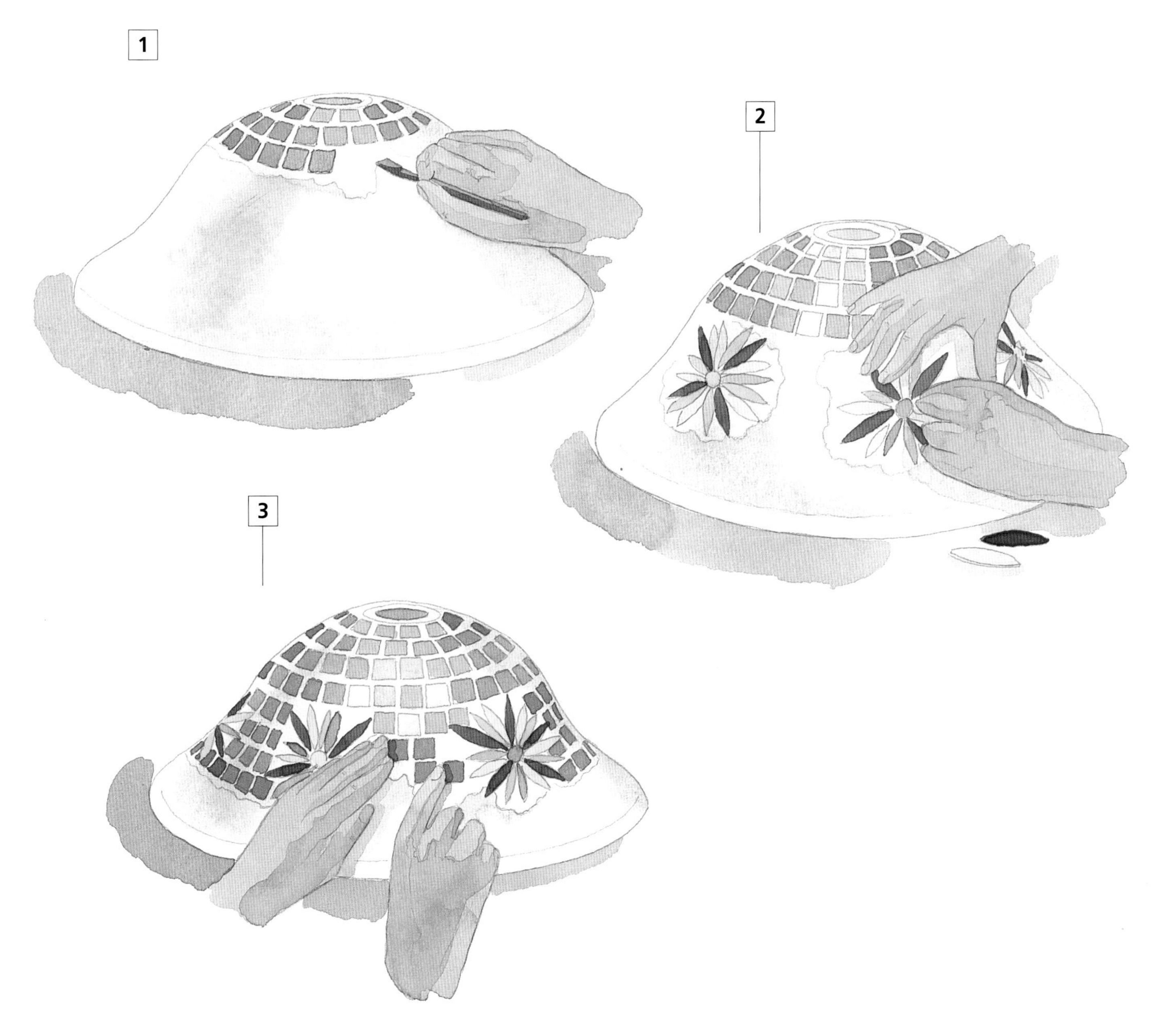

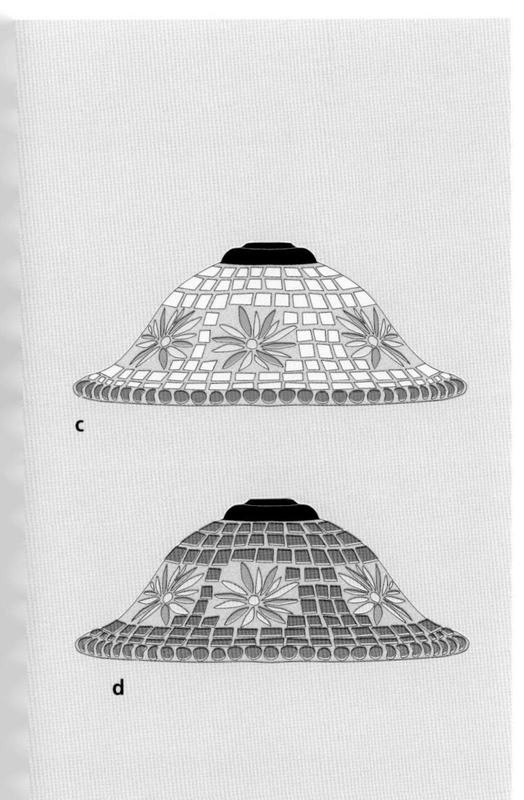

1 Begin at the top of the dome by squirting a bubble of clear bonding adhesive or clear silicone just beneath the circular pencil border you have drawn. Use the tip of the applicator tube to spread the adhesive into a thin layer. These adhesives dry very quickly, so only attempt to cover a small area at a time. Place the glass squares on the fixture in rows, leaving small spaces between each for grout. Work around the fixture from top to bottom for four rows.

2 Adhere flower petals to the fixture using the same method as in Step 3. Be sure to spread enough adhesive between the stained glass and the dome to form a solid bond so that the grout will not seep between the two and weaken the bond.

3 Fill in spaces between each flower with glass squares. You will not be able to fit squares between each flower petal, but these small areas will eventually be filled in with grout.

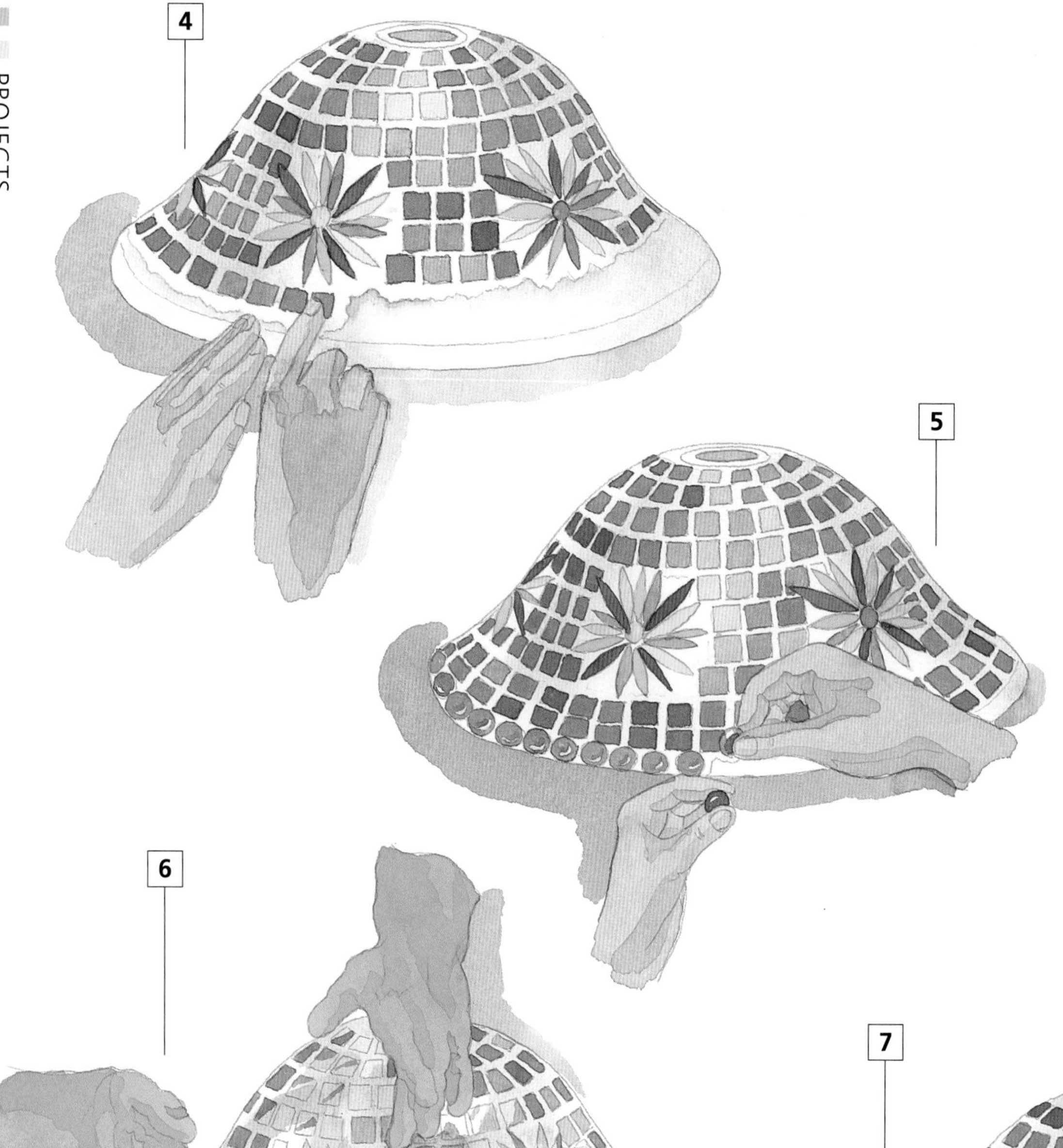

glass mosaic tiles

Vitreous glass is good for beginners. because it is thin, flat, and easy to cut. The uppermost side is smooth and flat, the underside is rippled for adhesion. As with ceramic, the usual way to cut glass titles is to quarter-cut them using nippers to nibble away the edges. Glass can be quartered in the same way as ceramic. Place the nippers on the edge of the piece and squeeze gently. After cutting glass, do not sweep up fragments with your fingers, because the shards are sharp and dangerous.

4 Add two more rows of glass squares below the flowers.

5 Glue the flat-sided marbles onto the dome to create a ring of colored gems around the bottom. These marbles are weighty, so you may need to secure them with masking tape while allowing them to dry. Leave to dry for at least one day before grouting.

6 While wearing rubber gloves, spread the prepared grout onto the fixture without going above the pencil border. The grout not only holds all of the glass in place, but it also gives definition to the piece. Fill every space between the glass pieces and the marbles.

7 Wipe the excess grout from the glass and then allow the grout to dry for about twenty minutes. Wipe off the remaining chalky haze with a clean dry rag and buff the glass pattern until clean and polished.

Gallery of lamps

1.

2

3.

1. Hap Sakwa's piece looks like a theater award, bringing together the classic and the kitsch.

2 and 4. Two pretty, homey designs from Rebecca Dennis and Paula Funt

3. The textured shade and pale grout highlight Tracy Graivier Bell's strikingly effective use of three-dimensional pieces.

4.

Candle Holder Glass Squares

TOOLS & MATERIALS

- Glass cylinder
- Stained glass in assorted colors
- Pencil
- Brown or white craft paper
- Scissors
- T square
- Glass scorer
- Running pliers
- Protective eyewear
- Work gloves
- Clear silicone or other clear quick-drying adhesive
- Sanded grout (dark gray or color of your choice)
- Newspaper or scrap paper
- Rubber gloves
- Disposable container
- Stir stick
- Sponge

Created by
Linda Oldham

A mosaic candle holder made of stained glass squares is a project that will allow you to practice scoring and breaking techniques before moving on to a larger and more complicated project like a light fixture or vase. Choose a clear glass cylinder to use as the base of your project. It can be a kitchen tumbler or drinking glass, or it can be a cylindrical flower vase of any height or diameter. Experiment with colors and patterns to achieve different effects.

- Create a series of candle holders to line up along a windowsill of fireplace
- Design a checkerboard candle using red and black or translucent and black glass squares.
- Use red and green for a Christmas theme, or blue and white for Chanukah.

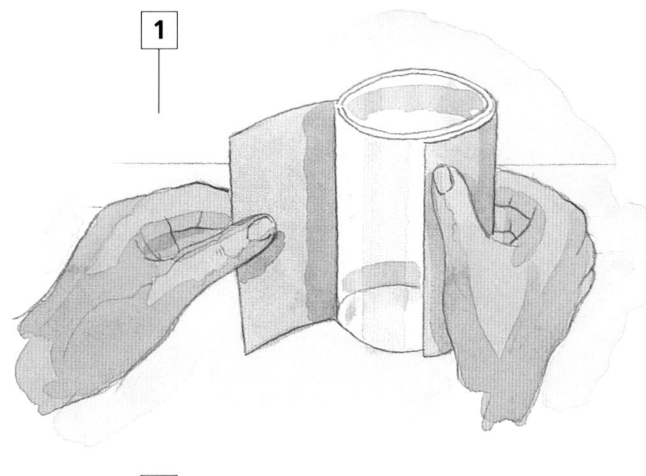

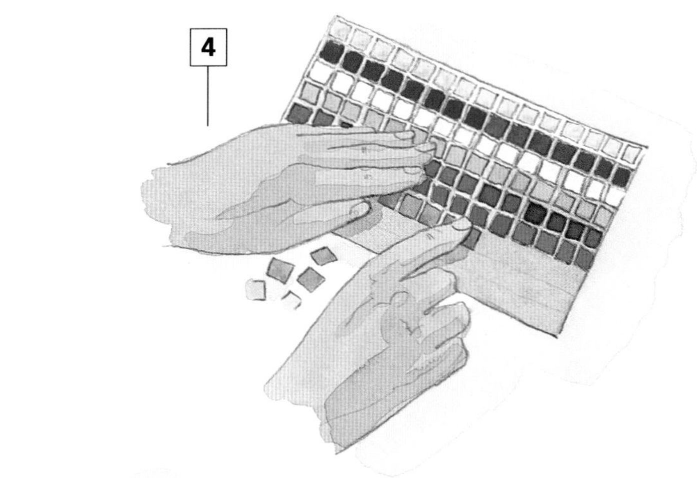

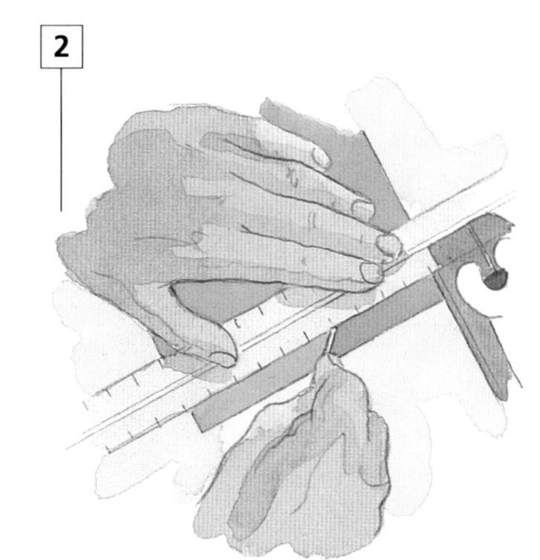

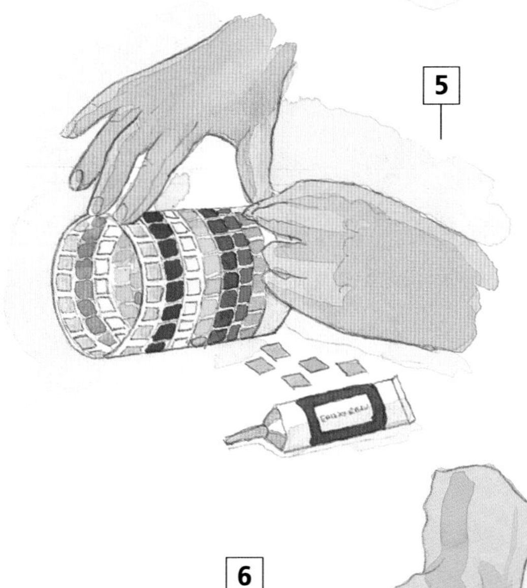

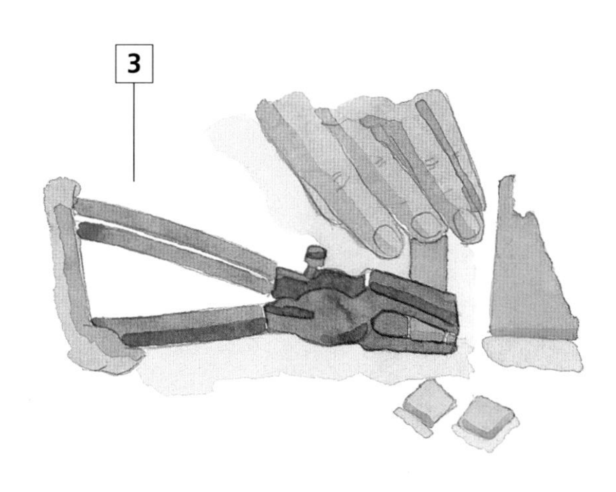

1 Create a paper pattern of the cylinder out of the craft paper by wrapping it around then laying it flat..

2 Score the stained glass into ½ inch strips using your T square as a guide. Adjust the glass a quarter turn, and score it again into squares. While wearing safety goggles and work gloves, snap the glass into strips using the running pliers.

3 Pick up each strip, and use the running pliers to snap it along the score lines into squares.

4 Arrange the squares on the craft paper in rows, leaving approximately ⅛ inch between each for grout. You can create a color design row by row, or you can place the squares by random color onto the pattern.

5 Drop a small bubble of clear adhesive onto the cylinder, and use the tip of the applicator tube to spread it into a thin layer. The adhesive will dry very quickly, so only cover a small section at a time. Be sure to cover the area completely so the grout does not seep under the glass during the grouting process. Press the squares onto the cylinder, and hold them in place for a few seconds until they are secure. Work around the cylinder until you have covered it completely. Allow to dry for twenty-four hours.

6 Place the cylinder on some paper or old newspaper, and prepare your grout. While wearing rubber gloves, apply the grout with your fingers. Wipe off the excess and allow your candleholder to stand undisturbed for approximately twenty minutes. Buff with a dry cloth.

Olive Branch Pot

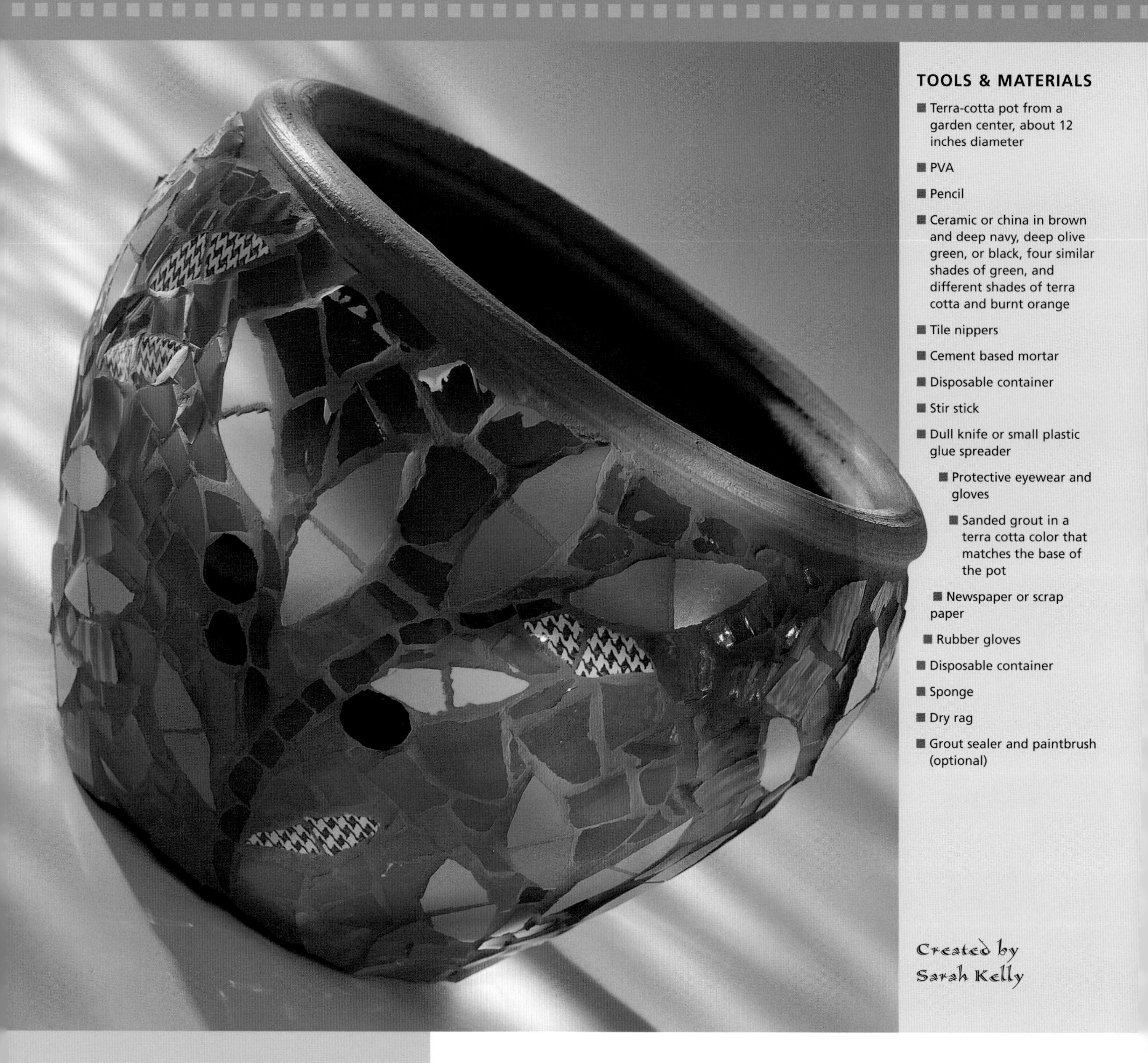

TOOLS & MATERIALS

- Terra-cotta pot from a garden center, about 12 inches diameter
- PVA
- Pencil
- Ceramic or china in brown and deep navy, deep olive green, or black, four similar shades of green, and different shades of terra cotta and burnt orange
- Tile nippers
- Cement based mortar
- Disposable container
- Stir stick
- Dull knife or small plastic glue spreader
- Protective eyewear and gloves
- Sanded grout in a terra cotta color that matches the base of the pot
- Newspaper or scrap paper
- Rubber gloves
- Disposable container
- Sponge
- Dry rag
- Grout sealer and paintbrush (optional)

Created by
Sarah Kelly

A mosaic by Antonío Gaudi in the Guell Colony Crypt in Barcelona inspired this design of green fronds and rich, dark olives on a background of burnt orange and terra cotta. This pot will give a lovely Mediterranean atmosphere to a garden or conservatory.

BEFORE YOU START

If the pot is rough and unglazed, prime it with a mixture of PVA and water (one part glue to four parts water) or coat it with a commercial waterproofing sealer available at any hardware store, so that the pot will not absorb excess moisture from the adhesive.

Don't use any tesserae material that has any strong or contrasting patterns, as these will interfere with the design of the olive branches. Try to keep any different colors quite close to each other in tone so that the contrast is not too glaring when you change from color to color around the pot.

1. Draw the olive branch design on with a pencil. If you are not sure of your design, practice drawing a few experimental fronds on a piece of paper first, then copy them onto the pot when you are happy with them.

2. Begin by cutting out a series of long, thin tesserae in brown with the nippers, wearing the protective gloves and eyewear as you work. Then cut out some circles for the olives,

1

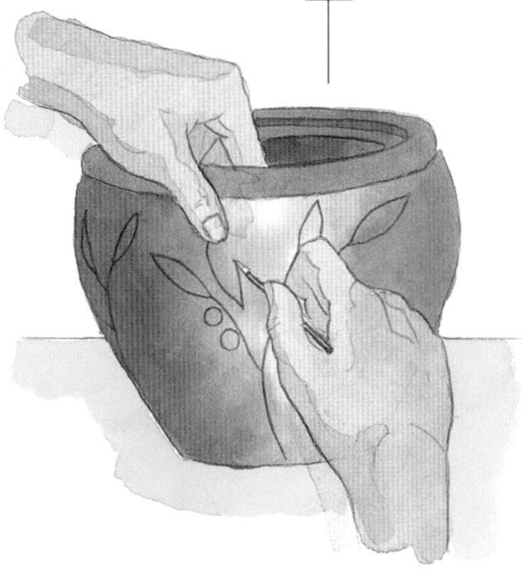

3

5

2

4

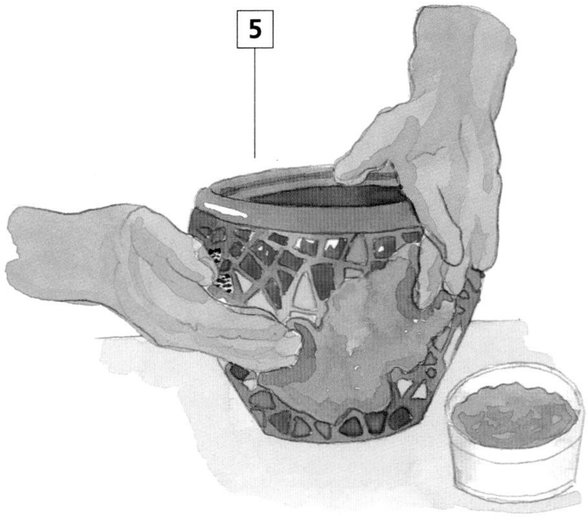

6

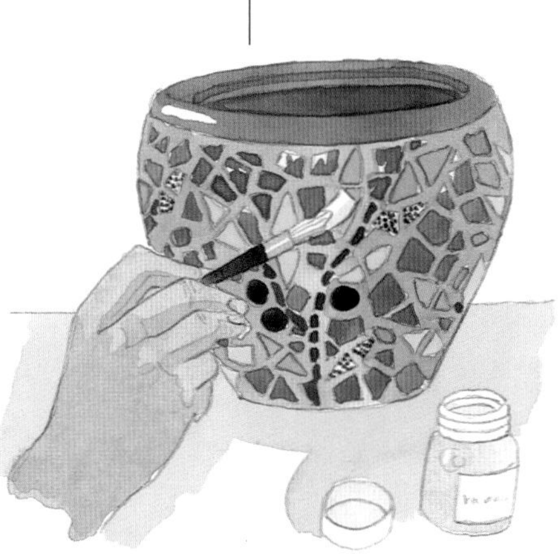

roughly 1¼ inches in diameter, from the navy, dark green, or black, then finally nibble some leaf shapes from the four different shades of green.

3 Mix the adhesive in the container with water and a spoonful of PVA for extra strength. Apply it with a knife or glue spreader to the line of one of your branches to a depth of about ⅛ inch and push in the thin brown tesserae. Add the leaves and olives to the branch in the same way. Mix the leaf colors as you go. You may need to break the longer leaf shapes into halves or thirds to accommodate the curve of the pot. Do one branch at a time and work around the pot.

4 When you have finished every branch, begin breaking up your selection of terracotta and orange-colored ceramics. Apply a layer of adhesive to a small area of the pot base, working from the edges of one branch to the next. Choose one of your shades and lay down a group of tesserae (about ten to twenty pieces). As you change color intersperse the odd tessera in the previous color with the new color at the beginning of each area. Take the mosaic right up to the underside of the top rim of the pot and leave a small space uncovered at the bottom, so that the tesserae don't run the risk of being dislodged when the pot is moved around.

5 Leave the finished mosaic to dry naturally for forty-eight hours. Put on the rubber gloves and mix up the waterproof grout with the coloring agent and water in the container. A good pale terra cotta is made by combining white grout with a mixture of brick and buff colored powders in quite large amounts. Try to match the color of your pot's base, remembering that the grout itself will look a lot lighter when it is dry. Rub the grout over your mosaic with your hands or your chosen tool, making sure all the gaps are filled.

6 Wipe off the excess with a dampened sponge and the remaining chalky haze with the dry rag after fifteen to twenty minutes. Remove any grout from the rim or the inside of your pot. Paint over two coats of grout sealer if you are going to put your pot outside.

Inspiration from nature

1. *Crevice* by Sonia King mirrors the shapes of mountain chasms and gorges.
2. Rebecca Dennis and Paula Funt use a natural base object shape to create decorative fruit.
3. King's flowing use of tesserae heightens the watery feel of her *Riverscape*.
4. Mary K. Guth creates a striking rose image from a shattered picture.
5. Philip Danzig's rampant lion is a powerful heraldic image.
6. *Primeval* by Sonia King, taken from rock strata with echoes of the primordial soup.

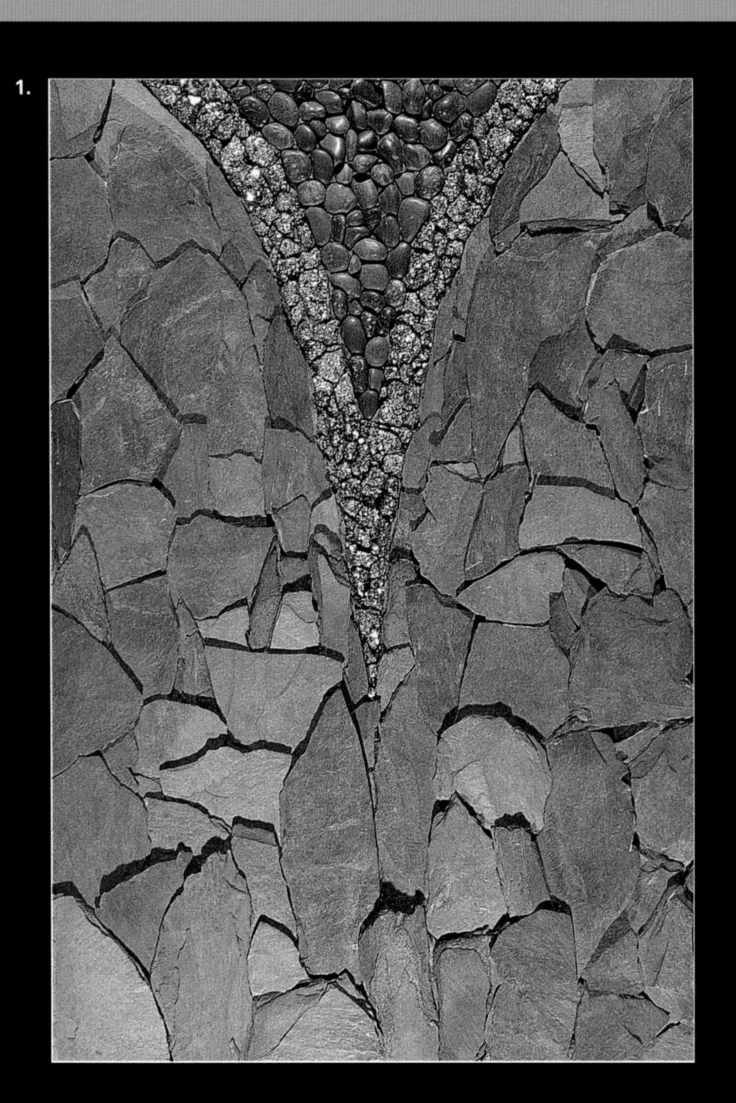

1.

2.

3.

4.

5.

6.

Mirror Fish

TOOLS & MATERIALS

- MDF or marine plywood between $^1/_2$ and 1 inch thick
- Jigsaw (optional)
- Mirror
- Clear and blue glass the same depth as the mirror
- Approximately thirty glass gems (clear and blue 'marble' style)
- One blue glass gem
- Sheets of silver and gold (or faux silver and gold) leaf
- Ceramic tile adhesive
- Piece of paper (14 x 10 inches)
- Pencil
- Tile or glass nippers
- Small spatula
- Protective eyewear
- Work gloves
- Picture hooks
- Newspaper or scrap paper
- Gray sanded grout
- Disposable container
- Rubber gloves
- Stir stick
- Dull knife
- Sponge
- Dry rag

Created by
Sarah Kelly

Extend the range of your mosaics by using a specifically cut base to decorate. If you don't want to use a jigsaw yourself, a friendly lumber merchant may do it for a small charge. This simple leaping fish shape is decorated with mirror, glass, and gems to mimic the effect of glittering scales and looks truly fabulous as it flashes in the light.

BEFORE YOU START

Prepare your glass and gems at least a day before you start work on the fish, as they need time to dry. Use the nippers to cut out two small sections of clear glass and a larger section of blue glass. Apply a thin layer of PVA or clear glue to one side only, making sure the surface is thoroughly covered. Stick the blue glass and one of the pieces of clear glass onto a sheet of silver leaf, then stick the remaining piece of clear glass onto a sheet of gold leaf. Do the same with the gems, dividing them fairly equally between the gold and silver. If you can't get hold of any marble-style gems, just use clear ones. Leave to dry until the white glue becomes clear.

Copy (or photocopy and enlarge) the fish design onto a piece of paper. The size of the fish is approximately 13 inches from nose to point of back fin and 9 inches from there to the point of the tail. Then, using the paper copy as a template, cut the fish shape out of the wood with a jigsaw (or get a lumber cutter to do it for you). Prime the surface of the fish, including the sides, with a mixture of PVA and water (one part glue to four parts water or according to manufacturer's instructions) and leave to dry.

TO HANG YOUR FISH

Screw picture hooks into the back of the fish, having first decided which angle they should be at to ensure the best hanging position for your fish. If your wood is quite thick and the mosaic very heavy, you may need to use mirror plates instead. You could try making other fish in slightly different sizes and hang them together to make a stunning shoal for a bathroom or children's room.

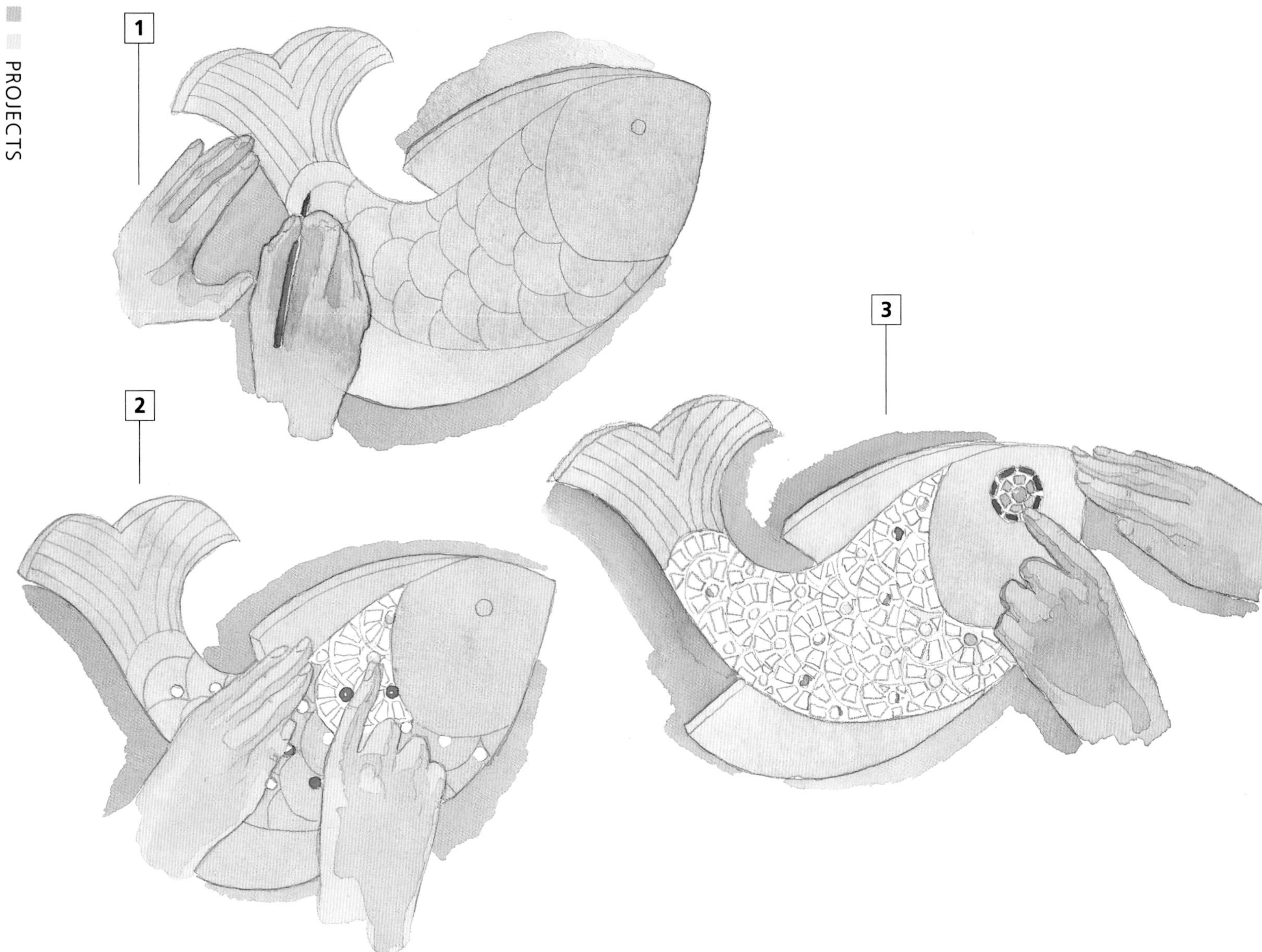

1 Use a pencil to draw the head, tail, and fins on the fish and to mark a position for the eye. On the body section, draw a series of fairly large overlapping scales following the curve of the fish's body and end in a single scale by the tail.

2 With the ceramic tile adhesive, stick a gem at the center of each scale on the first and second rows nearest the head. Put on the protective gloves and eyewear and use the nippers to cut random squares from the mirror to fit perfectly round the gem within each scale. To get these squares to fit a curve, you will have to nibble them so they are slightly wider at the top than the bottom, with the fattest part fitting against the widest part of the curve. Stick them down with tile adhesive, making any slight alterations to the position of the gems if necessary. Repeat this process along the rest of the body, making the tesserae bigger as the scales get fatter. Alternate the gold and silver gems as well as the clear and marble ones to add sparkle.

3 Stick down the blue glass gem for the eye, and surround it with a thin line of gold glass tesserae cut into small rectangles. Again, nibble the bottom edges away to shape the tesserae neatly around the curve of the gem. Do the same again with a second, thinner band of blue tesserae around the gold.

4 Cut lots of tiny little circles out of the gold and silver glass as well as a few from the mirror and the blue glass. They should be no more than ½ inch in diameter. Apply the adhesive to the surface of the fish's head, and stick the gold and silver circles in groups to give the effect of changing light on fish scales. Intersperse the odd individual or small patch of mirror circles amongst the silver and gold, as well as including a few random blue ones near the mouth of the fish.

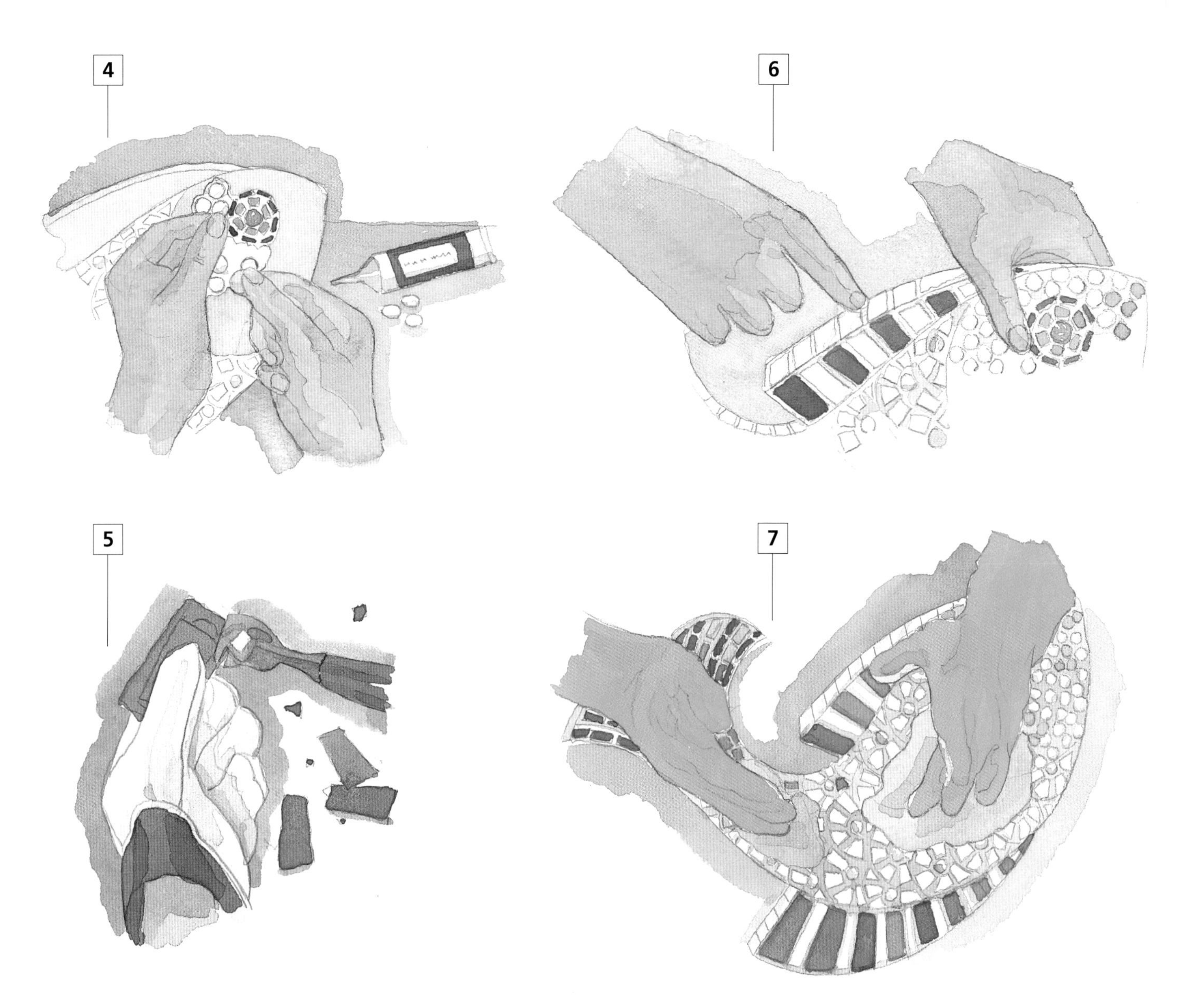

5 When the head is fully covered, move on to the fins and tail. For the fins, use alternating shapes of blue glass and mirror. To help you get these accurate, cut a strip with the nippers or glass cutter which will fit roughly over the area of fin you want to cover and place it over. Mark the exact shape you will need to cut on the glass with a washable pen, then nibble it into shape with the nippers. Cut each piece in order and then stick them down, alternating thick blue stripes with thin mirror ones. For the tail, cut tiny rectangular tesserae out of the blue glass and mirror, roughly 1½ inches long and ½ inch wide. Apply the tile adhesive over the tail area and lay a line of blue tesserae down one side of the tail, nibbling them if necessary to ensure a good fit. Repeat at the other side of the tail and then continue working inwards in this way, alternating the blue with the mirror. Try to gauge it so that your central and final line is not the same as either of the lines beside it.

6 Complete the fish by cutting mirror tesserae to fit around the sides. Make sure their tops lie just parallel with, or just under the top and bottom of, the fish. If any stick up past these lines they will interfere with the both the look of the mosaic and the fitting of the fish to the wall when it is hung. Apply a good bed of adhesive to the sides and stick the tesserae down. You will need to use narrower tesserae on the parts that curve to ensure a really firm fit. Work outward from any tight corners, filling them first.

7 Wait forty-eight hours for the mosaic to dry before grouting. Put on rubber gloves and mix the grout according to the directions on pages 30-32. The grout should be quite a neutral color so that it doesn't distract from the impact of the tesserae. Rub the grout in with your hands or knife, not forgetting to do the sides. Rub the grout into the spaces between the sides and the top and bottom of the mosaic as well. Wipe off the excess with a damp sponge, leaving the grout fairly intact between the top and sides to give a smooth, neat finish. Wait fifteen to twenty minutes for the grout to dry before carefully polishing with a dry rag.

Gallery of tableau

1.

4.

2.

3.

5.

1. Sonia King's *Watershed* uses a fountain-like flow of rainbow tesserae to create a feeling of motion.
2. In Sarah Kelly's *Balinese Girl* she uses three-dimensional tesserae to give depth to the headdress.
3. Phillip Danzig incorporates the Star of David in his candles' glow.
4. The tesserae add to the feathered effect in Sarah Kelly's *Owl*.
5. Hap Sakwa uses recognizable Hollywood icons in this Americana piece.

Teapot

TOOLS & MATERIALS

- Strong ceramic teapot
- Assorted plates, cups, bowls, or tiles in pinks and oranges, patterned and plain
- As above, with flower motifs in a variety of sizes
- Mosaic or tile nippers
- Protective eyewear and gloves
- Washable ink felt pen
- Ceramic tile adhesive or PVA
- Small plastic glue spreader
- White grout
- Grey grout
- Red grout coloring or acrylic paint
- Newspaper or scrap paper
- Rubber gloves
- Disposable container
- Stir stick
- Sponge
- Dry rag
- Container or small bucket

Created by
Sarah Kelly

BEFORE YOU START

Scour bargain shops and markets for a sturdy, attractively shaped teapot. The mosaic design can be adapted or simplified if you choose one that's a different shape to the one shown here. Fine bone china ones are not really suitable, as they might not be able to support the weight of the mosaic. The teapot needs to be smooth, flat, and simple without fussy details.

A picture of a brightly-colored piece of patterned fabric from India inspired the decoration on this slender, elegant teapot. Although no longer a functional teapot, it could nevertheless join a treasured collection of china or make an unusual ornament or vase for a vivid bunch of flowers.

1 Draw the design onto one side of your teapot with the felt pen. This basic design consists of an oval shape in the center with four petals coming from it. The remaining spaces contain a little "border" to the central oval and are then topped with a smaller flower medallion. The whole design is then enclosed in a teardrop. Make sure there is a space between the top of your teardrop and the top of the teapot. If you make a mistake, wipe it off with a damp rag and start again. If you're not sure whether this design will work, or you want to try out another one, practice first on a piece of paper, then copy it onto the teapot. Repeat the design on the other side.

2 Wearing the protective gloves and eyewear, cut out the flower designs from the plates, cups, or bowls with the tile nippers, then carefully nibble round them so you are left with flower medallions containing as little background as possible. Break some of the rest of the china into small tesserae to begin with, and break up more as you need it. Apply a coat of adhesive to your design. If you are using PVA allow it to become tacky. Choose a large, oval shaped flower medallion from your collection. To follow the curve of the side of the teapot, you will probably need to cut the medallion into quarters. Apply your chosen glue to each piece and stick it onto the center of your design. When this is firmly in place, work outward over the rest of the design using your own combination of pink and orange.

3 Once you have completed the design, nibble out a series of small circles in two similar shades of orange, or your chosen color. Apply a border of adhesive around the design and butter the nibbled circles with some more adhesive and then stick them down. Repeat the process on the other side.

4 When the designs on both sides are complete, mosaic the rest of the teapot (excluding the handle, spout, and lid) in pale pink or another light color, interspersing the pink tesserae with tiny flower medallions.

5 Choose some patterned china to decorate the handle, spout, and lid. Use the naturally beveled edges of your chosen plate, bowl, etc. around the outer edge of your lid to give a smooth finish. Use some more of the background color for the lid handle, topping it with a flower medallion big enough to sit comfortably over the edges of the tesserae round the outside. Use a series of flower medallions along the underside of the spout, starting with larger ones at the bottom and getting smaller towards the top. You may need to clip some of the larger ones into quarters to fit round the curves. If you have any beveled patterned edges left, use them round the top of the spout and work downward to cover the rest. If not, just use what you have.

6 For the handle, use some more of the background color. Stick large pieces down the outside of the handle and use smaller ones to cover the inside. This is quite difficult, but do persevere! Along the edges, which have now been widened by the addition of the tesserae top and bottom, glue strips of the patterned china, nipping them into tapering triangles where the spout meets the body of the teapot.

7 Allow the finished teapot to dry for at least forty-eight hours before grouting. Mix up a soft pink color by adding a small handful of gray grout to the white and then a little bit of red powder or red acrylic paint. Grout the lid and the pot separately and apply the grout carefully. Make sure that you work the grout into all the areas of the teapot. Smooth it round the top of the spout to give a neat finish. It may help to stick a piece of wadded tissue into the spout to stop any grout falling in. Carefully remove the excess grout with a sponge, using a smaller one to get into the difficult spaces. Wait fifteen to twenty minutes and then polish with a soft dry rag.

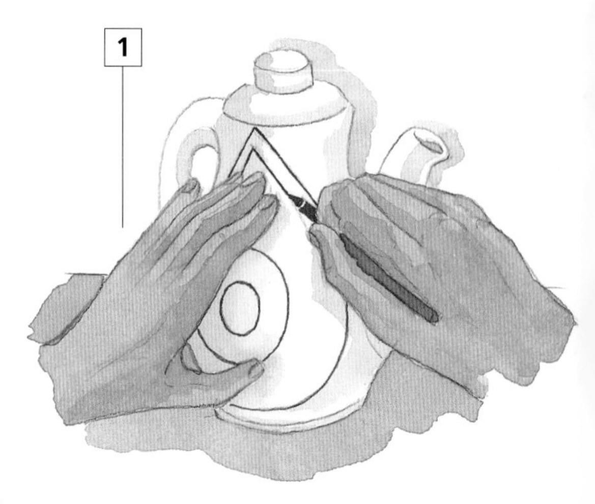

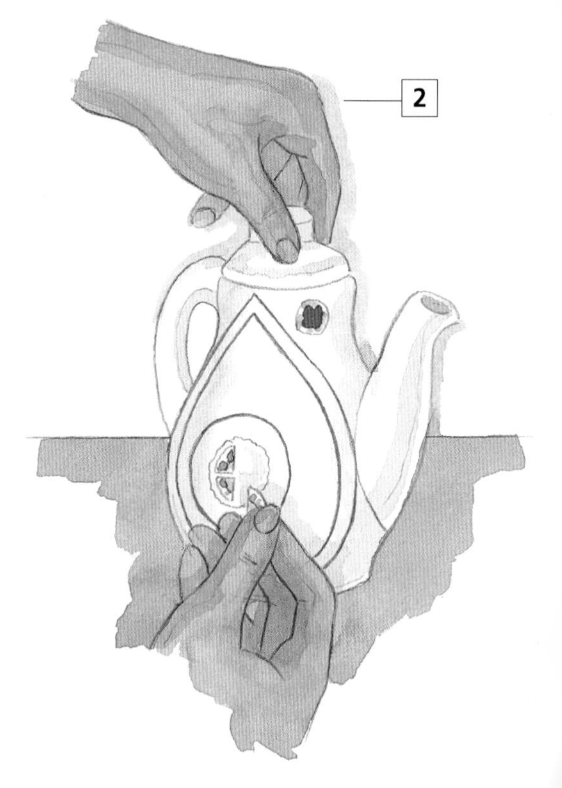

COLOR VARIATIONS

a Combine pale blue and primrose yellow, with maybe a little green, for a fresh, spring-like feel. Use pale yellow grout.
b Mix the pink with white instead of orange for a less exotic, more traditional look. Try pale pink grout.
c Try a black pattern on green background with a red grout for a stunning modern effect.
d A blue and white motif using blue flowers and various subtly different shades of blue china is very classic. Use pale blue grout.

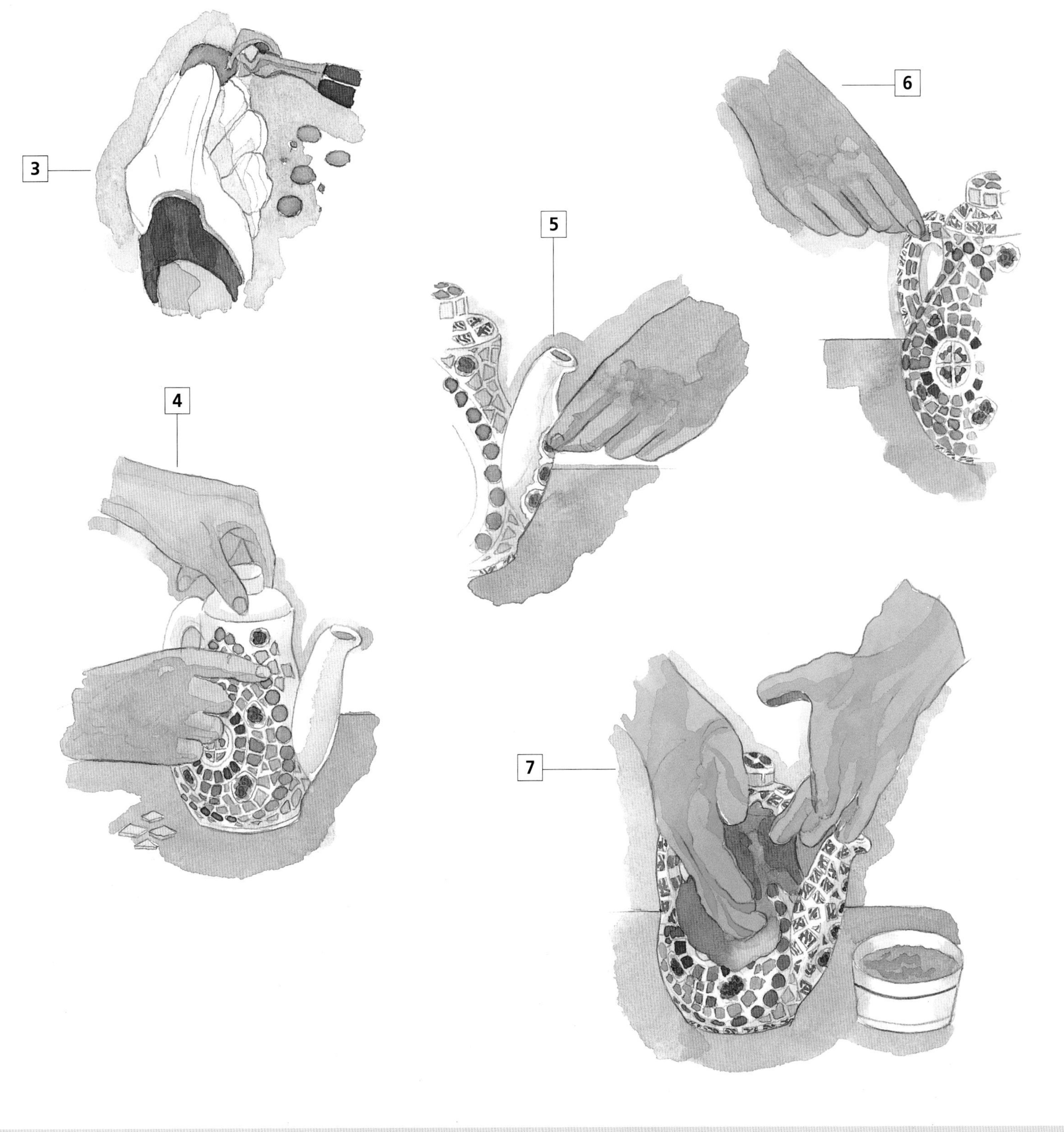
3
4
5
6
7

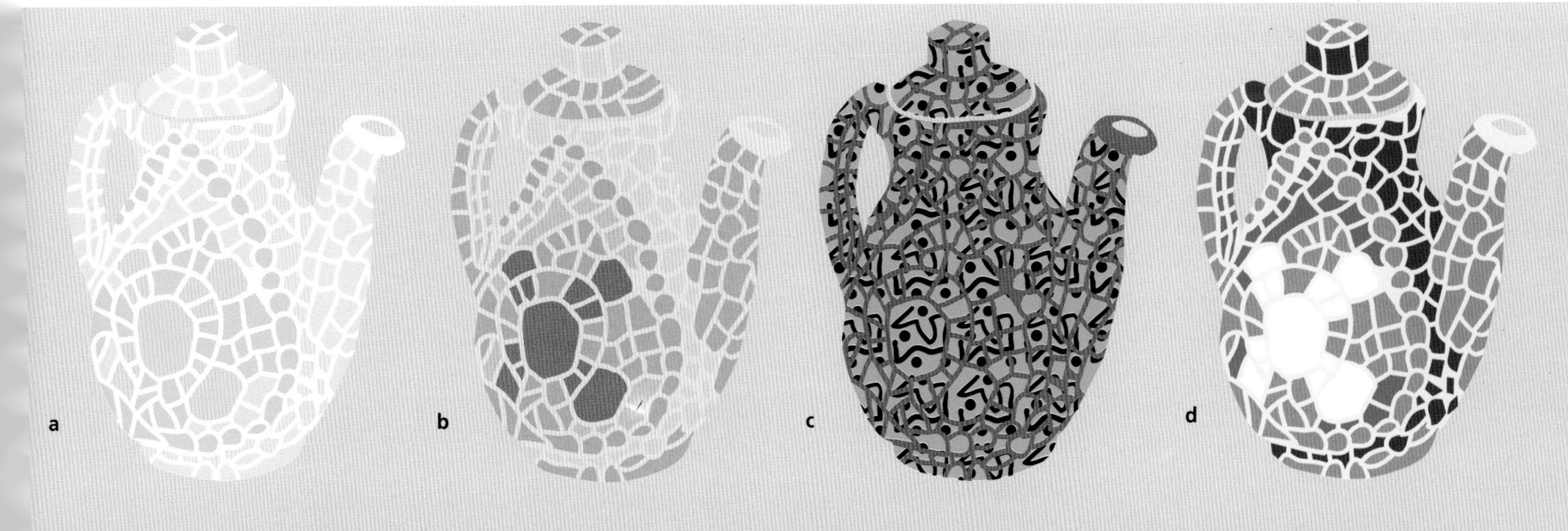
a
b
c
d

Mirror Frame

TOOLS & MATERIALS

- Mirror
- Wooden mirror frame
- White glue or waterproofing sealer
- Hanging brackets
- Glazier points or mirror mastic
- Assorted dishes
- 1 three-dimensional object
- Mosaic nippers
- Protective eyewear
- Work gloves
- Household cement or other strong bonding adhesive
- Dull knife or spatula
- Ceramic tile adhesive
- Grout
- Disposable container
- Stir stick
- Rubber gloves
- Newspaper or scrap paper
- Sponge or spatula
- Dry rag

Created by
Tracy Graivier Bell

This bright, cheerful mirror is a terrific starter project for working with dishes and china. When gathering dishes for this project, find several coordinating solid colors and patterns that work well together. This frame is made of five different plates in warm sunny tones. The plates have been nipped into small pieces and used in pattern groupings to give the final product a unified appearance and dappled swathes of color. The addition of a three-dimensional object, here a porcelain parrot head, adds interest and depth. Depending on its size, this mirror works well in a hallway, breakfast room, or bathroom. A zanier version will make a fun children's room mirror.

BEFORE YOU START

Choose a frame to use as the base form of your project. You can purchase a ready-made frame at most craft or gift stores, you can have a frame shop build one, or you can make one yourself out of narrow wood planks. For beginners, a flat frame surface is easier to work on than a curved one. If the wood is raw, waterproof it by painting it with a mixture of white glue and water (one part glue to four parts water) or coating it with a commercial waterproofing sealer available at any hardware store. Attach hanging brackets on the back of the frame before you begin.

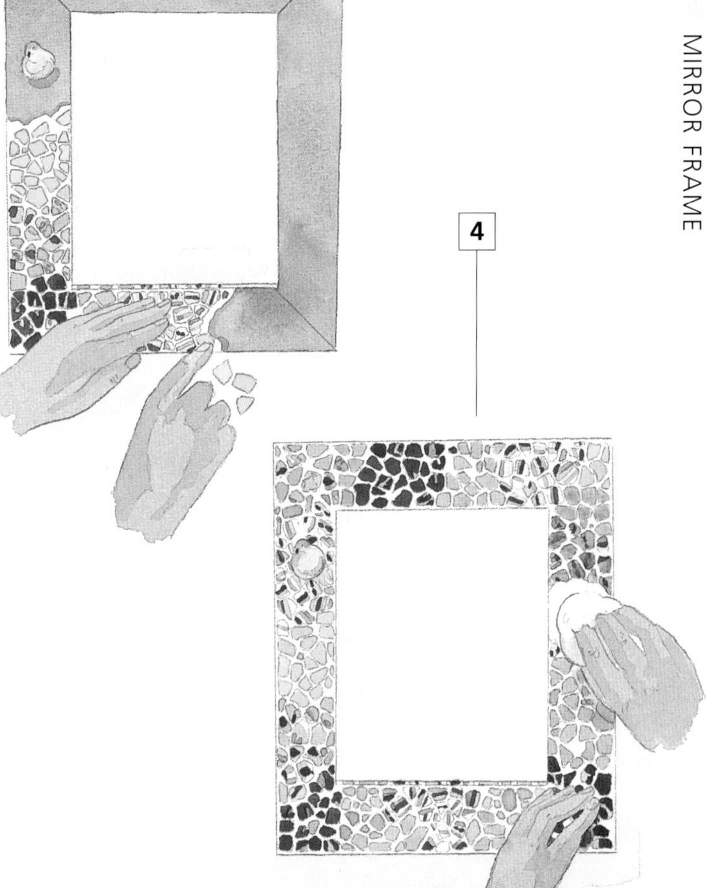

tip

- An oval frame made with old china looks very Victorian hung above an antique dresser.
- Install a piece of cork in the mosaic frame instead of a mirror to create a bulletin board for a kitchen, a playroom, or a child's room.
- Use your child's old baby dishes to create a mirror of memories. A great gift for a bride or groom!

Select your dishes and three-dimensional object. Use the mosaic nippers to clip the dinnerware into small irregular shapes. Always wear protective eyewear and work gloves when nipping, breaking, or smashing to protect yourself from shards and splinters.

TO USE YOUR MIRROR

Have a mirror cut to fit snugly into the frame. Install the mirror using either glazier points or mirror mastic, both are available at any hardware store.

1 Choose a place for the three-dimensional object on your frame. An off-center position works well for a figurine, while a medallion can be great top and center. Use household cement or another strong bonding adhesive to attach the object to the frame. Allow the adhesive a few minutes to set before proceeding with the next step.

2 Using a dull knife or spatula, spread a thin layer of ceramic tile adhesive onto a small section of the frame. The consistency of the adhesive is similar to cake frosting, and it remains moist for approximately half an hour after spreading.

3 Work section by section until the frame is completely covered with fragments. Remember that each fragment should fit comfortably into the space left by the surrounding pieces, so trim shards with your mosaic nippers when necessary. After the top of the frame is completely covered, use the same process to cover the edges. Be careful not to disturb the pieces you have already placed, as the ceramic tile adhesive will not be completely dry for forty-eight hours. When the mirror is installed in the frame, the inside edges will be reflected, so this is an especially important area to finish well. When the fragments are all in place, allow the frame to dry undisturbed for a few days before grouting.

4 Prepare the grout in a disposable container with the stir stick and carefully apply the grout while wearing rubber gloves. The full procedure is given on pages 30-32. Be sure to fill every space between the fragments. As the grout begins to set, vigorously wipe the excess from the fragments with and then allow the grout to dry for about twenty minutes. Wipe off the remaining chalky haze with a clean dry rag.

Gallery of frames

1. Tracy Graivier Bell uses larger tesserae here to give the frame some weight. The pottery bakery adds a touch of humor.
2. This interesting frame from Rebecca Dennis and Paula Funt shows how small, pale tesserae can subdue a striking or unusual frame.
3. Linda Benswanger uses broken plate to great effect on these frames.
4. Tracy Graivier Bell gives a springtime freshness to this frame with the pale tesserae dotted with patterned and floral pieces.
5. Rebecca Dennis and Paula Funt have created a crowning glory for this frame. The three-dimensional pieces pick out the points of the starburst.
6. Sarah Kelly's rich and shimmering frame beautifully contrasts with the reflective mirror.

1.

2.

3.

4.

5.

6.

Sconce

TOOLS & MATERIALS

- Terra-cotta wall sconce
- Assorted dishes and tiles
- Mosaic or tile nippers
- Protective eyewear
- Work gloves
- Cement-based mortar
- Disposable container
- Stir stick
- Dull knife or spatula
- Sanded grout (terra cotta or color of your choice)
- Newspaper or scrap paper
- Rubber gloves
- Disposable container
- Stir stick
- Sponge
- Dry rag
- Grout sealer
- Large paintbrush

Created by
Tracy Graivier Bell

tip

- Some sconces are molded with cupids or angels on them. Create your mosaic around the figurine, leaving it as a central focal point on your sconce.
- Perch a ceramic bird or squirrel on the rim of the sconce for an outdoorsy garden look.
- Use green and white tiles and dishes with ivy, vines, or floral patterns for the look of a summer garden.

A sconce is a versatile addition to any home or garden. It can be used for storing paper and pencil near a telephone or for growing your favorite hearty plant on a sunny fence or wall. A series of sconces mounted together and filled with lush plants provides a quick fix to a young garden. Find a terra-cotta sconce at a local garden center or hardware store. They are available in a variety of shapes and sizes, but look for one that is relatively smooth without intricate details and patterns. Choose dishes and tiles to reflect your décor, or use patterns to work within a floral theme. The instructions below call for cement-based mortar as the adhesive; however, if the sconce will be used indoors, feel free to substitute premixed ceramic tile adhesive.

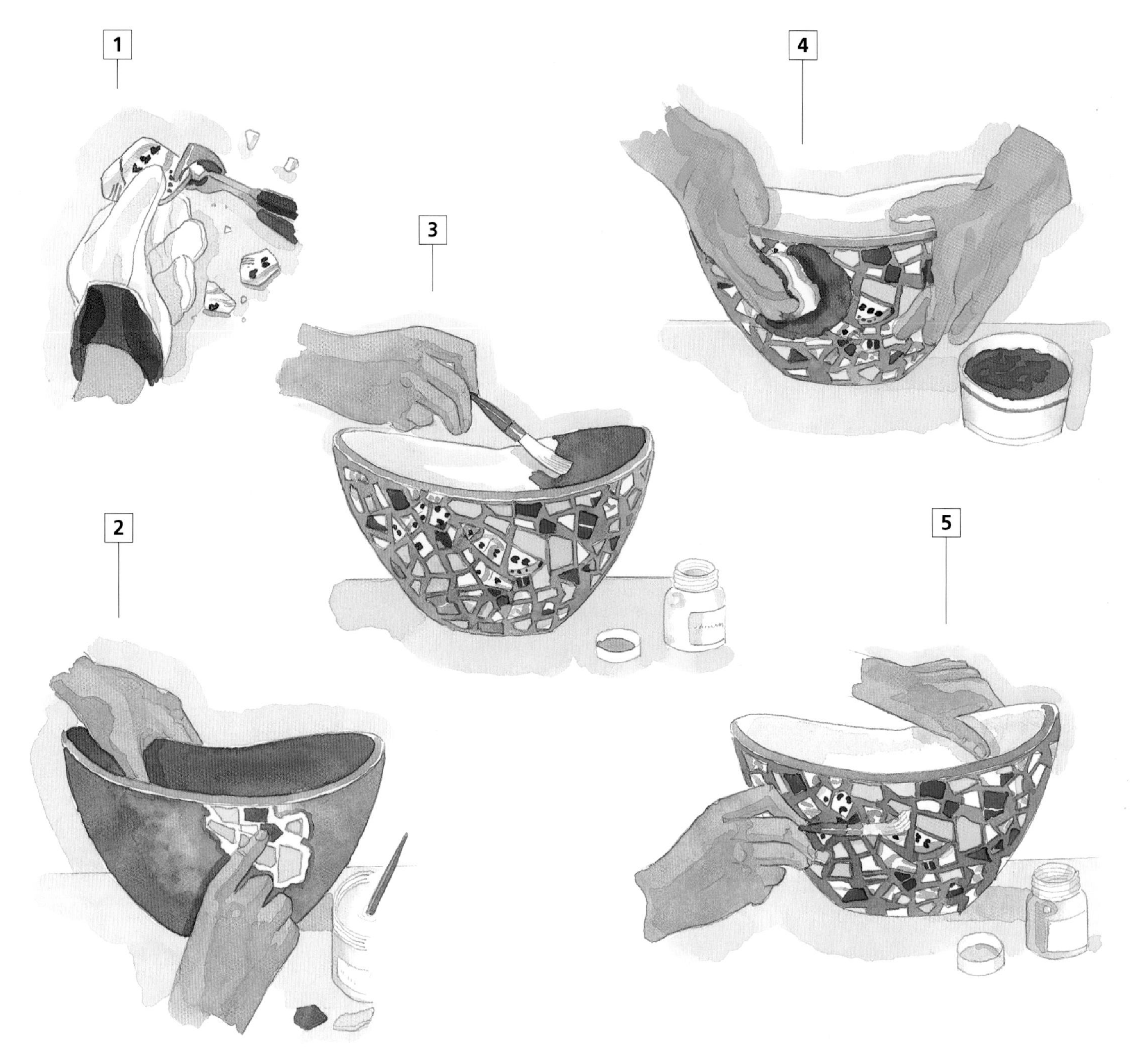

1 Use the nippers to clip the dinnerware into irregular shapes. Take into account the shape of the sconce and nip your materials into sizes that will fit comfortably around the curve. Always wear protective eyewear and work gloves when nipping, breaking, or smashing to protect yourself from flying shards and splinters.

2 Prepare the cement-based mortar in a disposable container according to the package directions. Using a dull knife or spatula, spread a thin layer of mortar, approximately ⅛ inch thick, onto a small area of the sconce. Press fragments into the mortar until that area is covered. Continue working section by section until the curved face of the sconce is completely covered with fragments. Nibble away at the shards with your nippers when you need to modify a piece of tile or dish to fit into a small space.

3 The inside of the sconce should remain undecorated with the smooth terra-cotta surface exposed. If the terra-cotta color is not pleasing to you, or clashes with your tesserae, then simply paint it with acrylic paint after the grouting process is complete. Allow the sconce to dry undisturbed for at least forty-eight hours before proceeding with the grouting.

4 Prepare and carefully apply the grout while wearing rubber gloves. Be sure to fill every space between the fragments. As the grout begins to set, wipe the excess from the fragments and then allow the grout to dry for about twenty minutes. Vigorously buff off the remaining chalky haze with a clean dry rag. If the wall sconce will be used outside, allow it to air dry for forty-eight hours before applying grout sealer.

5 In order to make the sconce weatherproof, brush the surface with two coats of grout sealer, a product available in any hardware or tile supply store.

Jeweled Trinket Box

TOOLS & MATERIALS

- Small circular ceramic trinket box, about 4 inches in diameter
- Glass gems in different shades of blue
- One larger blue glass gem
- Clear blue stained glass
- Silver leaf or faux silver leaf (not tin foil)
- Lots of silver beads
- Ceramic tile adhesive
- Small plastic glue spreader
- Fine tweezers (optional)
- Protective eyewear
- Work gloves
- Newspaper or scrap paper
- White grout (unsanded)
- Blue grout coloring powder or acrylic paint
- Rubber gloves
- Disposable container
- Stir stick
- Sponge
- Dry rag

Created by
Sarah Kelly

BEFORE YOU START

Find a small ceramic trinket box at a market or thrift shop. You could also use a wooden or plastic one, but make sure it is firm enough to support the mosaic. Select your blue gems. Mix turquoises and sapphires with petrol effect ones, and silvered opaques with transparents. You will need six for the lid and six for the side of the box, plus the larger one for the center of the lid. If you can't find a large one, another smaller one will do just as well. Next, use tile nippers or glass nippers to cut out a small section, about 3 inches x 3 inches, from the blue glass.

TO SILVER-BACK YOUR GLASS

Apply a thin layer of PVA to the back of each gem and onto one side of the glass, making sure every part of the surface is covered with glue. Press them onto the sheet of silver leaf and leave to dry overnight, or until the white glue has become transparent and can no longer be seen. Then gently peel them off the sheet. They should now be backed with the silver, which gives glass a much deeper, more lustrous look as well as making it really shiny.

A delicate combination of glass gems and colored glass backed with silver leaf and mixed with small silver beads makes this tiny trinket box almost a piece of jewelry in itself! A beautiful addition to any dressing table.

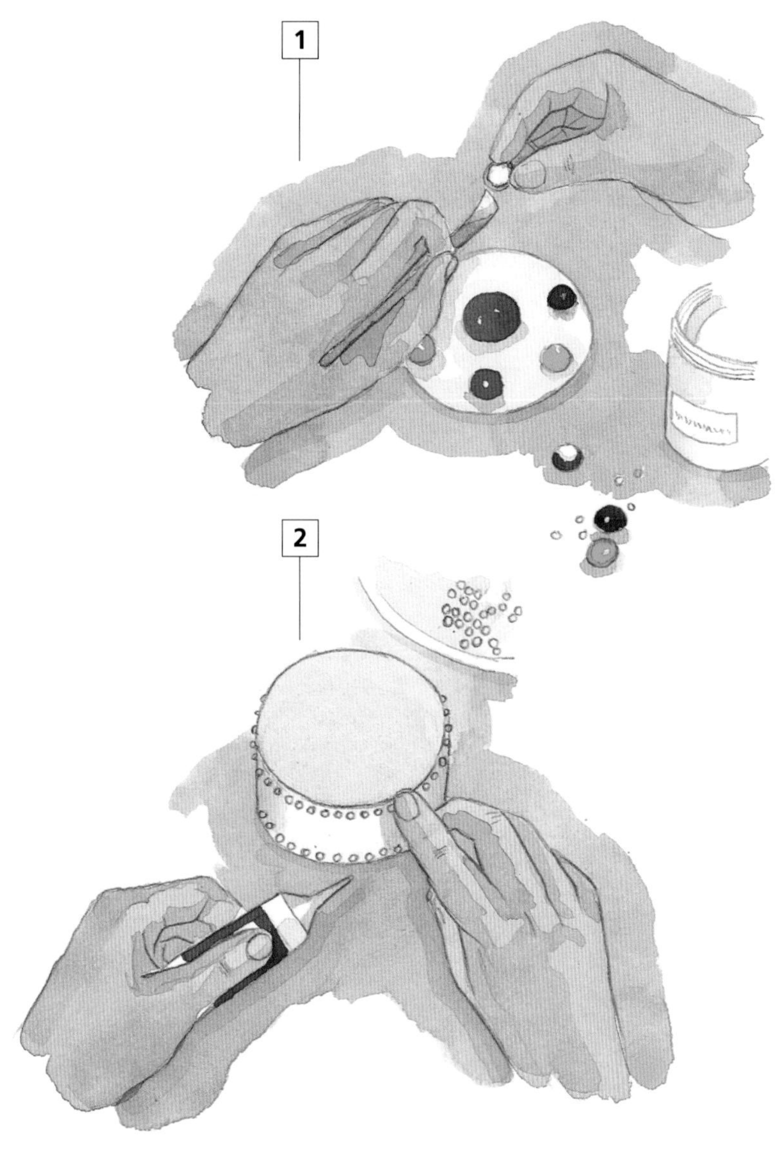

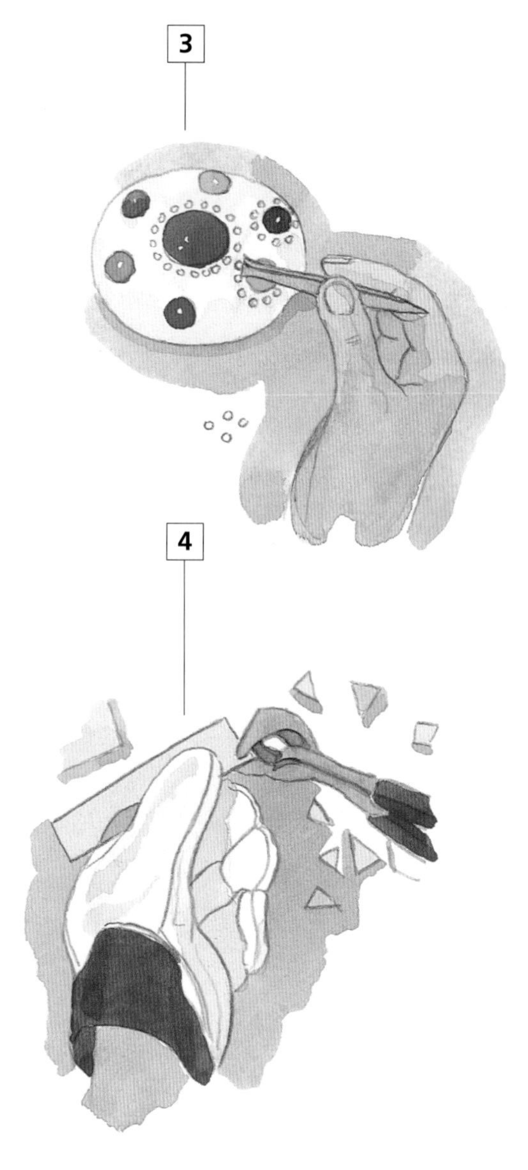

1 Begin with the lid and apply a layer of adhesive to the surface with the plastic spreader. While this is becoming tacky, apply a layer to the back of the large gem and then stick it into position in the center of the lid. Once this is firmly in place, apply an additional band of adhesive quite thickly around it; let it dry out a little, then surround it with a ring of the silver beads. It is too tedious to butter each bead individually, so the glue bed needs to be quite thick to hold them all firmly. Stick the beads down so that the holes point to the sides and are hidden from view.

2 Arrange a selection of six of the smaller gems evenly around the centerpiece, making sure that any duplicated colors are kept away from each other. Apply more adhesive to their backs and stick them down. Make sure you have left enough room round all sides to add a ring of silver beads. When they are all in place, surround them with beads in the same way as you did for the central gem. A pair of fine tweezers may come in handy for picking up and placing the beads.

3 Use your nippers to break the silver-backed glass into tiny random fragments, wearing protective gloves and eyewear. Re-apply adhesive to the base if necessary, then butter the glass pieces and fill the remaining spaces on the lid with them, silver side down. Use the tweezers again if you need to.

4 When the lid is finished, move onto the pot itself. Spread a thin band of glue (deep enough to hold beads) around the top edge of the pot and allow it to dry slightly. Stick a ring of beads right around this top rim, making sure that they do not come too high up and interfere with the fit of the lid. Wait for them to dry to a stage where they don't move when you touch them—keep an eye out for any slippages—then turn the pot upside down and repeat the process on the bottom edge. Again, make sure that the beads don't stick up too far and prevent the pot from standing flat.

5 Replace the lid on the pot and position your last six gems so that they correspond with the position of the gems on the lid, having first applied adhesive to the base and to the gems themselves. Frame each gem with a vertical strip of beads on either side, using the same method as before. When every gem has been

5

6

framed, fill in the spaces between each one using the glass fragments. You can also fill in the corners between each gem and the bead frame, but it's not vital as the gaps can be filled just as well with the colored grout. Allow the finished mosaic to dry naturally for forty-eight hours.

6 Put on rubber gloves and, using quite a lot of coloring, mix up a strong shade of blue grout according to the instructions on pages 30-32. Use your fingers to gently rub the grout over the lid and the pot, covering each one separately. Remove the excess with the dampened sponge and polish with a soft dry rag after fifteen to twenty minutes.

Gallery of boxes

1.

2.

3.

4.

1. A pretty little trinket box from the *Mosaicwares* designers, Rebecca Dennis and Paula Funt.
2. Mary K. Guth, *Rose Box* uses the repeated image of the rose's thorns to keep out unwelcome intruders.
3. Hap Sakwa's robust Americana pot shows that the outside can be just as exciting as anything you keep on the inside.
4. Hap Sakwa again fronts his piece with striking Hollywood iconography.
5. Rebecca Dennis and Paula Funt's delicately curved box in the style of a miniature dresser.

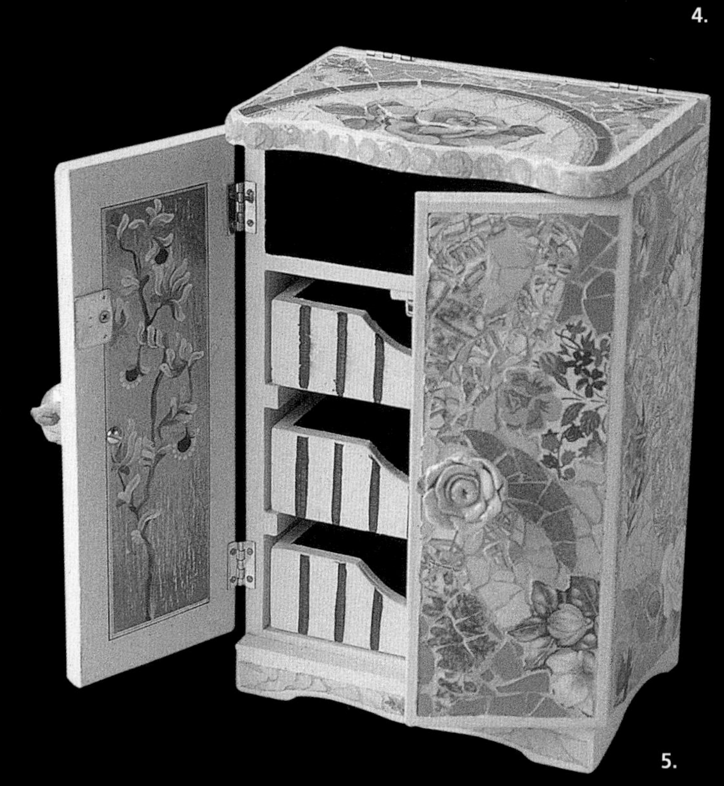

5.

Candle Holder Glass Strips

TOOLS & MATERIALS

- Glass cylinder
- Stained glass in assorted colors
- Pencil
- Brown or white craft paper
- Scissors
- T square
- Glass scorer
- Running pliers
- Mosaic, glass, or tile nipper
- Protective eyewear
- Work gloves
- Clear silicone or other clear quick-drying adhesive
- Sanded grout (black or color of your choice)
- Newspaper or scrap paper
- Rubber gloves
- Disposable container
- Stir stick
- Sponge
- Dry rag

Created by
Robin Oldham

A mosaic candle holder made of stained glass is even more beautiful when glowing from within. Choose a clear glass cylinder to use as the base of your project. It can be a kitchen tumbler or drinking glass, or it can be a cylindrical flower vase of any height or diameter. A table set with this centerpiece sets the scene for an intimate dinner for two or a festive holiday party. Slight variations in the width of the glass strips are expected and show that the candleholder is handcrafted.

- Use many different bright colored strips for a rainbow effect.
- Use glass strips in only one color with a contrasting color of grout:

  White glass with black grout

  Blue glass with white grout

  Almond-colored glass with dark brown grout.

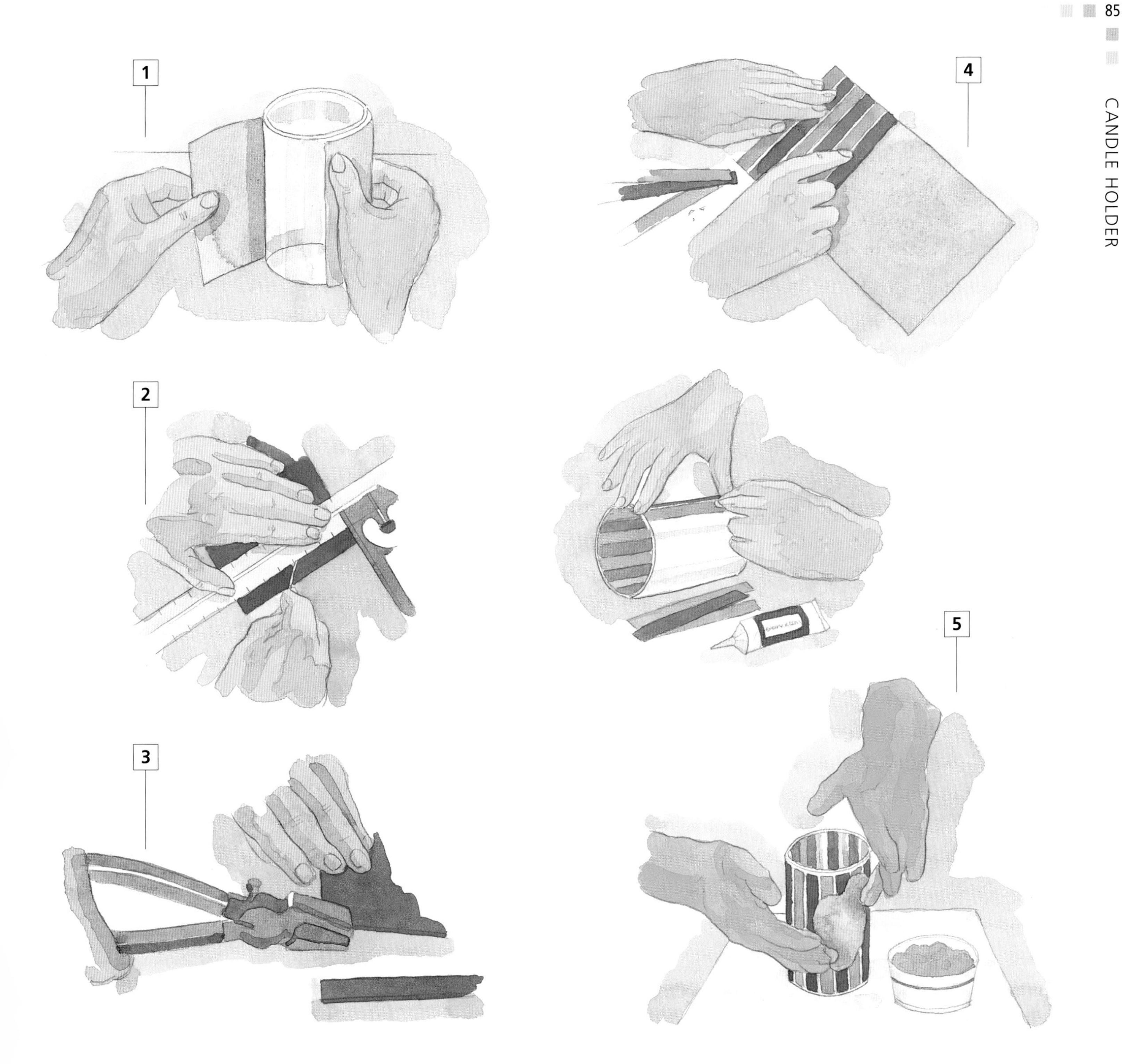

1 Choose a clear glass cylinder to use as the base of your project. It can be a kitchen tumbler or drinking glass, or it can be a cylindrical flower vase of any height or diameter.

2 Create a paper pattern of the cylinder out of the craft paper.

3 Use your T square as a guide to score the stained glass into ½ inch strips. While wearing safety goggles and work gloves, snap the glass into strips using the running pliers. Lay the strips onto the craft paper, leaving approximately ⅛ inch between each strip for grout. Adjust the length of the strips by scoring and snapping the individual pieces to fit the paper pattern or by clipping them with your nipper.

4 Drop a small bubble of clear adhesive onto a strip of stained glass, and use the tip of the applicator tube to spread it into a thin layer. Be sure to cover the strip completely so that the grout does not seep under the glass during the grouting process. Press the strip onto the cylinder, and hold it in place for a few seconds until it is secure. Work around the cylinder until you have covered it completely. Allow to dry for twenty-four hours.

5 Place the candle holder on some old newspaper, and prepare your grout. While wearing rubber gloves, apply the grout with your fingers. Wipe off the excess and allow the mosaic to stand for approximately twenty minutes. Buff with a dry cloth.

Chair

Covering a chair in mosaic is a slightly more ambitious project, but satisfying nevertheless! The smoother and finer your mosaic, the more practical your chair will be for sitting on, but it could also be used in a bathroom or bedroom to drape clothes or towels over or even as an unusual plant stand!

TOOLS & MATERIALS

- Sturdy wooden chair with a round seat
- A good quantity of tesserae incorporating patterned and plain blues and some white
- Craft knife
- Washable felt pen
- Tile nippers
- Ceramic tile adhesive
- Small plastic glue spreader
- Protective eyewear and gloves
- Blue acrylic or gloss paint
- Sanded grout in a vivid blue (or color of your choice)
- Newspaper or scrap paper
- Rubber gloves
- Disposable container
- Stir stick
- Sponge
- Dry rag

Created by
Sarah Kelly

BEFORE YOU START

Find or buy a plain wooden chair. Regular visits to markets and junk shops may yield good results. The chair needs to be quite sturdy, as the quantity of the mosaic over it will be heavy. It also needs to have as many flat surfaces as possible—not too many spindly bits. The design can be adapted to suit the shape of your own chair if you can't find one like this. Ideally the chair should be unpainted and not too heavily varnished. If it is, it would probably be a good idea to strip it first. If the wood is untreated, seal it with a dilution of PVA in water (one part glue to four parts water or according to the manufacturer's instructions). After these preparations, thoroughly score the surface of the chair with a craft knife to make a good key, or receptive base, for the mosaic.

FINISHING YOUR CHAIR

If there are any areas that you have chosen not to cover with mosaic, you can paint them using acrylic or gloss emulsion paint. If these areas are flush with any of your mosaic, stick some masking tape over the tesserae to protect them. If you are using gloss, prime the surface first according to the manufacturer's instructions. You can choose a color that matches the grout or the dark blue of the legs, or use another color of your choice.

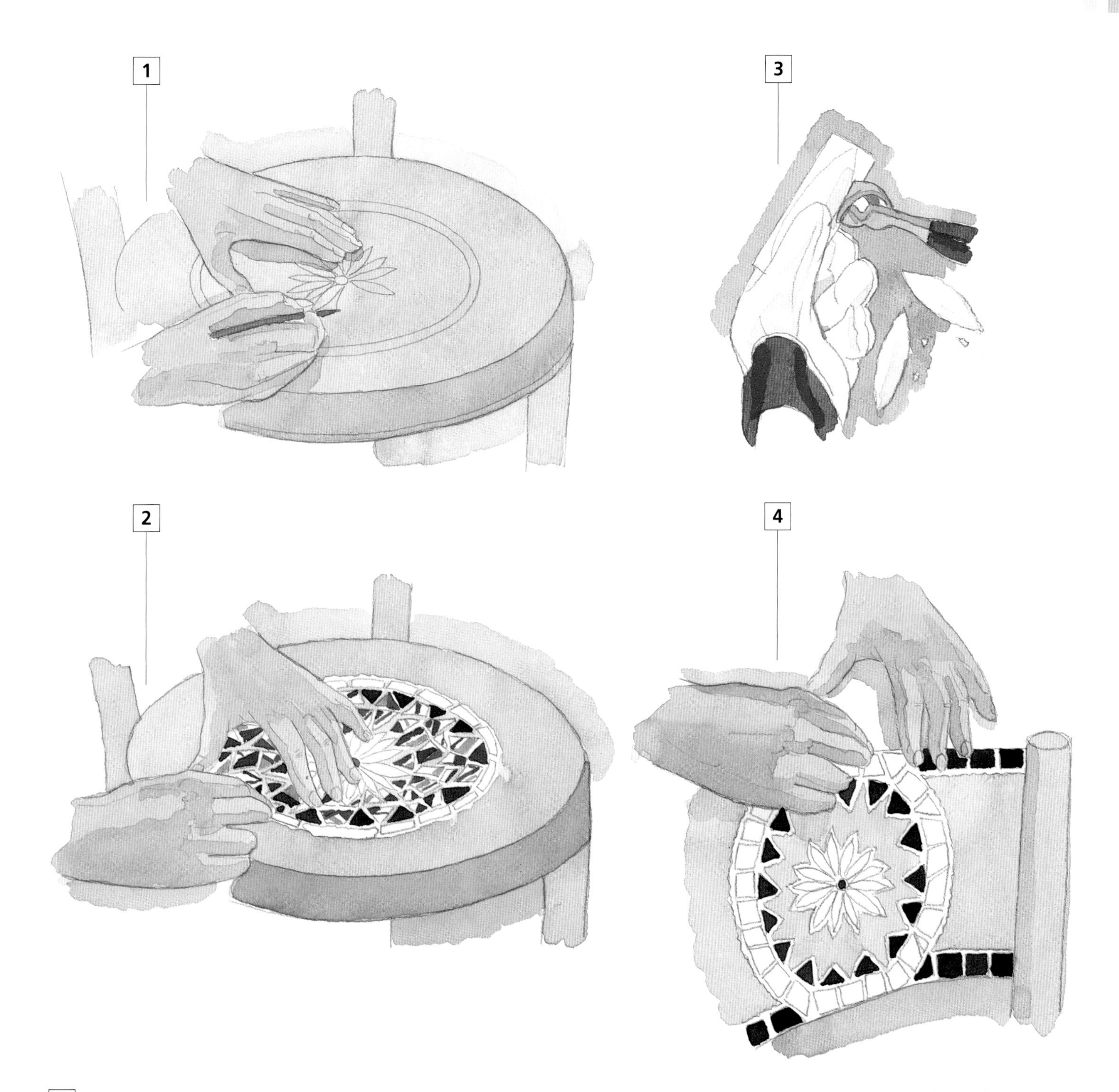

1 Draw the design on the flat surfaces of your chair with a washable felt pen. The design consists of a small twelve-petaled flower contained within a larger one. The points of the inside flower correspond with the "dips" in the outer one. The flowers are then contained within a banded circle. On the seat, alternating patterned and plain strips radiate out from the circle.

2 Put on the protective eyewear and gloves and using the tile nippers nibble out a small circle for the center of the first flower on the seat in dark blue, and then twelve thin petals in white. It is very important that you use tesserae that are the same depth to ensure smoothness, especially if you intend to use your chair to sit on.

3 Apply a layer of adhesive to the flower area on the chair then butter the individual tesserae and stick them into place. Fill the next flower design with a mosaic of random tesserae in patterned ceramic and complete the circle with plain dark blue tesserae placed between the petals. Finish it off with a band of white. Make the radiating lines on the seat a little wider at the top than the bottom so that they fit neatly round the central circle. Alternate dark blue lines with patterned ones and leave a space round the outside of about ½ inch for a white border.

4 Use the same techniques on a smaller scale for the flowers and circles on the front and back of the chair. Let the edges of the circle come flush with the top and bottom of the backrest. Add a border there in dark blue and fill the remaining space with patterned tesserae.

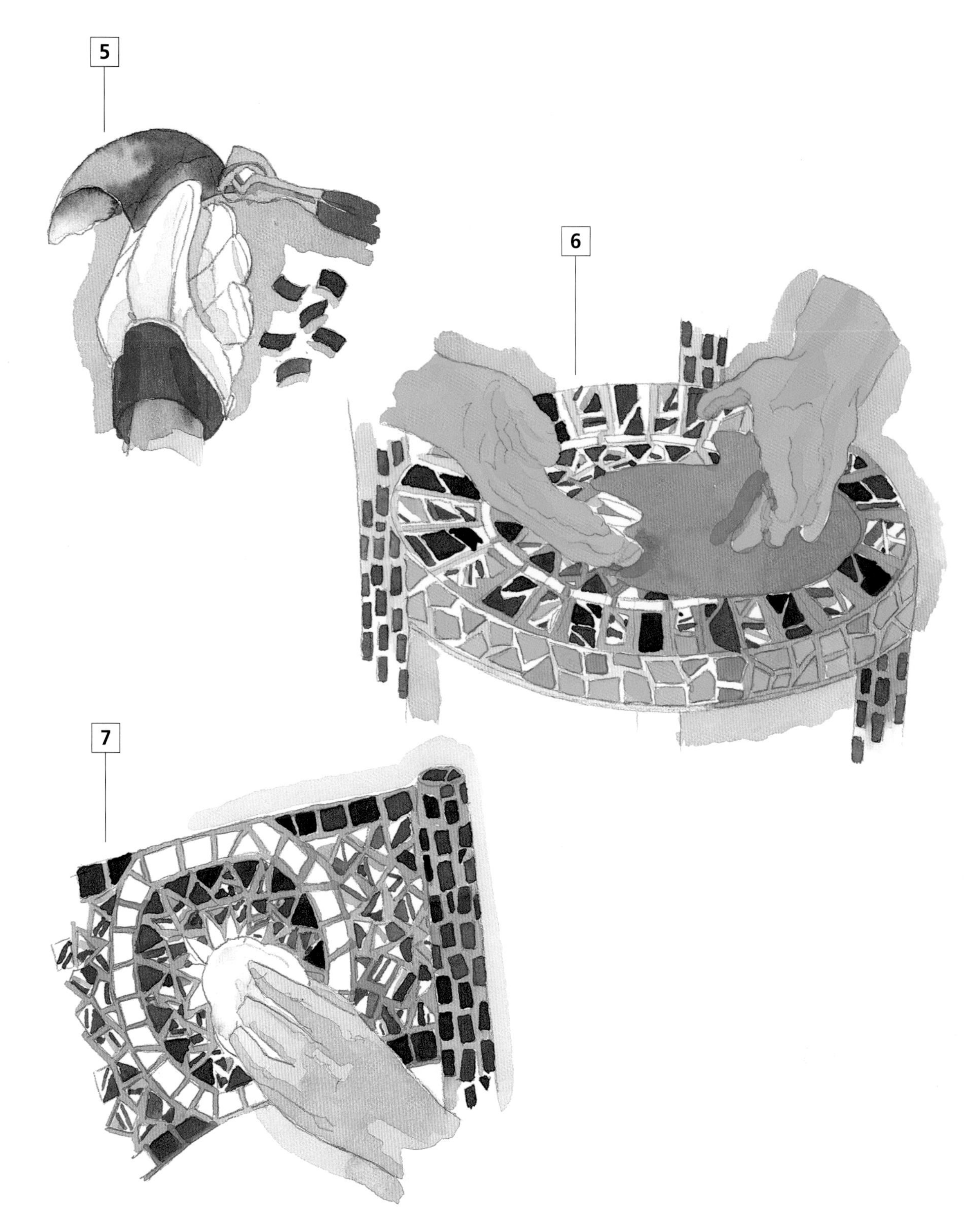

5 The spindles and legs of the chair are covered in a mosaic of dark blue tesserae. You will need to cut them quite small to fit comfortably round the curve of these areas. Similarly curved tesserae taken from cups or bowls will also help here. Even though it is difficult, try to make sure you do the insides and tops of the legs as well as you can. You don't need to mosaic under the seat.. Take the mosaic down the legs to about ½ to ¾ inch from the bottom and use circular medallions for the tops of the chair spindles.

6 When the chair is completely covered, leave it to dry naturally for forty-eight hours before grouting. Put on the rubber gloves and mix up a vivid blue grout according to the instructions on page 30-32, using a fair amount of powder or paint to get a strong color. You will need a lot of grout to cover the whole chair. Apply the grout thoroughly with your hands or your chosen grouting tool, making sure you rub it really well into every part of your mosaic.

7 As soon as the whole chair is fully covered, begin wiping off the excess immediately with a damp sponge. Wipe off the remaining chalky haze with a dry rag and paint the unmosaiced areas if you like.

Gallery of larger furniture

1. Mary K. Guth, *Wingback chair*. This piece is wickedly witty with the doves' wings creating the 'wingback'.
2. Mary K. Guth *Lunch Chair*. A chair made, not for lunch but from lunch. Note the cup-handle edging and inlaid spoons.
3. Mary K. Guth *Female Image Vanity*. A mosaic sideswipe at the stereotypical female icons. Note the dolls set into the drawers as handles.
4. Tracy Graivier Bell uses a bird theme too, but hers are more mischievously subtle.
5. Rebecca Dennis and Paula Funt's pretty dressing table mirrors the curves of the table within the mosaic design.

Decorative Plates

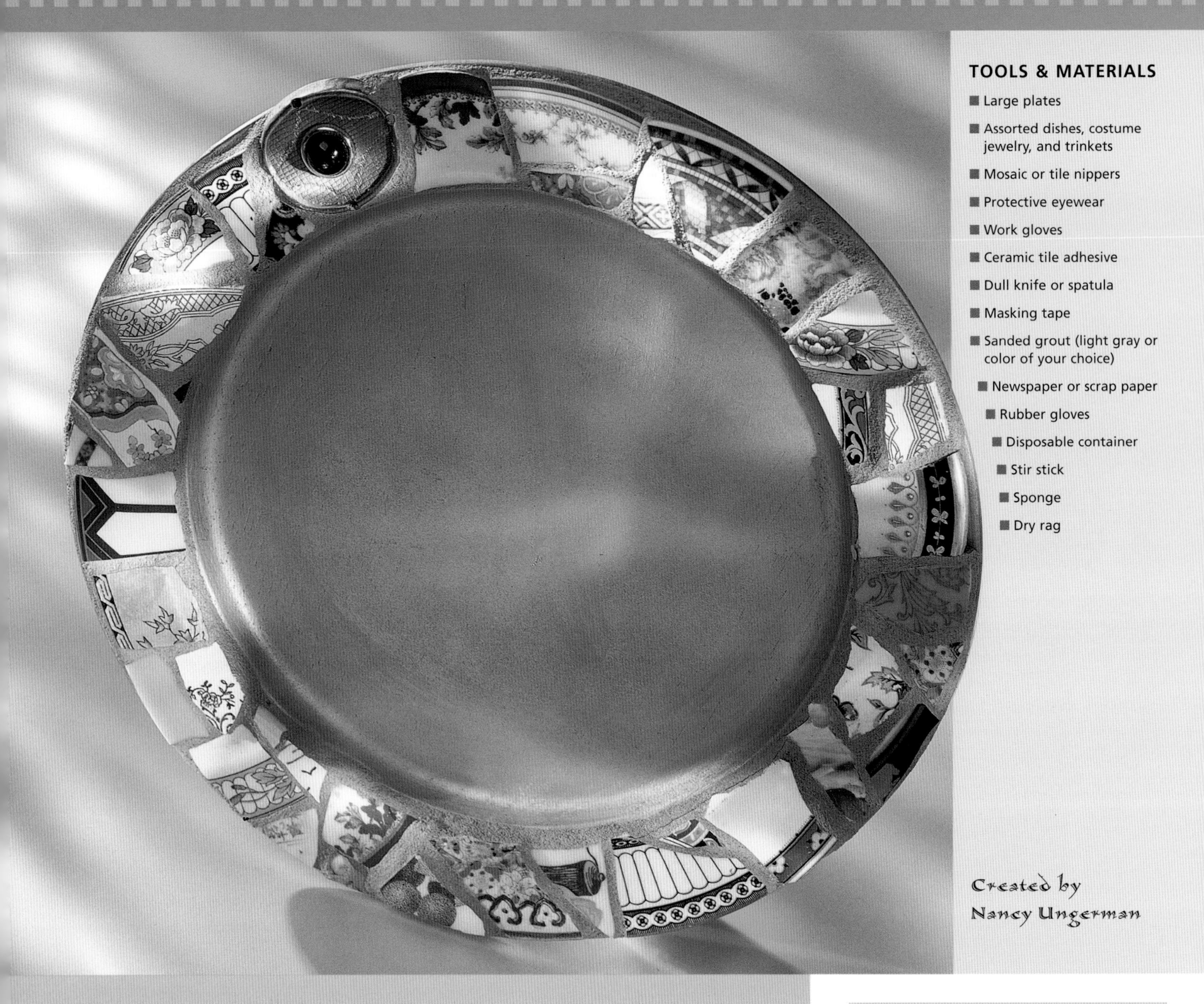

TOOLS & MATERIALS

- Large plates
- Assorted dishes, costume jewelry, and trinkets
- Mosaic or tile nippers
- Protective eyewear
- Work gloves
- Ceramic tile adhesive
- Dull knife or spatula
- Masking tape
- Sanded grout (light gray or color of your choice)
- Newspaper or scrap paper
- Rubber gloves
- Disposable container
- Stir stick
- Sponge
- Dry rag

Created by
Nancy Ungerman

These spectacular decorative plates can be used under any china to set a striking dinner table. The mosaic on the rim of each plate is made of a variety of broken dishes and old brooches and trinkets. Find a set of 'service plates' or 'chargers' approximately twelve inches in diameter, to use as the base of your project. They can be made of wood, hard plastic, or glass and are generally available in kitchen stores and department stores. You can use colors and patterns to accentuate your own dinnerware, or use a multicolored and random palette as pictured here for universal appeal.

tip

- For a more conservative look, limit the amount of colors you use on the plate borders but leave in lots of texture for interest.
- Use black shiny plate forms for a sleek dramatic look.

BEFORE YOU START

If your plates are made of raw wood, paint the front and back of each plate with acrylic paint, and then waterproof them by applying a mixture of white glue and water (one part glue to four parts water) or a commercial waterproofing sealer. These are available at any hardware store.

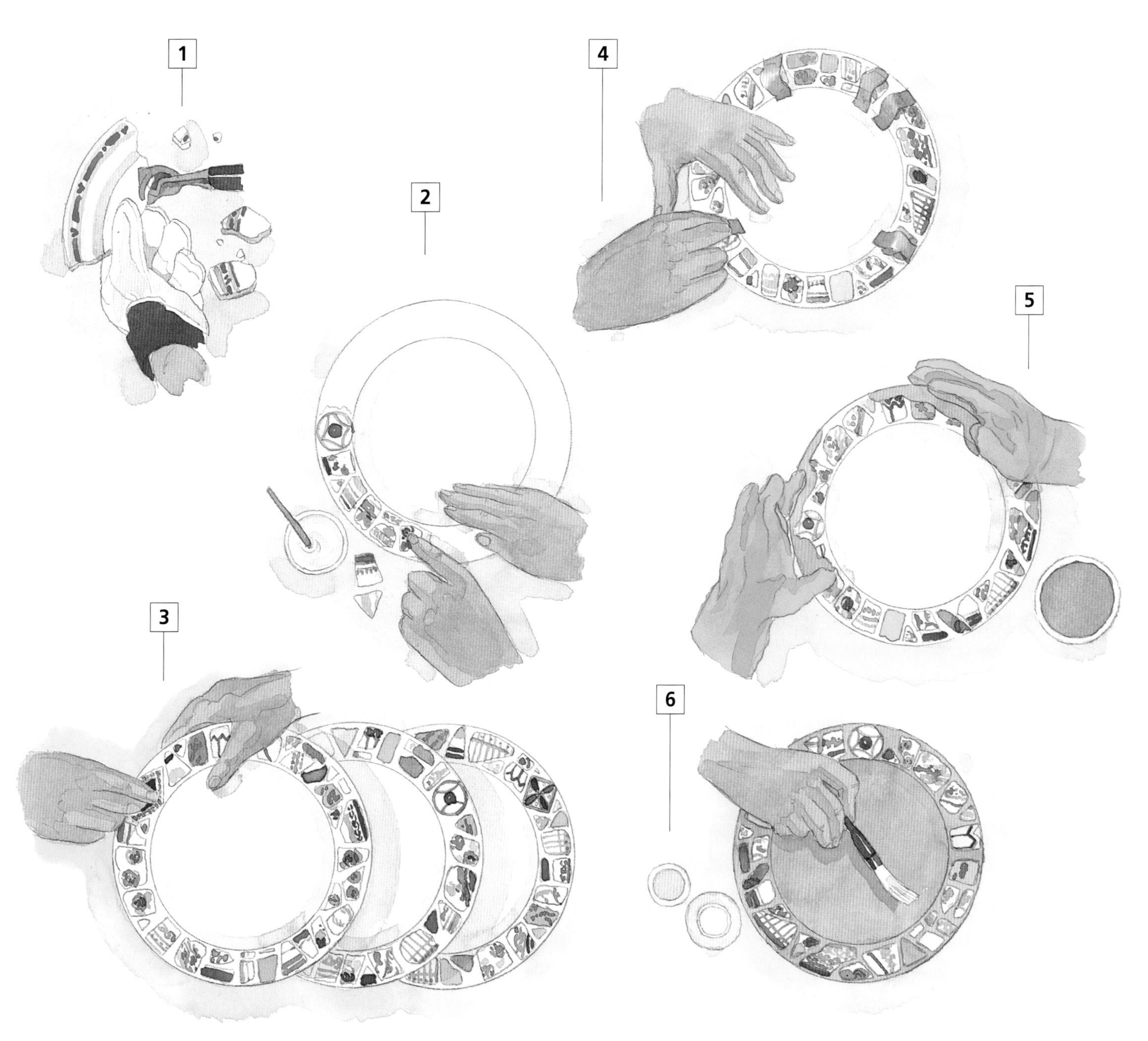

1 Use the nippers to clip the assorted dishes into irregular shapes. Always wear protective eyewear and work gloves when nipping, breaking, or smashing to protect yourself from shards and splinters.

2 Using a dull knife or spatula, spread a thin layer of ceramic tile adhesive onto a small section of the rim of a plate. Press fragments and memorabilia into the wet adhesive. Work section by section until the rim of the plate is completely covered with mosaic. Remember that each fragment should fit comfortably into the space left by the surrounding pieces, so trim shards with your nippers when necessary. Work section by section until the rim of the plate is completely covered with mosaic items.

3 Repeat this process with all the plates in your set. Follow the same general color and pattern scheme within the set, but try to find some unique pieces of memorabilia to incorporate so that there is something interesting and unusual on each one. Allow to dry for forty-eight hours.

4 Use masking tape to cover any intricately patterned jewelry or trinkets before applying the grout. The grout will not damage the memorabilia, but it can be difficult to clean from all the cracks and crevices.

5 Place the plates on some old newspaper, and prepare your grout. While wearing rubber gloves, spread the grout onto the plate rims, covering them completely, as if you are icing a cake. Wipe off the excess grout and allow the plates to stand undisturbed for approximately twenty minutes. Buff the chalky haze with a dry cloth.

6 In order to make the plates completely waterproof, allow them to air dry for forty-eight hours and then apply two coats of grout sealer, a product available in any hardware or tile supply store.

Tortoise

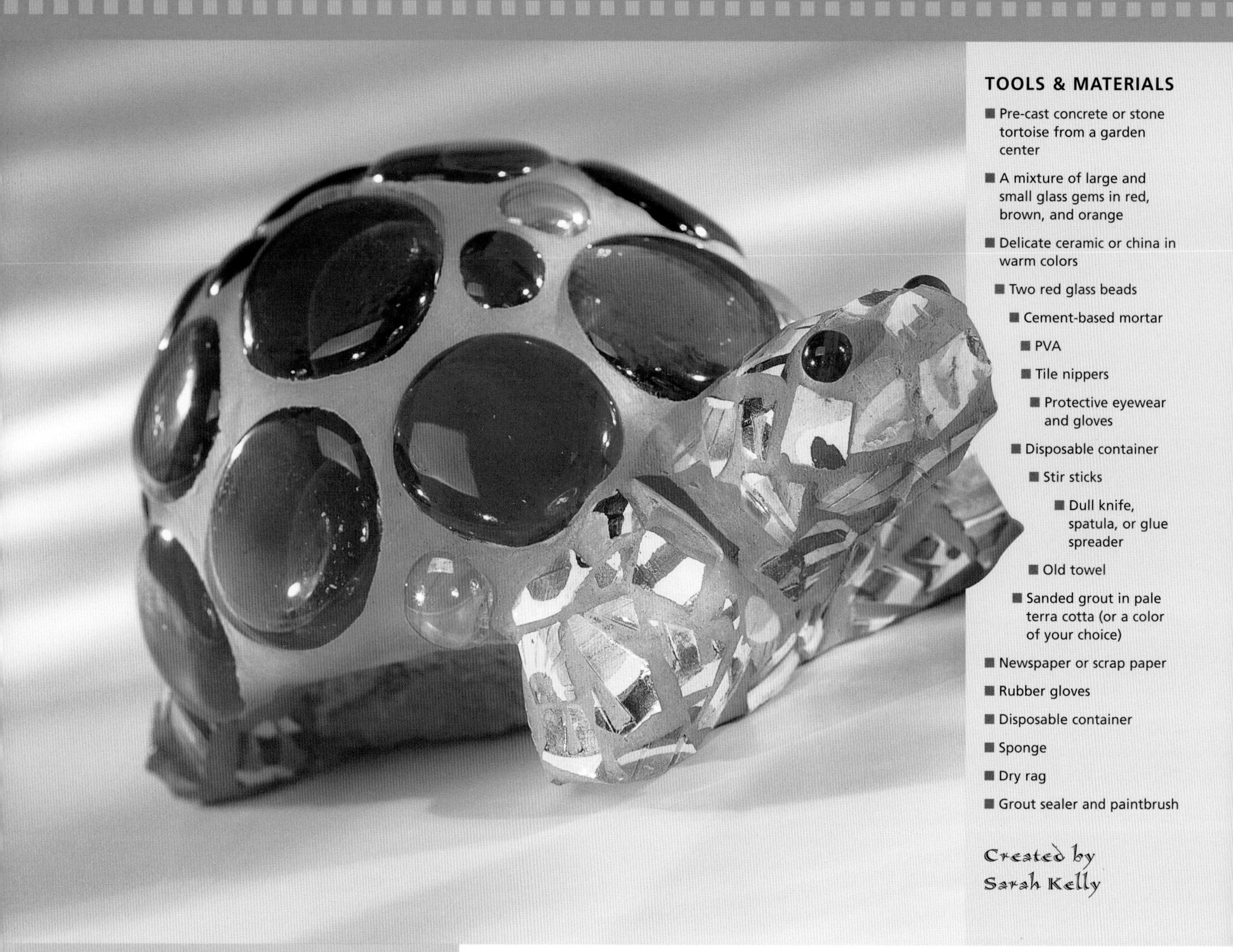

TOOLS & MATERIALS

- Pre-cast concrete or stone tortoise from a garden center
- A mixture of large and small glass gems in red, brown, and orange
- Delicate ceramic or china in warm colors
- Two red glass beads
- Cement-based mortar
- PVA
- Tile nippers
- Protective eyewear and gloves
- Disposable container
- Stir sticks
- Dull knife, spatula, or glue spreader
- Old towel
- Sanded grout in pale terra cotta (or a color of your choice)
- Newspaper or scrap paper
- Rubber gloves
- Disposable container
- Sponge
- Dry rag
- Grout sealer and paintbrush

Created by
Sarah Kelly

This cute little tortoise would look good on a paved area in the garden, on a wall, or peeping out from some foliage. It can also be displayed inside as a decorative ornament or used as a doorstop, as it is quite solid despite being so pretty.

BEFORE YOU START

Choose some patterned ceramic or china in colors that match or compliment the gems. As the surfaces of the tortoise's head and legs are quite small, you will find it easier to work in ceramic, which is relatively fine and delicate. Put on the protective eyewear and gloves and use the nippers to break the ceramic into small random tesserae.

COLOR VARIATIONS

a Make different shades of green with pale green, pale yellow, or gray grout.
b Use different shades of yellow/orange with a lilac-blue grout.
c Try dark blue and purple shades with terra-cotta-colored grout.
d Try dark blue shell, turquoise body, and blue or terra cotta grout.

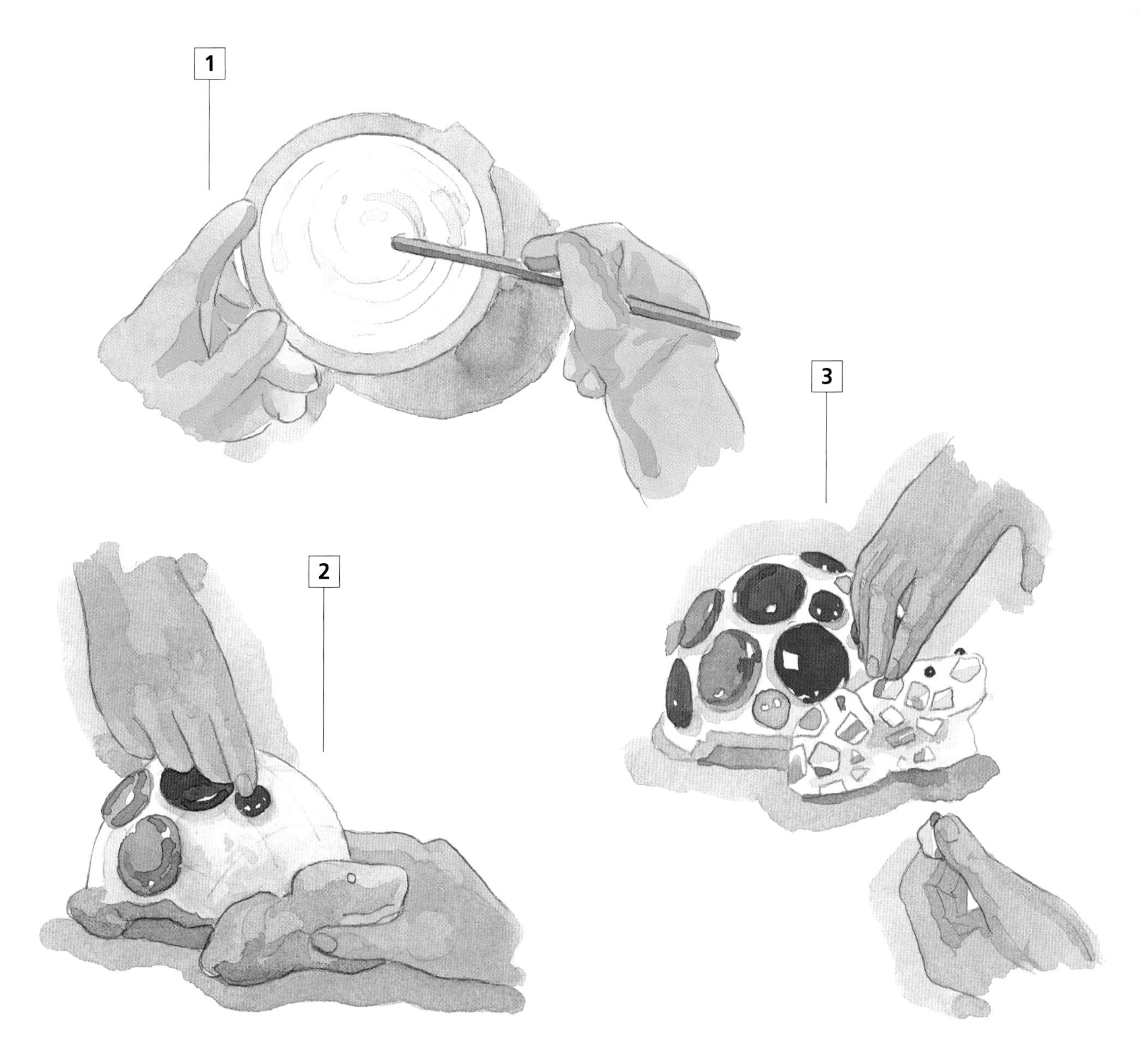

1 Mix the mortar with water in the container, using the stir stick. The adhesive needs to be quite thick but still pliable. Add a spoonful of PVA to the mortar and cover the shell of the tortoise with a layer about ¼ inch deep.

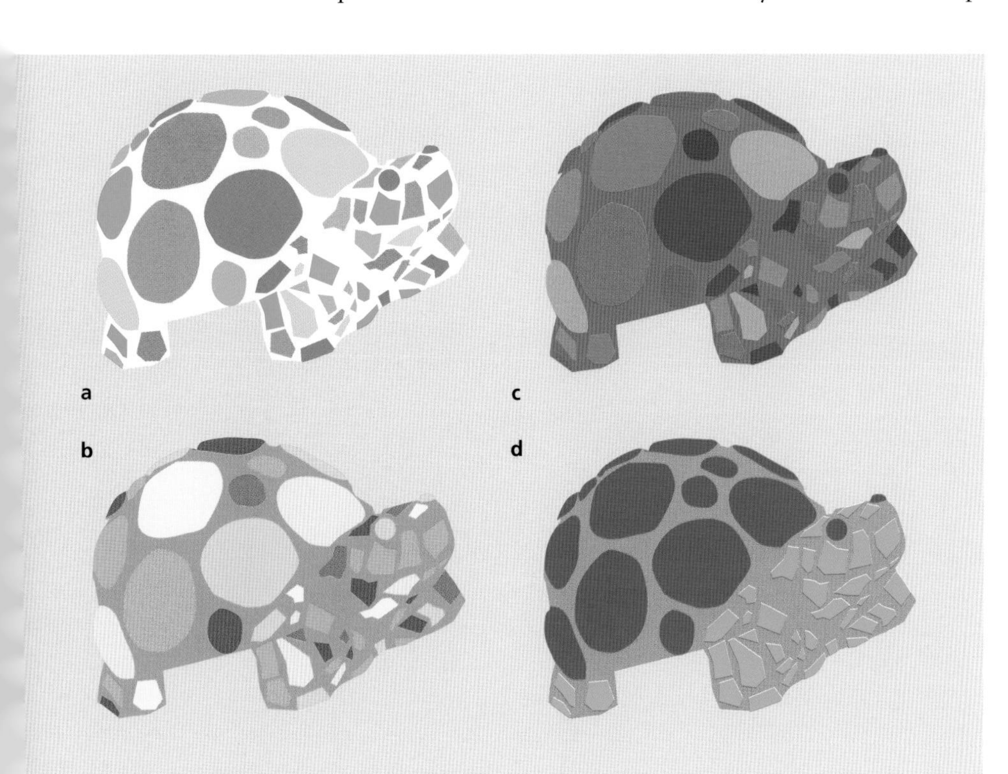

2 Start by pushing the larger gems firmly into the mortar, putting them as close together as you can. Use the occasional small gem in the spaces where you can't fit a larger one. You may need to jiggle the arrangement around a bit the more gems you stick down. Aim for as even coverage as you can, without any large and irregular gaps.

3 Cover the top and sides of the tortoise's head with a layer of mortar. You don't need to make it as thick as the previous layer—about ⅛ inch will do. Push the two glass beads on either side of the top of the head for eyes, then press the ceramic tesserae over the rest of the head, filling any awkward little gaps and crevices first. Save the underside areas for later.

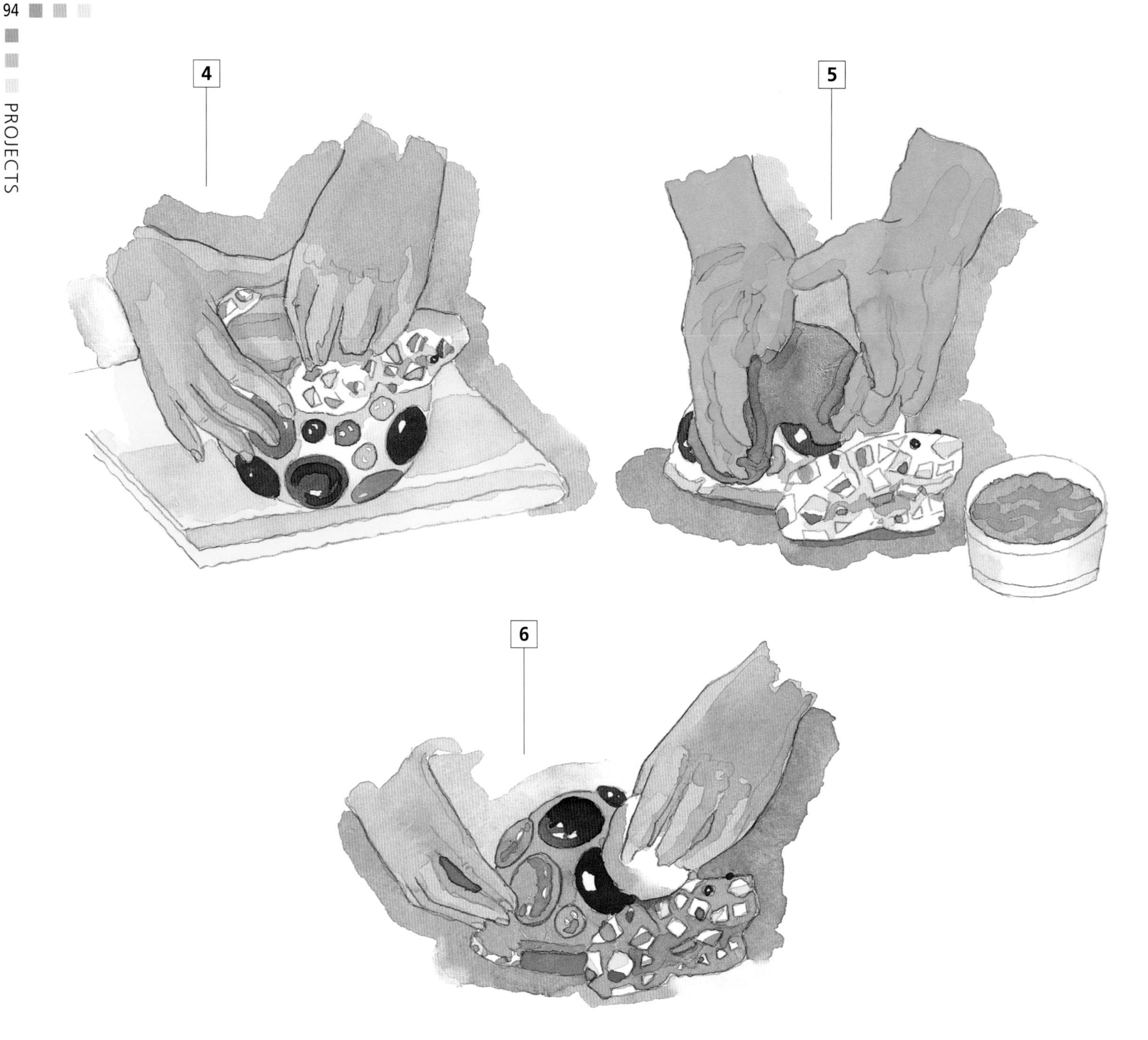

4 Repeat the process with the ceramic tesserae over the legs and tail. Wait until the top of the tortoise shell is dry enough for the gems to be held firmly in place, then turn the tortoise over, rest it on an old folded towel and mosaic the underside of the head and any parts of the legs and tail you had trouble reaching before. Don't go quite to the bottom with the mosaic; leave a gap of about ⅛ inch above where the tortoise will sit flat on the ground. Don't mosaic the bits that the tortoise stands on, or any part of the casting that is not part of the tortoise shape and can't be seen when it is standing up.

5 Leave the finished tortoise to dry naturally for forty-eight hours before grouting. Put on rubber gloves and mix up some terracotta-colored grout, or a color that will complement your particular choice of gems and tesserae. If you can't find a ready-made terracotta-colored powder, make your own by mixing red and yellow powders to make a reddish orange, then darken it using a tiny bit of blue—don't use black, it will kill the color. Rub the grout thoroughly into the surface, filling all the gaps between the gems and all the edges of the mosaic on the tortoise's underside. Extend the grout a little way onto the uncovered parts of the base, bordering the mosaic with grout for extra strength and durability.

6 Wipe off the excess immediately with a slightly dampened sponge and wipe off the chalky haze that will appear after fifteen to twenty minutes using a dry rag. If your tortoise is to go outside, wait forty-eight hours for it to dry and seal it with two coats of grout sealer.

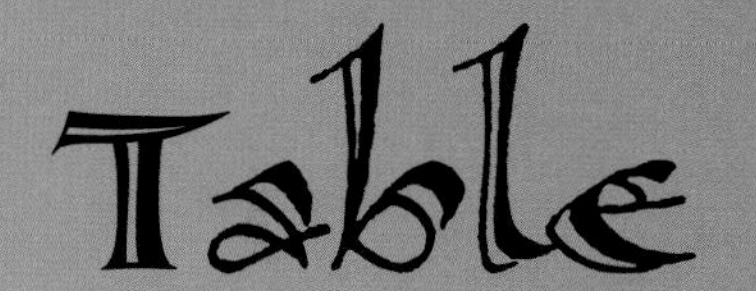

Table

TOOLS & MATERIALS

- Wood table, approximately 14 inches x 14 inches
- White glue or waterproofing sealer
- Assorted solid colored tiles, patterned dishes and trinkets
- Carbon paper
- Pencil
- T square
- Tile cutter
- Mosaic or tile nippers
- Hammer
- Heavy paper bag
- Protective eyewear
- Work gloves
- Ceramic tile adhesive
- Dull knife or spatula
- Paintbrush
- Paint or wood stain
- Sanded grout (terra cotta or color of your choice)
- Newspaper or scrap paper
- Rubber gloves
- Disposable container
- Stir stick
- Sponge
- Dry rag

Created by
Nancy Ungerman

tip

- Will the table be functional, or will it be purely decorative? If it will be used, then opt for flat pieces of tile and dishes to create a level surface.
- A wrought iron table base is very durable and ideal for use indoors or outside.

This small contemporary table is decorated with an abstract face reminiscent of the cubist style. The solid half of the table, the table border, and the face are made of ceramic tiles, the features of the face are made of trinkets and memorabilia, and the background around the face is made of patterned dishes. This square table can be functional as well as decorative when used next to a chair or sofa.

BEFORE YOU START

Find a wooden table to use as the base of your project. If the wood is raw, waterproof the tabletop by painting it with a mixture of white glue and water (one part glue to four parts water) or coating it with a commercial waterproofing sealer from any hardware store.

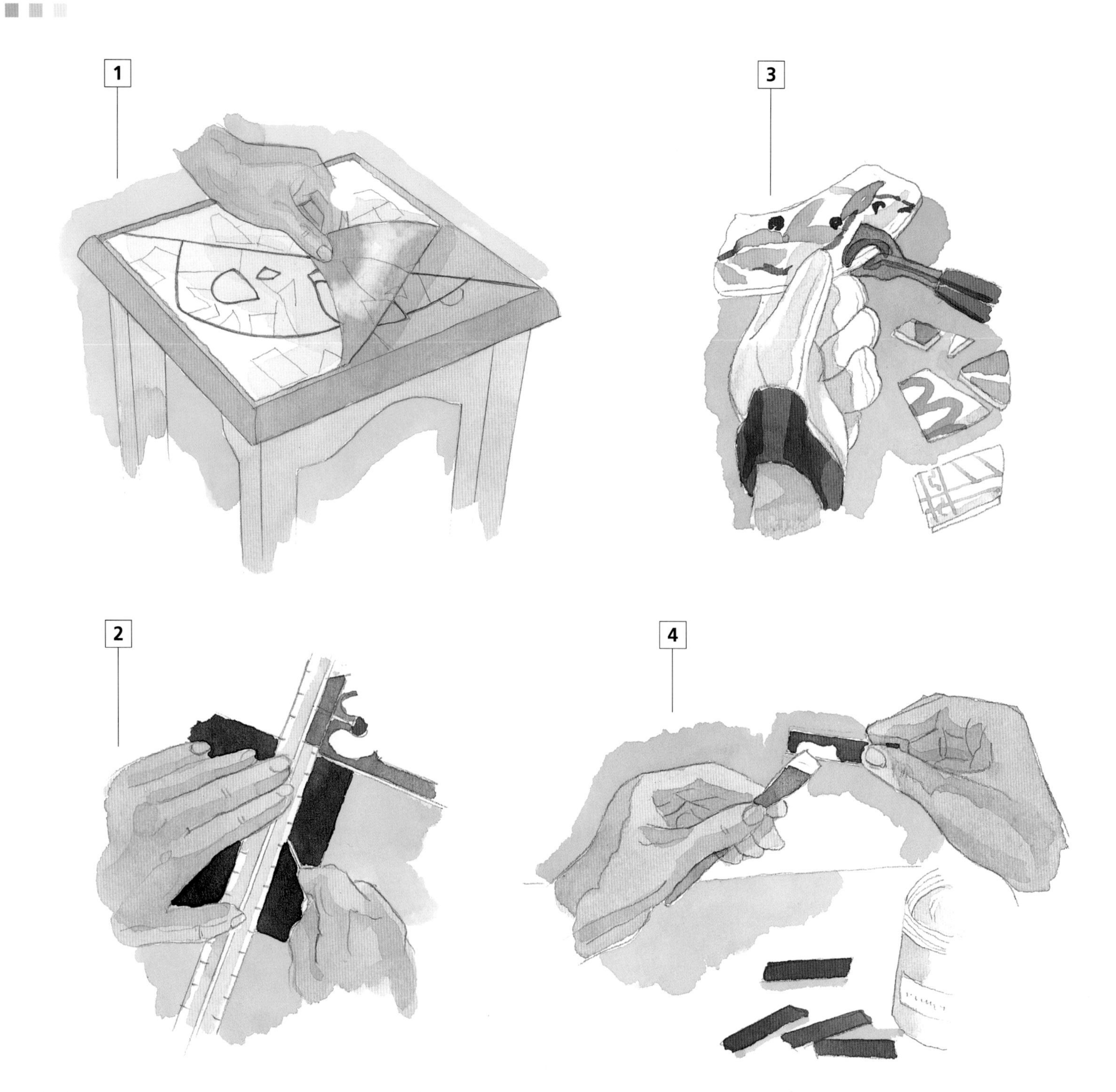

1 Follow the pattern shown in the main photograph or draw your chosen pattern to the correct size for your table and trace it onto the tabletop using carbon paper.

2 Place the T square firmly on top of a border tile, and use the scoring wheel of the tile cutter to score it into strips. Snap the tile along the score lines with the tile cutter. Repeat this score-and-snap technique until you have plenty of strips for two rows of border tiles. Break these strips into uneven lengths.

3 Use the nippers to clip the dishes into irregular shapes. Smash the ceramic tiles in a heavy paper or thick plastic bag with a hammer. Check the pieces frequently to see how you are doing. The broken pieces should be a variety of sizes ranging from ½ inch to 2 inches in diameter. Always wear protective eyewear and work gloves when nipping, breaking, or smashing to protect yourself from flying shards and splinters.

4 Using a dull knife or spatula, butter the back of the border tile strips with a thin layer of ceramic tile adhesive approximately ⅛ inch thick. Press the buttered strips in straight rows around the edges of the tabletop. Use your nippers to clip strips that are too long. If possible, lay a second row of tile strips around the sides of the table to give a clean finish to the edge.

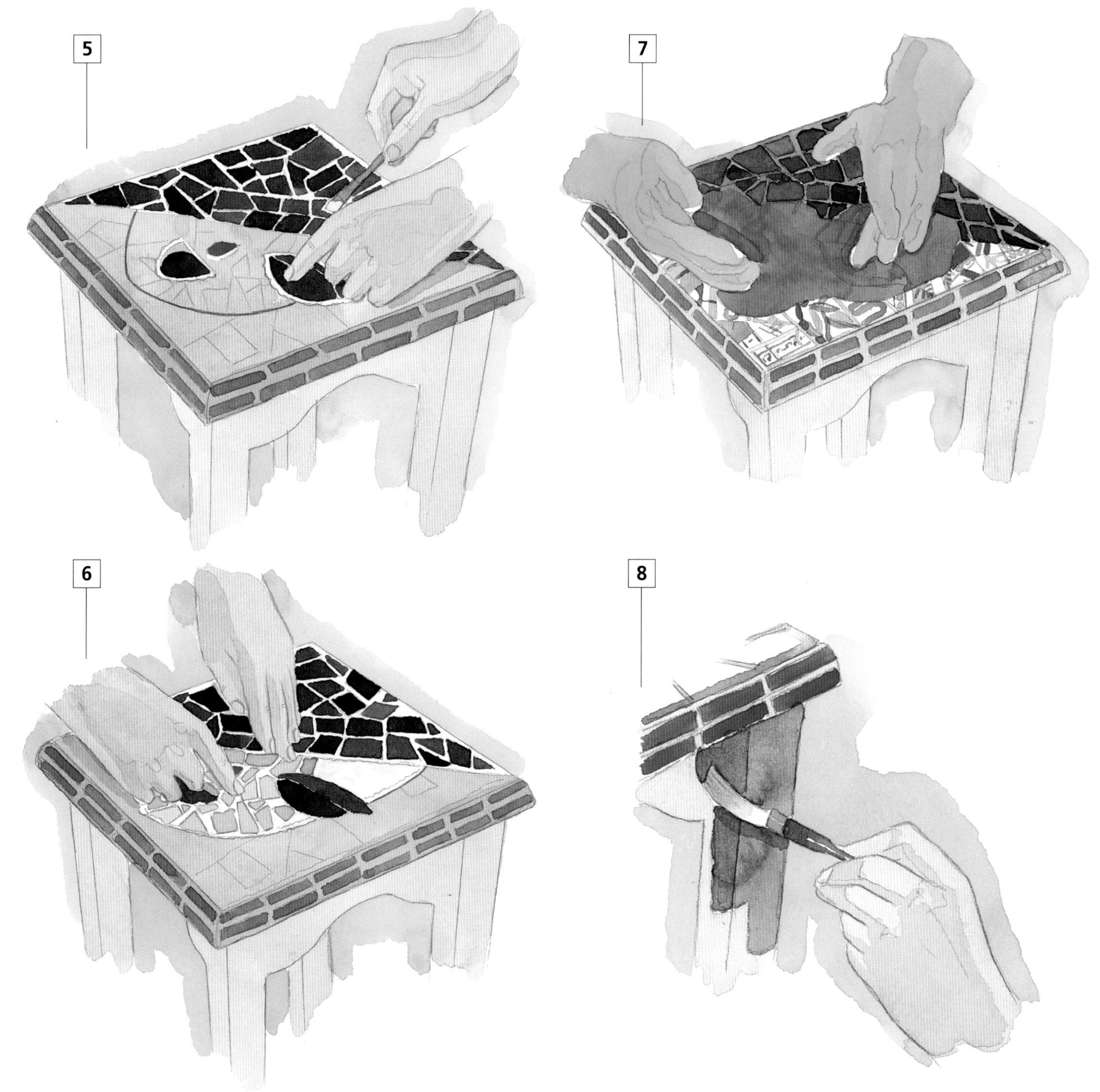

5 Spread ceramic tile adhesive onto a small area of the tabletop in the triangular solid-colored section. Press pieces of broken tiles into the adhesive. Continue spreading adhesive and adding tiles until this area is completely covered in fragments. Then spread adhesive onto the back of the memorabilia to be used for the facial features. Press the eye, nose, and mouth into place.

6 Spread adhesive onto the face area of the template. Press solid-colored ceramic tile shards into this area around the facial features. Remember that each fragment should fit comfortably into the space left by the surrounding pieces, so trim shards with your nippers when necessary. Fill in the background around the face with the broken dishes using the same technique. Allow the table to dry undisturbed for at least forty-eight hours before grouting.

7 Prepare and carefully apply the grout while wearing rubber gloves. Full procedure is given on pages 30-32. Be sure to fill every space between the fragments. As the grout begins to set, wipe the excess from the fragments and then allow the grout to dry for about twenty minutes. Vigorously wipe off the remaining chalky haze with a clean dry rag.

8 Tint the wooden table legs with stain or watered-down acrylic paint (one part paint to two parts water) or use a clear varnish if you prefer the look of natural wood.

Gallery of tables

1. Linda Benswanger creates a jumble of color and pattern with her broken pottery tabletop.

2,4,7 and 8. A selection of tables from the Mosaicwares designers Rebecca Dennis and Paula Funt.

3. Mary K. Guth's *Washington DC Table* has a center of focus on the 'President and First Lady' image on the tabletop.

5. Tracy Graivier Bell uses a central broken plate motif to focus attention on the center of the table.

6. Mary K. Guth's *Flower Table* is darkly inviting.

1.

2.

5.

6.

3.

4.

7.

8.

Vase

TOOLS & MATERIALS

- Glass vase
- Stained glass in 4 colors, 1 for background and 3 for flowers and leaves
- Glass scorer
- T square
- Running pliers
- Mosaic, glass, or tile nippers
- Protective eyewear
- Work gloves
- 2 flowerpots, cans or other stable objects
- Clear silicone or another clear quick-drying adhesive
- Sanded grout (charcoal gray or color of your choice)
- Newspaper or scrap paper
- Rubber gloves
- Disposable container
- Stir stick
- Sponge
- Dry rag

Created by
Linda Oldham

This tall graceful vase is made of opaque stained glass. The pieces of symmetrically cut oil-glass (which looks like a puddle of oil … shimmering pinks and blues on a black background) and dark grout provide a striking backdrop for the bright hand-nipped flower petals and leaves. Perfect for a bouquet of spring flowers! Flea markets and garage sales are good places to start your search for a glass vase to use as the base. Any shape will do, but look for one with clean lines and without much decoration. The simpler the vase, the better.

- A background of light-colored glass, hence less color contrast, will create an understated and subtle effect.
- Try nipping out different petal shapes to create these flowers:
  - Pansy
  - Tulip
  - Iris

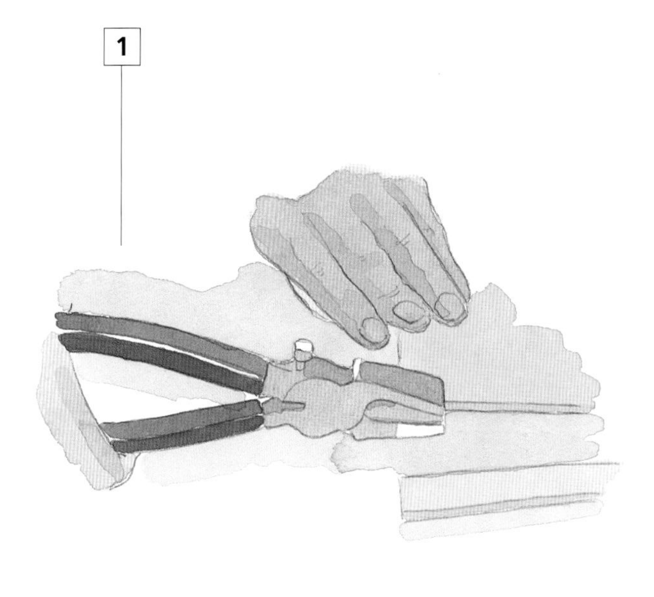

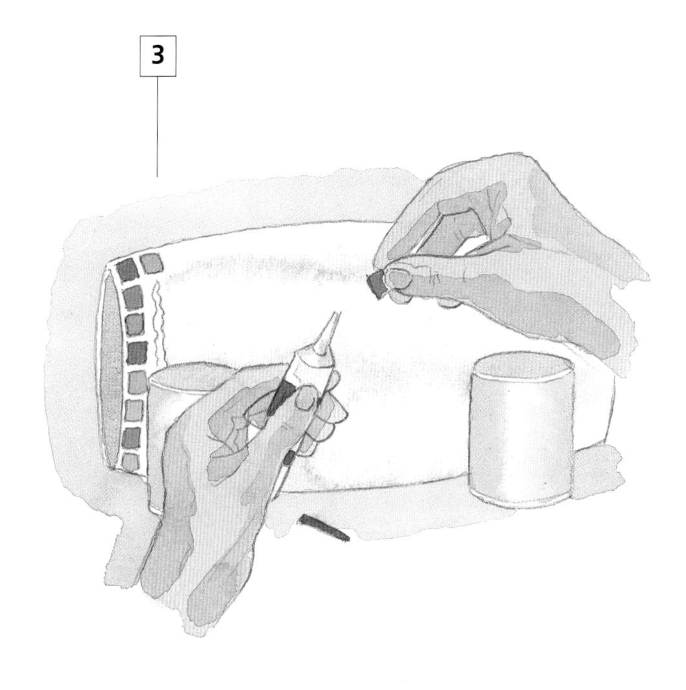

1 Using the T square as a straightedge, score the stained glass into ½ inch strips. Adjust the glass a quarter turn, and score it again into squares. Using the running pliers, snap the glass along the score lines in one direction into strips and then repeat in the other direction into squares.

2 Nibble away at the other three colors of stained glass with your nippers to form petals and leaves, laying them on your worktable to check their arrangement. Always wear protective eyewear and work gloves while scoring, breaking, and nipping glass to avoid injury from tiny glass shards.

3 Lay the vase on its side so that it is horizontal. The stained glass pieces tend to slide down if you work on a vertical surface. Use flowerpots or cans to stabilize the vase so it won't roll while you are working. Begin at the top of the vase by squirting a bubble of adhesive just beneath the rim of the vase. Use the tip of the applicator tube to spread it into a thin layer. These adhesives dry very quickly, so only attempt to cover a small area at a time. Place the glass squares on the vase in rows, leaving small spaces between each for grout. Work around the fixture from top to bottom for two rows.

4 Adhere the petals and leaves to the vase using the same method as in step three. Be sure to spread enough adhesive between the stained glass and the vase to form a solid bond so that the grout will not seep between the two. This vase is tall and slender and has one flower on the center of each side. If your vase is larger or rounder, you may choose to add a third or even a fourth flower.

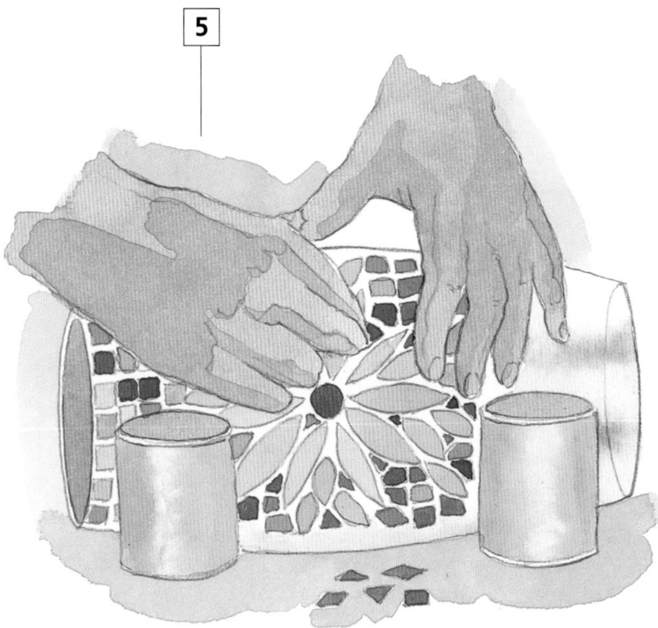

5 Fill in spaces between the flowers with glass squares, taking care to keep the rows straight. You will not be able to fit squares between each petal and leaf, so nibble away at some pieces of background glass to make irregular shapes to fill the empty spots. Continue adding rows of glass squares below the flowers until you reach the bottom. Allow to dry for twenty-four hours before applying the grout.

6 While wearing rubber gloves, spread the prepared grout onto the vase as if you are icing a cake with your hands. Refer to pages 30-32 for instructions on preparing grout. Fill every space between the glass. Wipe the excess grout from the glass and then allow the grout to dry for about twenty minutes. Buff off the remaining chalky haze with a clean dry rag.

COLOR VARIATIONS

a Try a pink flower on the oil glass background and a dark grout.

b Use a red flower on a light oil glass background with a pale gray grout.

c For a summery look, try a yellow flower on orange background. Use cream-colored grout.

d A purple flower on dark green background with pale green grout will give an exotic look.

a

b

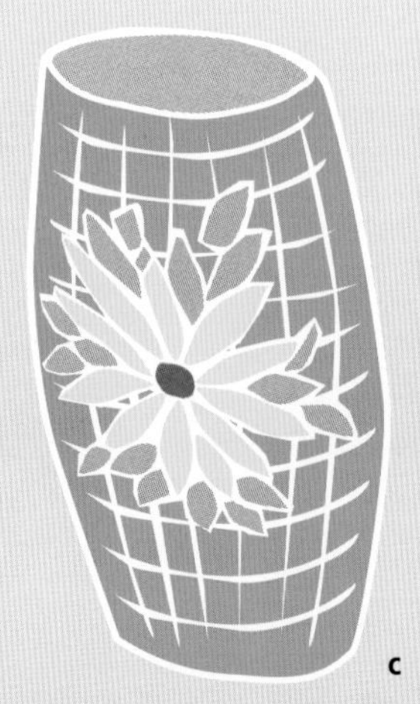
c

d

Gallery of vases

1.

2.

3.

1. Linda Benswanger gives a slightly Roman feel to this modern vase.
2. Hap Sakwa takes the traditional and enlivens it with the novel. Take this traditional urn-shaped vase covered in bright plastics and American icons, for example.
3. Hap Sakwa's spiky vase has an oriental feel.
4. Tracy Graivier Bell uses strategically placed three-dimensional objects to enhance this everyday plant pot.
5. Mary K. Guth uses doves as handles on her *White Vase*.

4.

5.

Cup Handle Mirror

TOOLS & MATERIALS

- Rectangular piece of MDF or plywood 1 inch thick
- Rectangular mirror
- PVA
- Thick cloth (i.e., a dish cloth)
- Assorted white cups
- Mosaic nippers
- Protective eyewear and gloves
- Ceramic tile adhesive
- Dull knife or spatula
- Sanded grout (light gray)
- Rubber gloves
- Newspaper or scrap paper
- Disposable container
- Stir stick
- Small rubber grout spreader
- Sponge
- Dry rag
- Varnish
- Old paintbrush
- Screw-in picture hooks or mirror plates

Created by
Sarah Kelly

Create a strikingly quirky three-dimensional effect around a mirror with a selection of cup handles around the edges and parts of the cups on the face of the frame. This makes an ideal garden mirror.

BEFORE YOU START

Try to find an off-cut of medium density fiberboard or plywood at a lumber merchant as this is usually cheaper than getting a piece cut specially. Aim for a size of roughly 15 inches by 12 inches. Choose a piece of mirror which will lie in the center of the wood leaving a border of about 4 inches all round with a slightly bigger space at the bottom. Prime the wood using a mixture of PVA and water (one part glue to four parts water or according to the manufacturer's instructions). Then place the mirror onto the wood in the desired place. Mark the corners with a pencil and then remove it. Apply a layer of ceramic tile adhesive to the marked area on the wood and replace the mirror over it. Cover it with a thick folded cloth and press gently to stick it down.

TO HANG YOUR MIRROR

Slide your hands under the mirror and carefully turn it over. If the mirror is to hang in a bathroom or another damp place, apply a coat of wood varnish to the back according to the instructions on the tin. If not, just screw in the picture hooks and attach some string or wire to hang it. Finished mosaic pieces can often be very heavy, especially if they are quite big, so if your mirror is particularly heavy, you should hang it using mirror plates. Make sure you attach them to an area where there is a gap in the handles so you can get the screwdriver through when you screw it into the wall.

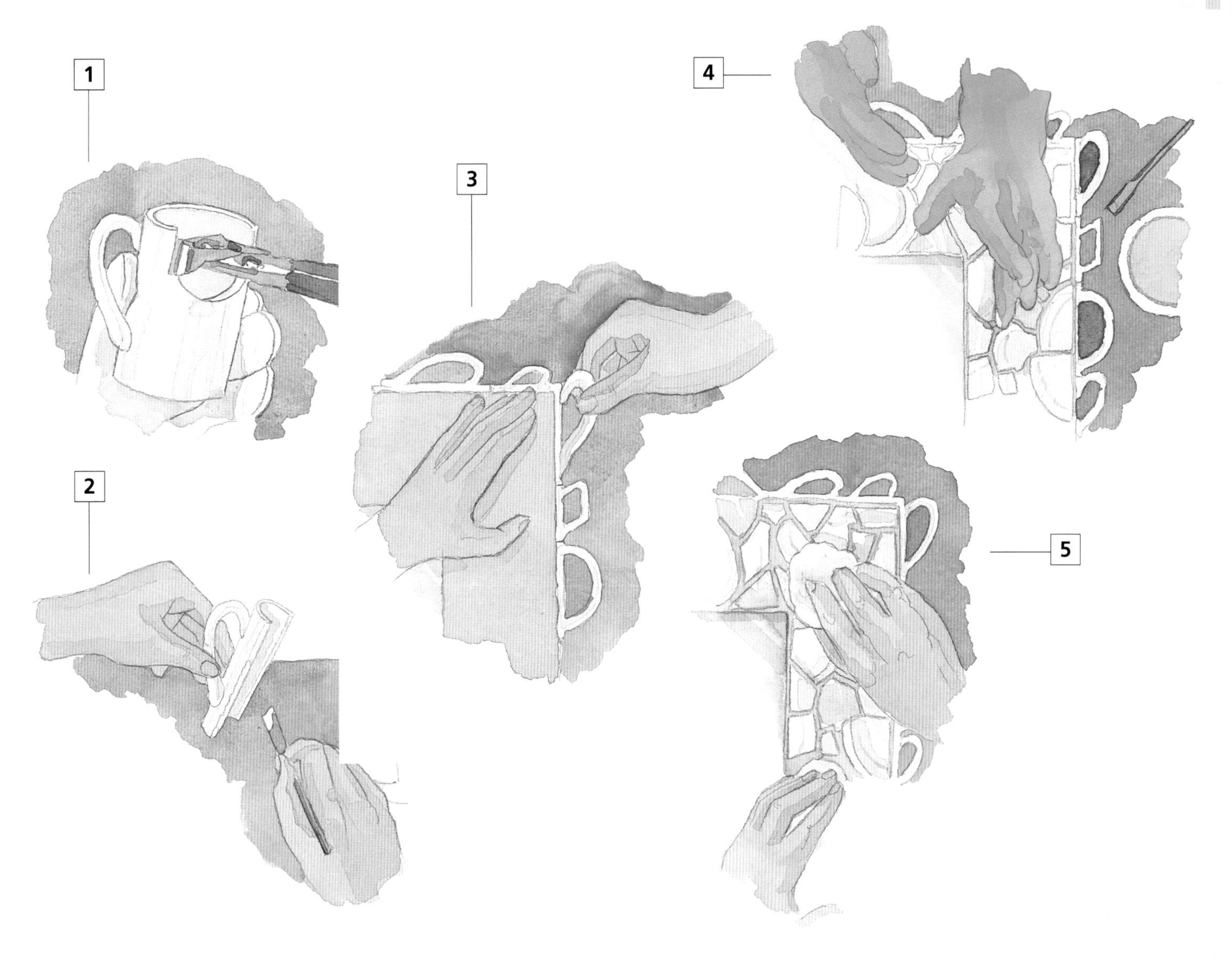

1 Use the tile nippers to carefully cut out the handle sections of your white cups. Wear protective gloves and eyewear while doing this. You will need the whole handle area, not just the handle itself, so it is advisable to have quite a few cups at your disposal in case of accidents! You will need about twenty to twenty-five cups (plus emergency extras) but this will vary depending on the size of your wood. Try to collect cups with a variety of handles in different sizes and shapes, as this will make a much more interesting design.

2 With the mirror base flat on your work surface, arrange the handles round the sides of the wood and move them around until you get an interesting layout. Mix shapes and sizes and the direction they point in. Trim any bases that stick up over the front of the wood. When you are happy with the layout, leave the handles where they are and, taking one at a time, butter it with tile adhesive using the knife or spatula, then lay it down. Fill in any gaps with small pieces from the rest of the cups.

3 When all the handles have been stuck down, you can begin to mosaic the front of your mirror. Use the offcuts from the cups you have taken the handles from and cut them into random pieces with the nippers, again wearing the gloves and eye wear. To add interest to your mosaic, you can also use the circular bottoms of the cups, either intact or cut in half. Apply tile adhesive to a small section of the wood and press the pieces in. Work round the rest of the mirror in the same way. Try to mosaic the edges as neatly as possible so nothing sticks out—the ceramic pieces can be sharp.

4 Allow the finished mosaic to dry for forty-eight hours. Wearing the rubber gloves, mix up a quantity of light gray grout in the disposable container and apply it over your mosaic. It may be difficult to get it between the handles, so make sure the gloves are thick enough to prevent cutting them on any jagged ceramic edges. Take care not to pick the mirror up by the handles at any time as they will not be able to support the weight.

5 Wipe the excess grout off the surface of the mosaic with a slightly dampened sponge, taking lots of care around the handles. You may even need to use a smaller sponge round this area. Leave to air dry for a further 20 minutes polish the mosaic with a clean dry rag.

Inspiration from everyday

1. Patty Goya's *Cowboy Boots* are 'stitched' in broken plate and adorned with commemorative pottery.
2. Mary K. Guth's *Large Folding Screen* incorporates well-known views from around the world with caged dolls.
3. Cleo Mussi has created a traditional piece using Islamic floral designs.
4. Mary K. Guth's *Mouth Box* actually contains a full set of teeth.
5. Hap Sakwa's Americana vase draws on images from stage and screen.
6. Mary K. Guth's *Guitar* is decorated with gold ceramic, Elvis, and a souvenir from Reno. Decidedly kitsch and wonderfully decorative.

2.

1.

3.

4.

5.

6.

Cat

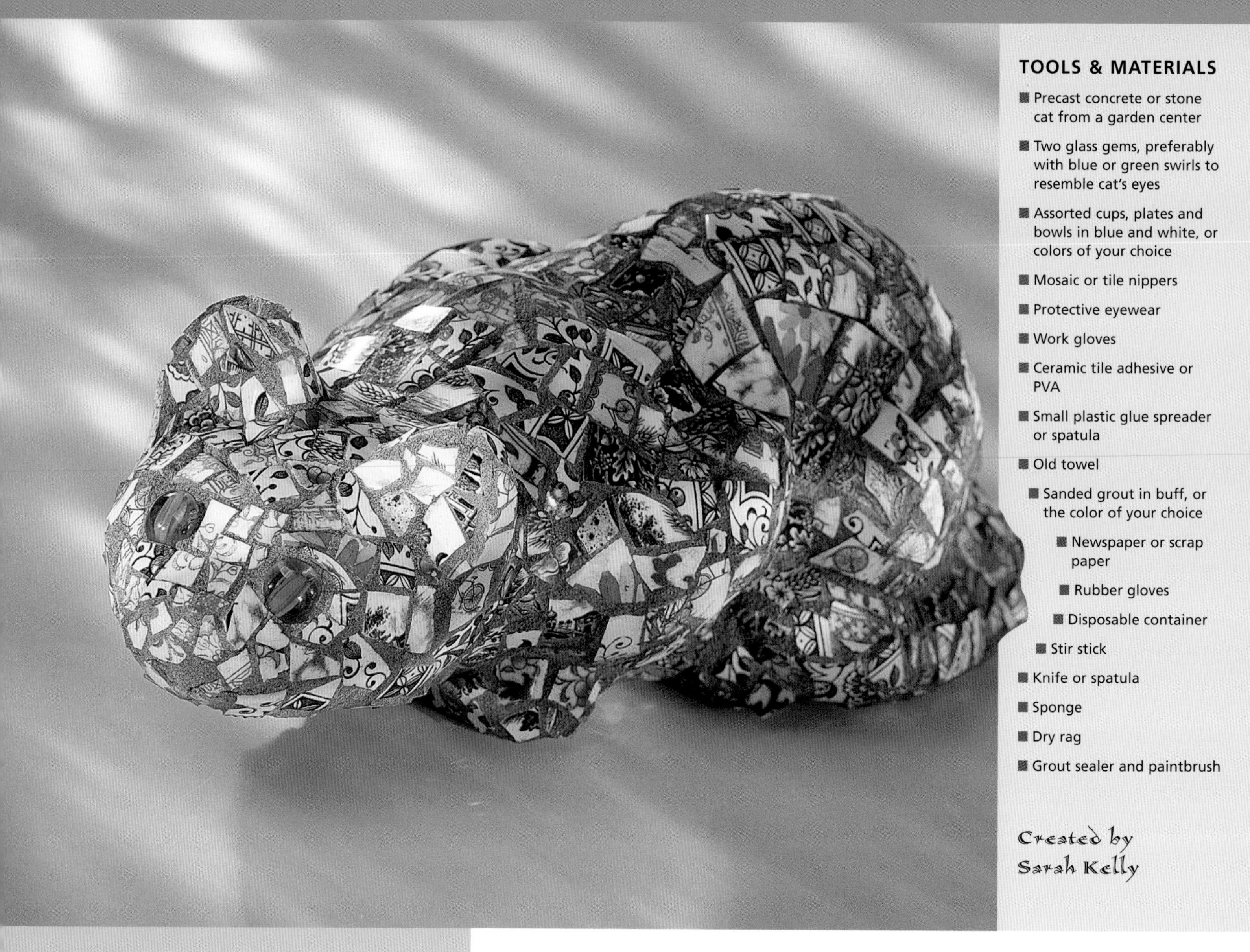

TOOLS & MATERIALS

- Precast concrete or stone cat from a garden center
- Two glass gems, preferably with blue or green swirls to resemble cat's eyes
- Assorted cups, plates and bowls in blue and white, or colors of your choice
- Mosaic or tile nippers
- Protective eyewear
- Work gloves
- Ceramic tile adhesive or PVA
- Small plastic glue spreader or spatula
- Old towel
- Sanded grout in buff, or the color of your choice
- Newspaper or scrap paper
- Rubber gloves
- Disposable container
- Stir stick
- Knife or spatula
- Sponge
- Dry rag
- Grout sealer and paintbrush

Created by Sarah Kelly

Transform a concrete cat from a garden center into a delightfully chunky decorative object for the house or garden. You can use colorful, patterned tesserae all over for a kitsch look or experiment with realistic cat colors and markings such as stripes and spots.

BEFORE YOU START

Try to choose two flat-bottomed glass gems that are similar in size or design to make a convincing pair of eyes. If you can't find any marble types then use ordinary ones in blue, yellow, or green. As the surface of the cat is generally quite curved, it's best to use china cups or bowls that curve in a similar way. This will enable the tesserae to stick better. If your china is flat, you will need to cut the pieces quite small to fit the curves snugly.

tip

- Check each area periodically to replace any tesserae that may have slipped. If your tesserae keep slipping, allow the base coat of PVA to dry for a bit longer before you stick them.

1 Apply a good dollop of adhesive over the existing eyes of the cat base. If you are using PVA, allow it to become tacky before gluing on the two flat-bottomed glass gems. Wearing the protective gloves and eyewear, start cutting small tesserae from the china. Beginning with the cat's face, apply a layer of adhesive to the surface, wait a few minutes then butter each tessera with adhesive and stick them round the eyes and then round the rest of the face down to the bottom of the chin. Do the insides of the ears next and, still using small pieces, complete the tops and backs of the ears until you reach the cat's body.

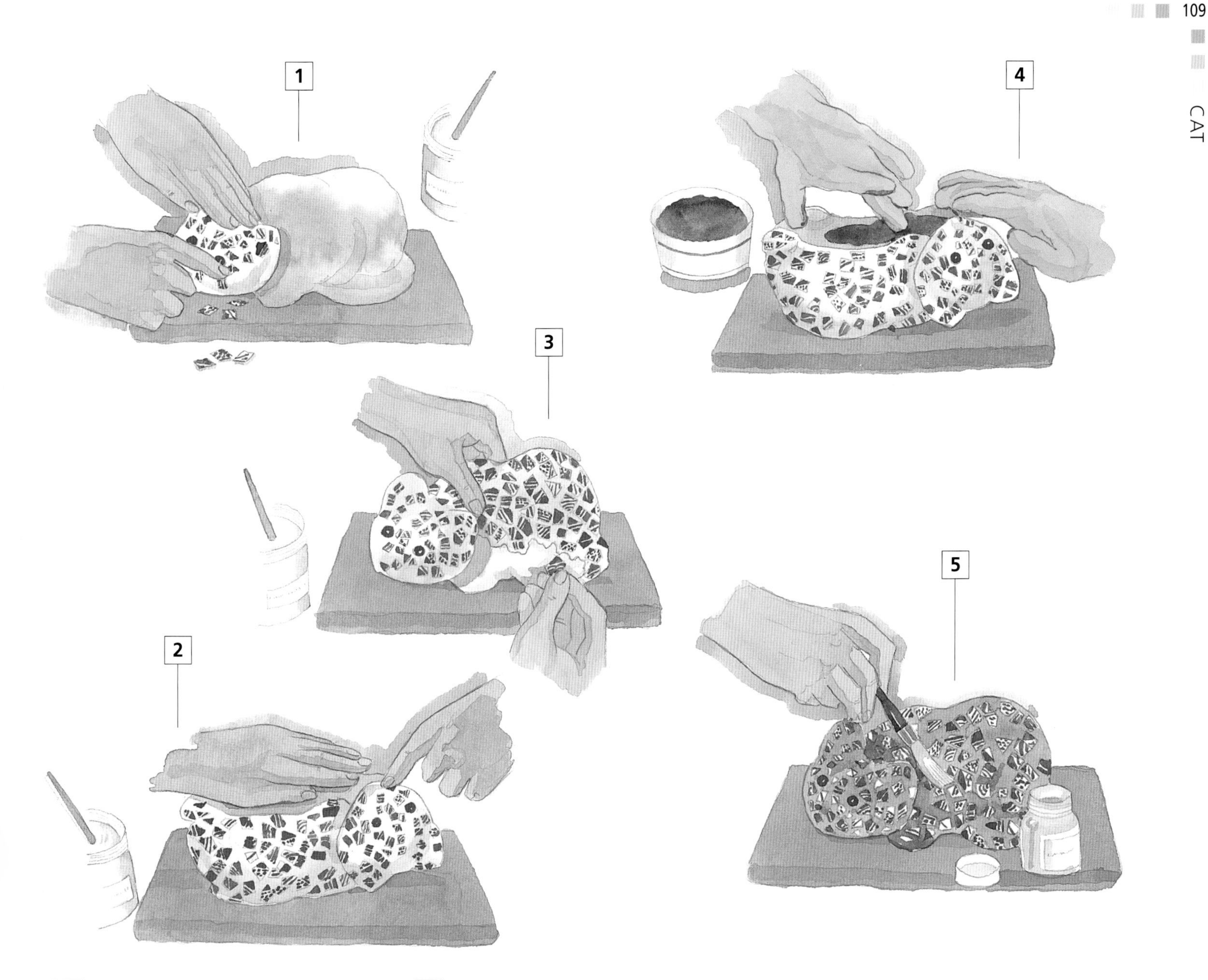

2 Using slightly larger tesserae, follow the same method to cover the cat's back. Do as much as you can comfortably, then make a padding with your towel on the work surface and gently tip the cat onto one side, making sure there are no still-drying tesserae on the other side that may get dislodged in the process. Carry on working in the same way to cover the legs and tail. Work outward from any difficult crevices and take the tesserae down to about ½ inch from where the cat would sit when it is resting flat on the surface. Tesserae on the edges of objects are quite vulnerable and if you take them right down to the bottom of the cat they will be much more prone to falling off whenever the cat is moved.

3 Allow this side to dry thoroughly (preferably twenty-four hours or at least overnight), then carefully turn the cat over on the towel and repeat the process. When you have finished this side, turn the cat onto its back and do the underside of the chin and neck. Don't mosaic the base of the cat. Leave to air dry for forty-eight hours before grouting.

4 Color the cement-based grout with buff colored powder suitable for coloring cement, following the procedure given on pages 30–32. The colors are usually quite intense so you don't need to add too much. Carefully apply the grout to the cat while wearing rubber gloves. Tip the cat onto its sides and back as before in order to grout it thoroughly. Make sure you grout round the tesserae on the edges of the cat, extending the grout onto the base a little way to give these pieces a bit of added protection. When the surface is completely covered, begin to remove the excess with the sponge, then polish with a soft rag after twenty minutes or so to remove the residue.

5 If you want your cat to sit outside, apply a couple of coats of grout sealer after letting the grout air dry for forty-eight hours.

Spiral Pebble Pot

TOOLS & MATERIALS

- Terra cotta or earthenware pot.
- Small, smooth, rounded pebbles
- Pencil
- Cement based mortar
- PVA
- Dull knife or plastic glue spreader
- Newspaper or scrap paper
- An old towel
- Disposable container
- Stir stick
- Sanded grout
- Black grout-coloring powder
- Rubber gloves
- Disposable container
- Sponge
- Dry rag
- Grout sealer and paintbrush

Created by
Sarah Kelly

tip

- You may need to give some of the white pebbles an individual clean with a damp rag to remove any discoloration. Be aware that particularly porous white pebbles may permanently absorb some of the grout color.

Use smooth white pebbles to create a spiral pattern on a contrasting background of black. This pot will make a hardy and attractive addition to a small garden or patio. Fill it with a plant with bright red flowers to suit the strong coloring and design.

BEFORE YOU START

If your pot is unglazed (with a matte appearance), seal it using a dilution of PVA in water (one part glue to four parts water or according to the manufacturer's instructions). Leave to dry.

FOR THE FINISHED PIECE

If your pebbles are very small and your pot quite large, the gaps between each of your tesserae should be quite tiny so you may be able to get away without grouting at the end. If this is the case, you should color your mortar with some of the black grout-coloring powder in the same way you would color grout. If not, just grout as normal.

COLOR VARIATIONS

a Reverse the colors for black spirals on a white background and use very pale gray grout.

b Use sandy colored pebbles on a terra cotta or darker brown background. Match the grout to the background color.

c Try sandy color spirals on a blue gray background with a pale grey grout.

d Use patterned pebbles on white background with white grout

a

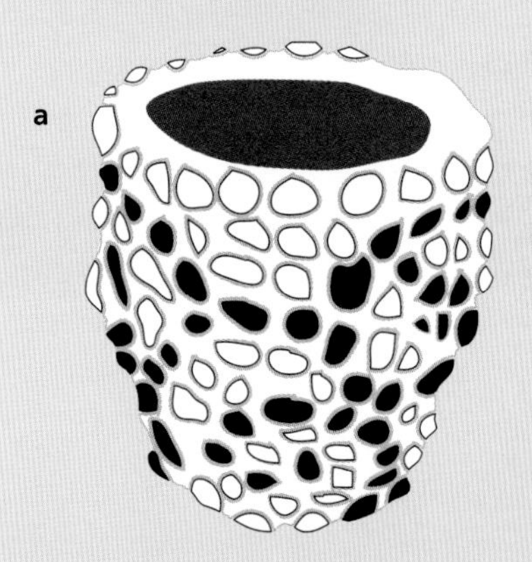

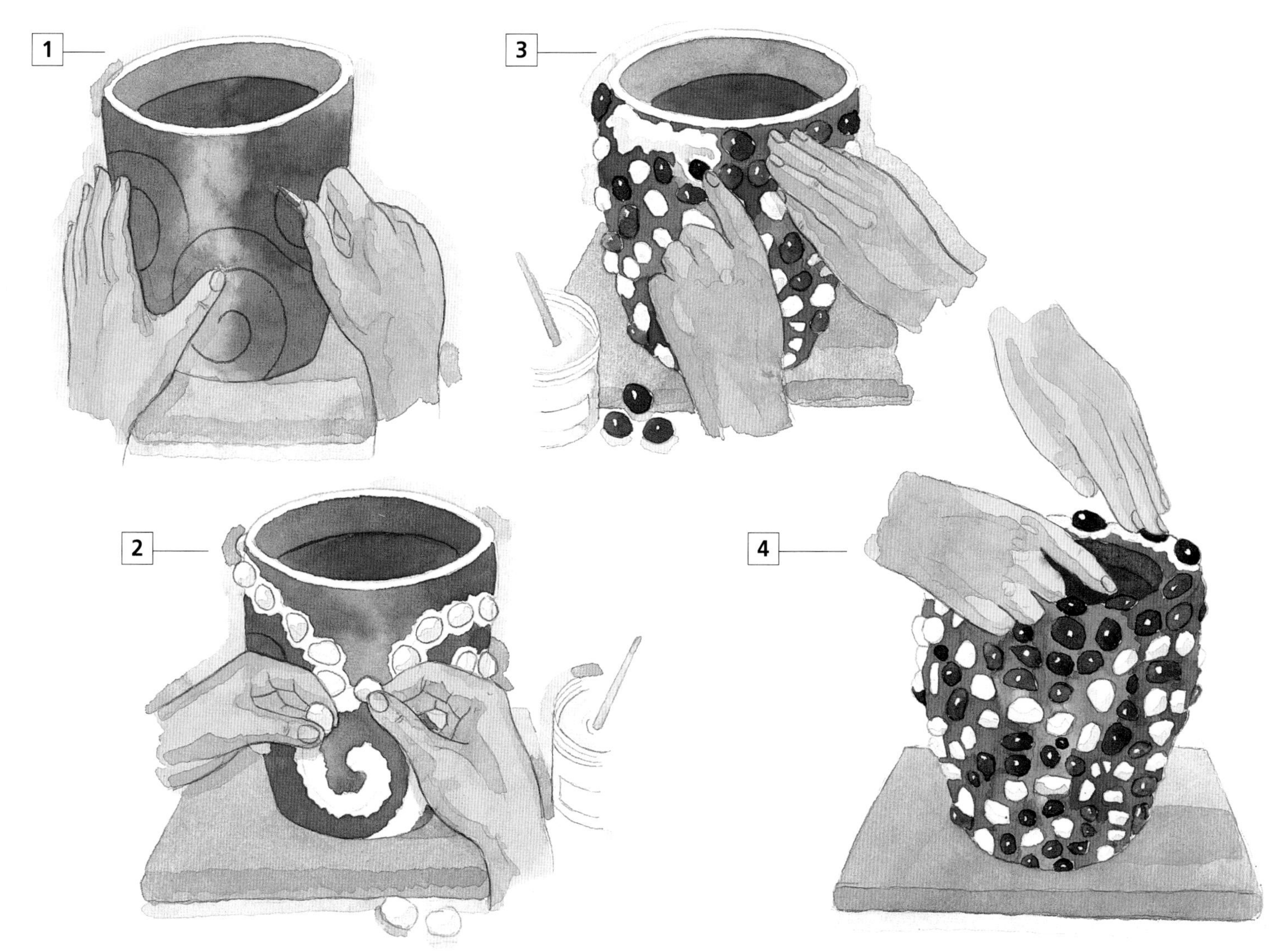

1 Use a pencil to draw out a pattern of spirals round the pot. Make sure they don't get too tight, especially if you are using a small pot. You will need to be able to fit at least one line of black pebbles between each spiral of white pebbles. When you are satisfied with your design, mix up some adhesive with water. Add a spoonful of PVA to strengthen the bond.

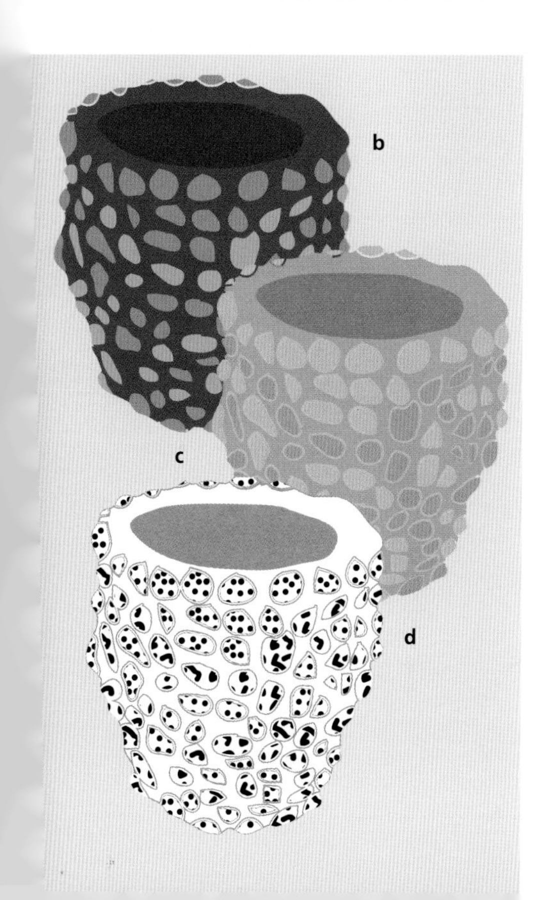

2 Using the knife or glue spreader, apply a layer of adhesive to one of the spirals. The adhesive needs to form a good bed for the pebble to sit in, so you will need to make it about $\frac{1}{4}$ to $\frac{1}{2}$ inch deep, depending on the size of your pebbles. Starting from the center, begin sticking a line of white pebbles, flattest side down, along the line of the spiral. You may find it easier to lay the pot on its side while you're working so that the pebbles don't slide off. An old towel should be folded and placed underneath to protect the pot and help to keep it in place.

3 When the spiral is finished, carefully fill the gaps with adhesive. Fill in the gaps with the black pebbles. You may need to jiggle both sets of pebbles around slightly to ensure a good fit, especially if they are quite large. Don't be afraid to replace individual pebbles to get a better fit.

4 Gradually work your way around the pot in the same way, doing one spiral at a time and filling in surrounding areas as you go along. It's important to complete each area while the adhesive is still pliable enough make any corrections. As you turn the pot, make sure the area underneath is dry enough to rest on the towel without disturbing any of the pebbles. If your pot has a rim, lay some more black pebbles over this when you have finished the main design.

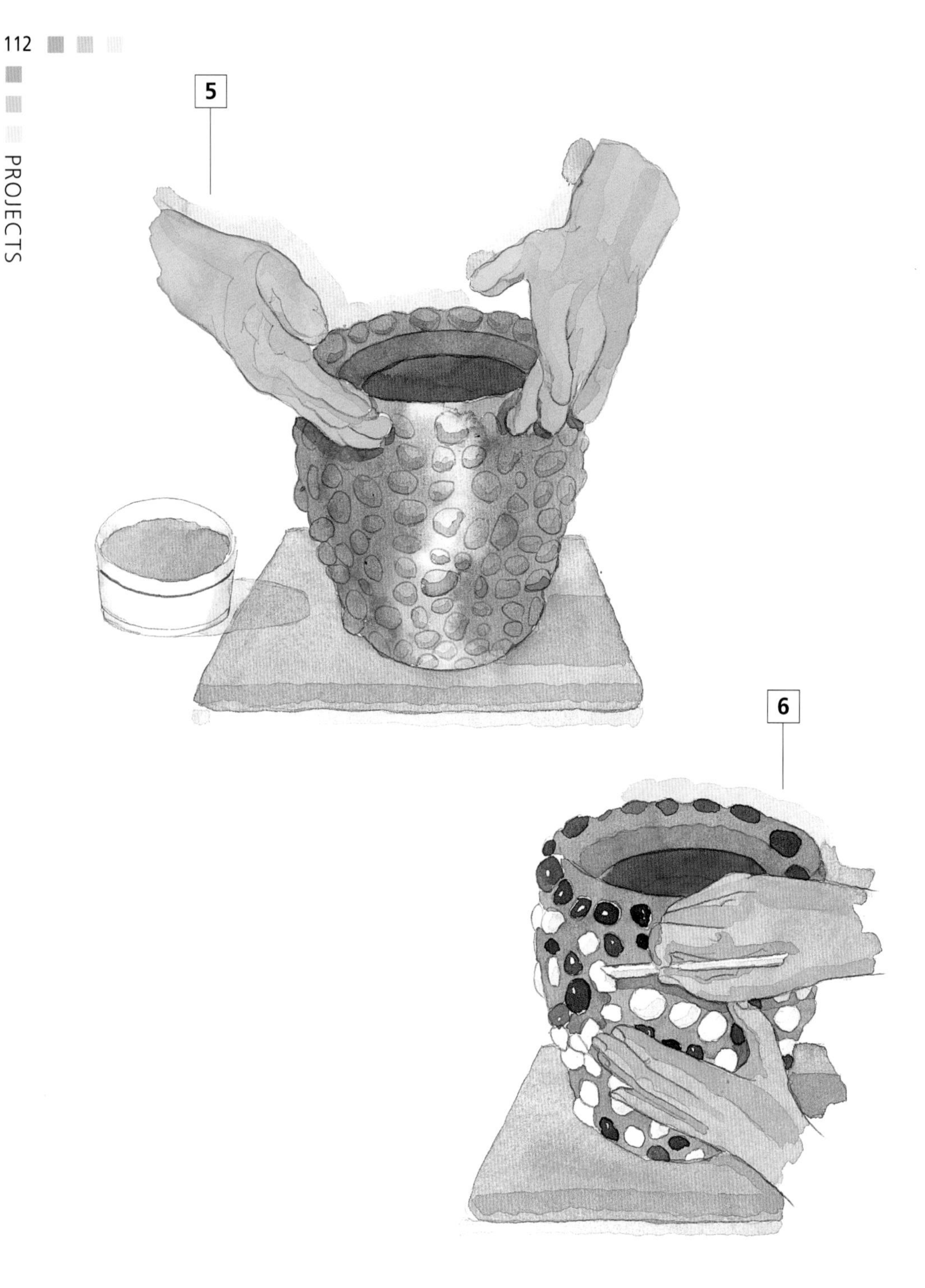

5 When the pot is completely covered allow to dry for forty-eight hours. If you need to grout it, put on the rubber gloves and mix the grout, adding a little black grout-coloring powder as described on pages 30-32. With black powder, the color can often look a lot darker when it is applied than it does in the pot, so be aware of this when you are mixing. Rub the grout over the surface of the pot using your hands. Apply only a thin layer to let the individual shapes of the stones to stand out, or a lot more if you want them to just peek out from a smoother surface. Take the grout right over the top of the pot to cover all of the original surface—a band of color at the top will detract from the impact of the black and white design.

6 Rub off the excess grout immediately with a damp sponge. You may want to excavate some of the pebbles a bit more if they are getting lost. Use the point of a knife then smooth the sponge over again. After fifteen to twenty minutes, polish the whole pot with a soft dry rag. If your pot will be used outside, wait forty-eight hours for the grout to dry, then brush two coats of grout sealer over it and allow to dry.

1. Sarah Kelly and Kaffe Fassett created this beautiful black swan for exhibition at the annual Royal Chelsea Flower Show in London, England.
2. Carlos Alves' Mermaid mural brings a maritime theme to a poolside wall.
3, 4, 5, 6 and 7. Cleo Mussi's outdoor pieces include big cats resting in the undergrowth, natural themes such as birds and bees, and even the occasional sun god.

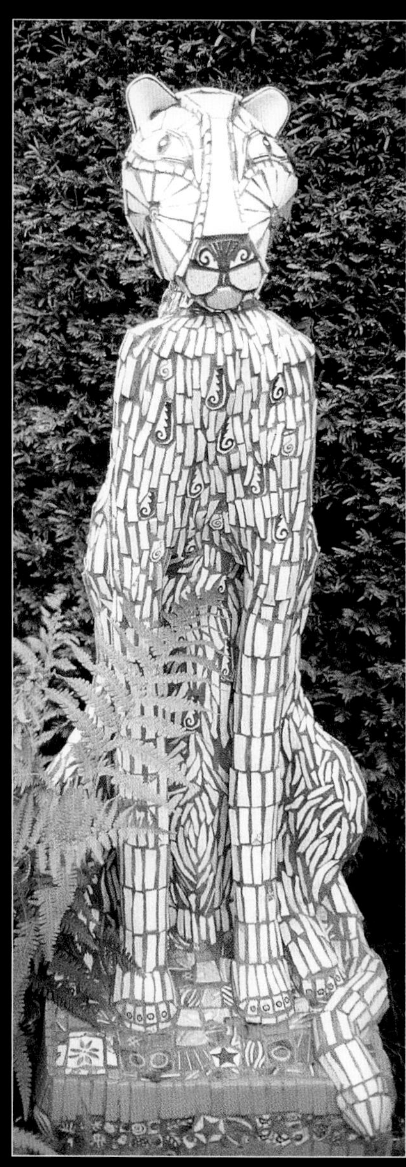

3.

Gallery of garden pieces

1.

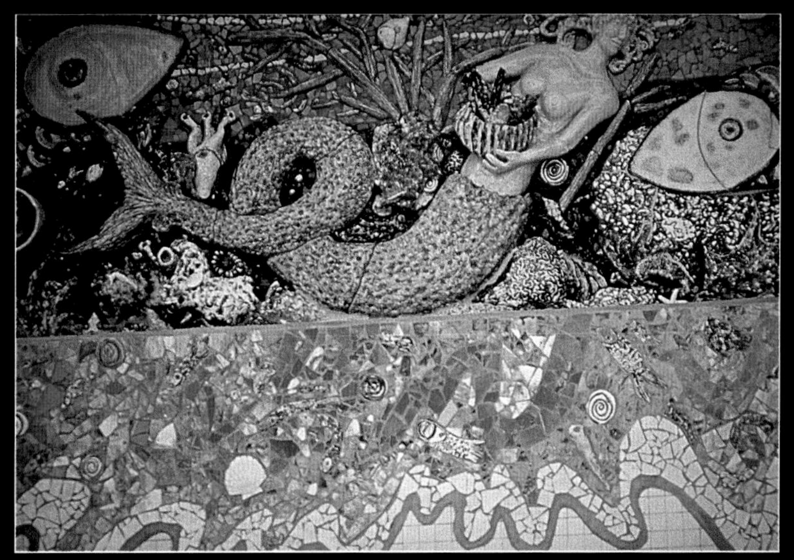

2.

6.

4.

5.

7.

Star Pot

TOOLS & MATERIALS

- Compasses or a circular template, such as a small cup
- Attractively shaped, blue glazed ceramic pot
- Ceramic or china in different shades of blue, pale dusky pink, soft peach, light golden yellow, and pale terra cotta
- Paper
- Scissors
- Washable felt pen
- Masking tape
- Ceramic tile adhesive or PVA
- Small plastic glue spreader
- Tile nippers
- Grout in pale terra cotta (or color of your choice), sanded or unsanded
- Newspaper or scrap paper
- Disposable container
- Stir stick
- Sponge
- Dry rag

Created by
Sarah Kelly

The base of this pot is such a beautiful color that only a simple band of mosaic has been added to it. The colors used both complement and gently contrast with it and were inspired by a picture of a Moroccan room. The star motif itself was also inspired by a piece of Moroccan design.

COLOR VARIATIONS

a Make all the stars different shades of your chosen color along with the rest of the motif, so each one is totally different from its neighbor.
b Try orange, red, and green on a warm green pot, with a green or terra cotta grout.
c Use pinks and whites on pink pot with pink grout.
d Use blues, oranges, and yellows on a dark blue pot, with a dark blue grout.

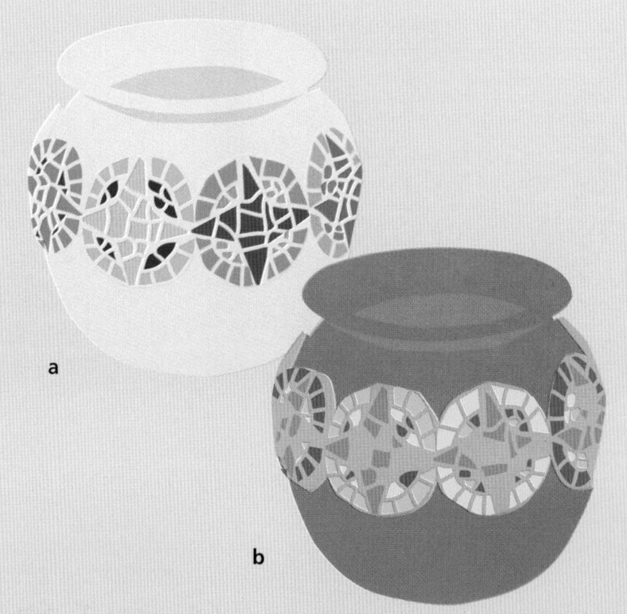

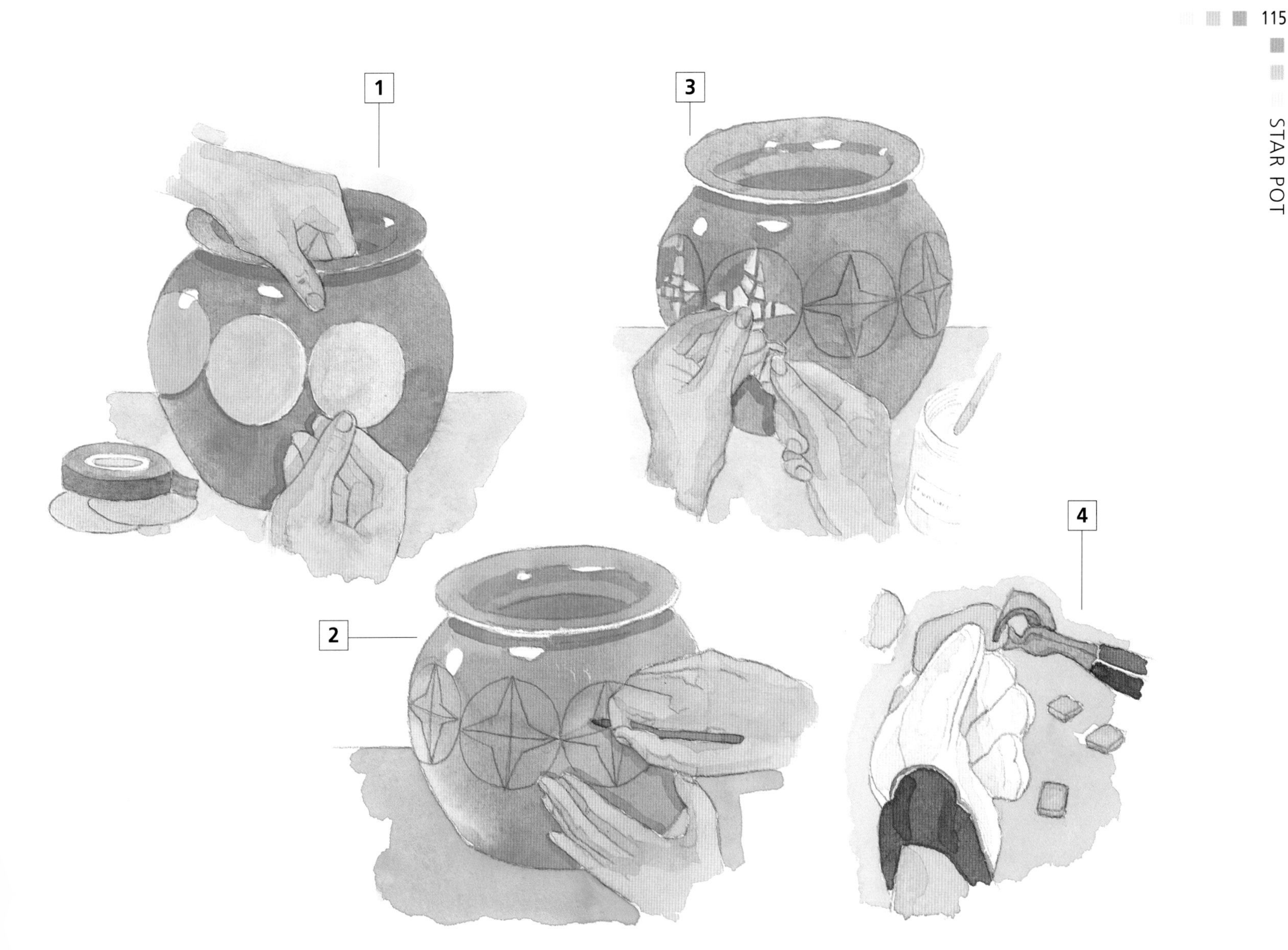

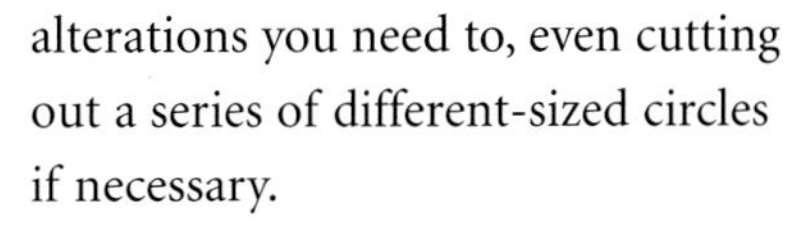

1 Plan your design by using the compass (or cup) to draw out a number of circular templates on a piece of paper. Cut these out and stick them around the pot in the desired position using tiny rolled-up pieces of masking tape on the back. They should fit together in a continuous band, so make any alterations you need to, even cutting out a series of different-sized circles if necessary.

2 When you are happy with the layout of the paper circles, draw round them carefully with the felt pen and then remove them. Inside the circles draw a star with four points. The easiest way to do this is to draw a cross and draw the star points round it. Make sure the points are flush with the edges of the circle. Then draw a narrow border around the inside of the circle, letting the star points break through it.

3 Choose a pale blue for the stars. This color should remain constant throughout the design, so make sure you have enough to go around. Put on the protective work gear, and break the ceramic into quite small, random tesserae using the nippers. If you are using PVA, apply a layer to one circle on the pot and leave it to become tacky. Apply your chosen glue to the back of each tessera and stick them carefully onto the star design, making sure you keep the shape as true as you can, although obviously some variation is part of the charm of mosaic!

4 Choose one of your warm colors for the border. Break the ceramic into small squares or rectangles, nibbling them a little thinner at the bottom so that they fit round the circle as smoothly as possible. Try to use the naturally shallow or beveled parts of tesserae on the outside of the border where it meets the surface of the pot if possible, so that the difference in height of the surfaces is not too dramatic. Apply the glue in the same way as before and stick the pieces as close together as possible.

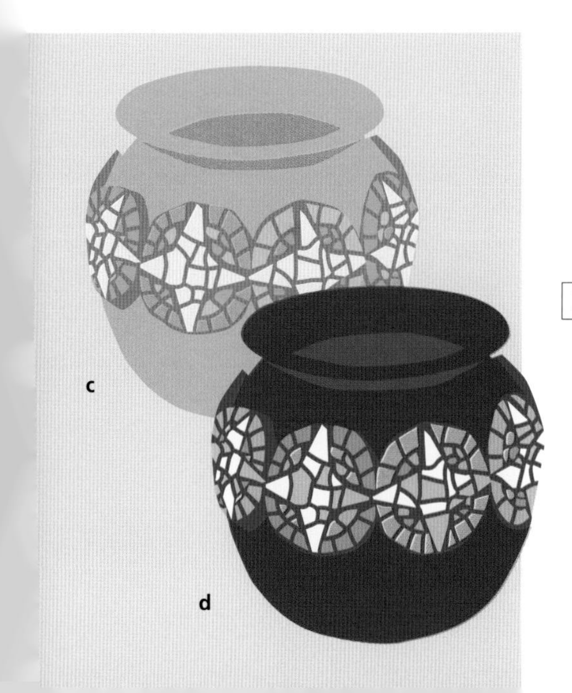

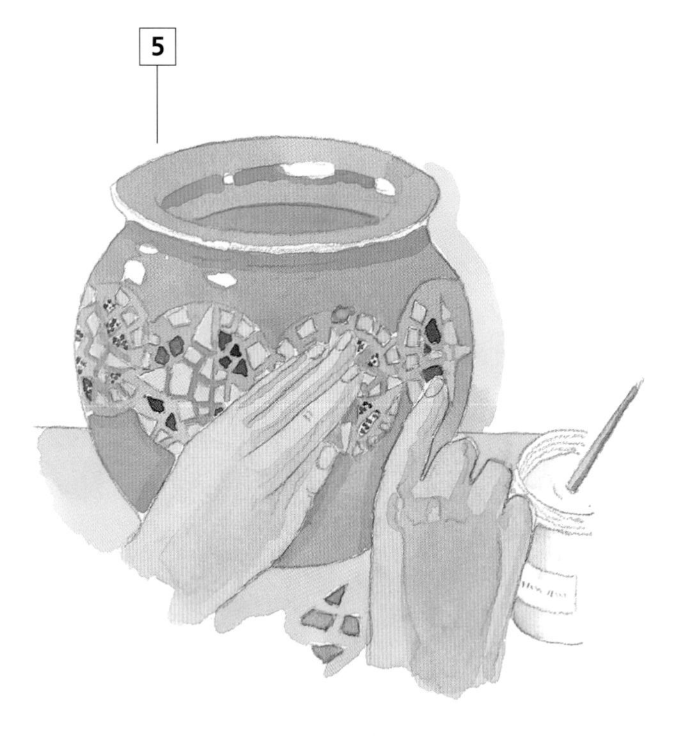

5

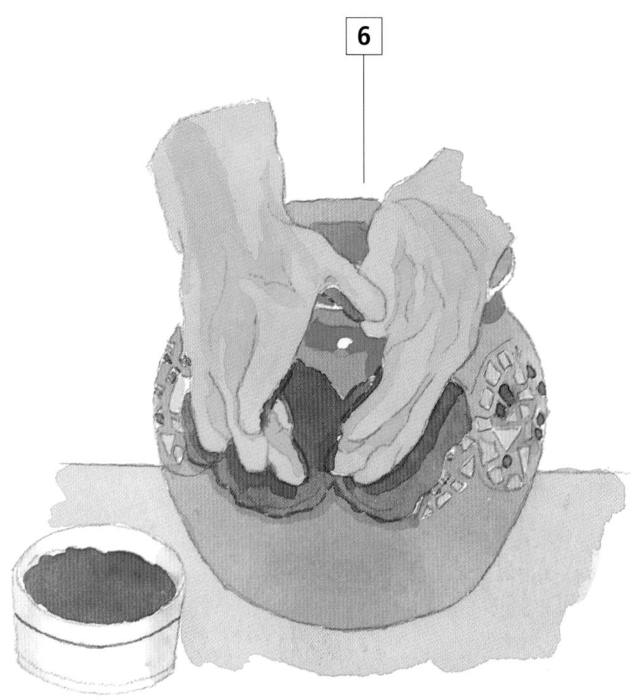

6

5 Fill in the remaining space of the circle with a blue that contrasts with the one that you used for the stars. Try to aim for a shade that goes well with the border color as well. You can use either patterned or plain tesserae, varying them as you work round the band. Continue working in this way around the rest of the band. Change your choice of shades subtly for the borders and circles as you go, but keep to the same general color scheme. When the band is completely finished, leave the mosaic to dry naturally for forty-eight hours.

6 Prepare the colored grout according to the instructions on pages 30-32. Tips for making a good terra cotta color are given in the Tortoise project on page 67. Apply the grout wearing the rubber gloves. Take it round the edges of the circles so that they have a smooth contact with the pot, but try not to smear too much onto the pot itself. Wipe away the excess with the dampened sponge, including any on the surface of the pot, and then wait fifteen to twenty minutes before polishing away the chalky haze with a dry rag.

1.

2.

1. Mary K. Guth creates a classic, ancient, almost biblical look with these pale doll parts.
2. An unusual percolator from Patty Goya incorporates the use of the item in the design with the cup motif.
3, 4, 5 and 6. An entire selection of Hap Sakwa's vases, pots, and vessels. Dazzlingly colorful and wonderful to look at, the colorful Americana theme never falters in this creative mosaic artist's work.

3.

4.

5.

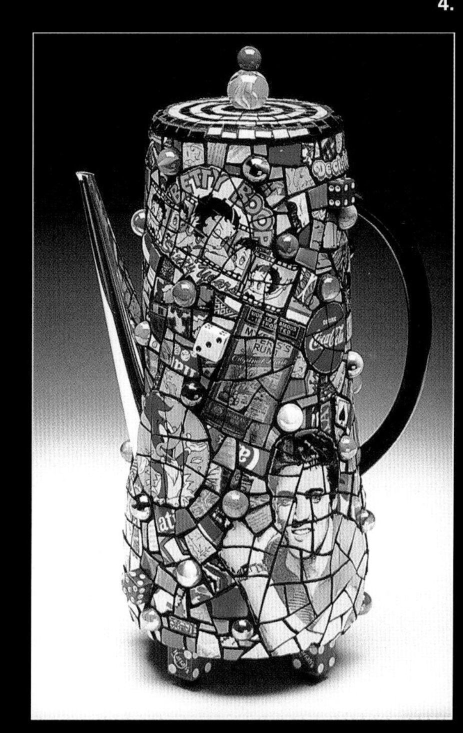

6.

Contributors

The Contributors

The artists whose work is featured in the gallery sections of this book have a wide range of education and experience in the arts. Some have studied and received higher education degrees in the fine arts, while others have become mosaicists through serendipity or happenstance. Regardless of how diverse their backgrounds, the commonality is that each artist has found the medium fulfilling and gratifying. After each project description in this book, you will see an array of artists' work that may inspire your own. Remember that the mosaic process is always the same, no matter how large or small the substructure of the piece. Some work is contemporary, bold, and bright. Other work is traditional, fine, and delicate. Some work is organized and carefully arranged, while other work is random, capricious, and whimsical. Over time and with experimentation, you will develop your own style, the parameters of which will be defined by the materials you enjoy working with and by your own color and design preferences.

SARAH KELLY

"It is entirely logical for me now to be working in mosaic but a few years ago I wouldn't even have considered it."

Sarah Kelly has always been a hoarder of bits and pieces and, as a commercial illustrator, used this magpie tendency in collages that were detailed and realistic with a painterly feel to them. She particularly enjoyed creating something out of something else and the fact that the finished pieces had dual interest—the piece itself and the elements it contained. Sarah's collage style prompted a client to request a cut paper mosaic effect for a project they were developing. Sarah was not impressed with her first attempt but had caught the mosaic bug. She bought her first bag of tesserae soon after and has never looked back.

Sarah loves the qualities that assorted tesserae give to even the plainest areas of her work. This has encouraged her to explore increasingly abstract designs that let the tessersae arrangements speak for themselves. Sarah finds beauty and inspiration in most mosaic styles, from Ancient Greek and Roman to Gaudí's stunning creations. She marvels at the intricacies of Islamic mosaic and was nearly reduced to tears by the beauty of some Byzantine work in Istanbul, Turkey.

Sarah feels that she hasn't even begun to scrape the surface of this vast and versatile medium and is bursting with ideas for mosaic work in the future.

CARLOS ALVES

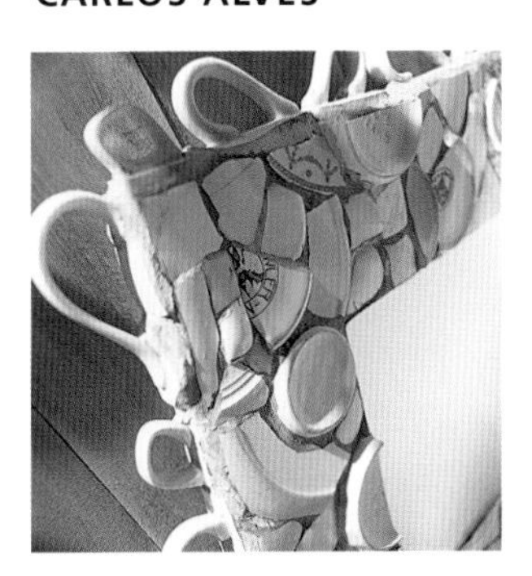

"The great wall of china" is Carlos Alves' cluttered stockpile of thousands of pieces of pottery, porcelain, dishes, lamp bases, figurines, ceramic doorknobs, trinkets, and memorabilia, just waiting to be smashed and recycled into one of his Folk Mosaics. He also designs and makes his own tiles to incorporate into his work. Born in Hialeah, the "Little Havana" of Miami, to a Czechoslovakian-Cuban mother and Puerto Rican father, Alves' passion for life and art goes hand-in-hand with his Latin heritage. Alves began his love affair with art at age ten when he started using clay to make ceramic flowers at home. Unbeknownst to him, his father was selling the flowers over the years and eventually presented him with the accumulated proceeds to pay for his university education. (Alves has a Bachelor of Fine Arts degree from the University of Miami and a Master of Fine Arts degree from Illinois State University.)

The restored, hip, art deco district of South Beach, Florida is currently home to Alves where his rich body of work is abundant, both in the private and public domain, throughout the state. The South Florida Arts Center is the site of one of his early installations, where his broken tile mosaic floors creep up the walls and into doorways and studio entrances. The Calle Ocho, or 8th Street, station of Miami's Metromover public transportation system is home to an ensemble Alves installation. On the north side of the station is Ventana Solar (Solar Window), a mural of broken crockery and bric-a-brac collected from merchants up and down Calle Ocho. Alves wants his art to be a reflection of the neighborhood, and this mural represents a Cuban colonial window to the area as well as a homage to freedom.

Alves also created a "Map of Florida" mosaic floor installation for the United States Department of Interior at the Everglades National Park and is currently working on a floor for the Miami Children's Museum. Other commissions include the front porch, mirrors, floors, chairs, tables, and elevator at the renovated Marlin Hotel; tables, bar, and restrooms at singer Gloria Estefan's restaurant, Larios on the Beach; and innumerable bathrooms, kitchens, floors, and swimming pools in private homes and commercial spaces.

Alves has also installed his mosaics around the world: floors, bathrooms, and a driveway for clients in London; a 29,000-square-foot loft, including floors, ceilings, walls, tables, chests, and chairs, and an erotic Kama Sutra inspired kitchen and dining area in New York City; a restaurant in Toronto; commercial and residential interiors in Hong Kong. Smaller pieces, such as game boards, candlesticks, and urns, have been included in Alves' shows around the world since 1985.

When asked where he expects to be in ten years, Alves says that he doesn't think of the future … he believes in living for the here and now. Carlos Alves may choose to live for the present, but his durable and exuberant Folk Mosaics will survive for many years.

REBECCA DENNIS & PAULA FUNT

A great pair of legs was the beginning of sisters Rebecca Dennis and Paula Funt's impressive line of mosaic home furnishings. Rebecca loved the wrought iron base but wasn't so enamoured with the top of a table she had received as a gift. A few broken tiles and a mosaic sunflower later, the table looked great. Paula, who studied interior design, began helping Rebecca create more tables and other items. Their first studio was Rebecca's garage, then an artist friend's workshop, then the basement of a building, and now they are settled into an enormous studio workspace in Toronto that is home to their thriving business, "Mosaicwares."

Dennis and Funt use custom made wooden and wrought iron substructures to support a vast product line which includes mosaic encrusted cake stands, mirrors, clocks, lamps, trays, vanities, armoires, tables, chairs, wastebaskets, tissue boxes, and much much more. They have turned the ancient art form of mosaic into a thriving business venture with a production, management, and sales staff of almost 50 people. "Every piece we design is totally different from another and takes between one and two weeks to produce," says Funt. The team buys plates that are chipped and cracked and cut out the parts they want. Their suppliers are major china distributors and antiquers who bring in plates by the carload. With their eclectic array of vintage china, Dennis and Funt have created a modern design medium that is clearly not a passing trend. Pieces of Staffordshire floral china may show up next to a 1960s plate border, and it is exactly those quirky combinations that make their art so appealing. Through trial and error the sisters have perfected their art and make pieces that are timeless, durable, and unique. Rebecca and Paula give accolades to their parents for instilling in them the ambition, energy and business skills that have carried them to this point in their careers. Both women worked in the family lumber business until father Harry sold it in 1990. Rebecca says she often calls her dad to say thanks for teaching her, without really teaching her, how to run a business. The sisters also credit their dad with showing them how to work with materials and follow a plan. "'You can do it' is our motto," says Rebecca. Clearly, they have.

PHILLIP I. DANZIG

Phillip I. Danzig is an architect who came to mosaic-tile making in mid-career and holds that his architectural training has been surprisingly valuable. It taught him to examine the visual and cultural environment of each site, to listen to those who use the space, and to master the techniques of the work.

Following graduation, Danzig spent a year working in England and then made the "Grand Tour" of Europe. He visited the countryside of England and Holland, savored Paris, and journeyed through Germany and Austria to the former Czechoslovakia, the former Yugoslavia and, of course, Greece. But it was while returning to England, through Italy, that he encountered the great golden mosaics of Ravenna, that were to influence and resonate in his own work.

Although inspired by the great European public spaces and grand palaces, Danzig sought to reduce the importance of the elitist artist and to champion a more democratic subject matter and working method. He has been influenced by the turn-of-the century architect Louis Sullivan, Los Tres Grandes of the Mexican mural movement (Rivera, Orozco, and Sequieros), and by the rise of an indigenous, streetwise community mural movement in the United States.

Danzig's first public work was directing the creation of 350 sand-cast plaques for the May Matthews Park, in New York's Hell's Kitchen, in 1970. He saw himself, at first, as instructor to a loose gang of urban youth who had to be asked, invited and cajoled into expressing themselves in their own neighborhood park. This was part of a program sponsored by CityArts, the urban arts organization. When September arrived and the kids went back to school, Danzig found he was some 50 plaques short. How could he finish the project when the "clients" he was supposed to work with had left? Anyway, he reasoned, he was not the image-maker, he was merely the architectural "facilitator." The project manager, however, insisted the work be done. So Danzig had to reinvent himself as urban artist. But he soon realized, to his surprise, that he had a real graphic flair and that the work was richly rewarding. He initiated the use of cracked dinner dishes in his work at this time.

The following summer, Danzig joined forces with the Chilean sculptor and community artist, Pedro Silva, and began his work in mosaic tile at the General Grant National Memorial, in New York City. His responsibility was the creation of some 400 linear feet of images, in cracked tile, on the outside facing of a sinuous, curvilinear bench. The other artists, and most of the 2,000 community volunteers who created the bulk of the tile images, produced a wonderful medley of natural images. But Danzig's training as a functional architect led him in a different direction. He designed a portrait of General Grant as a tribute, then a portrait of Grant's horse, Cincinnatus, and a 250 foot image of the General's, "Stars and Stripes," plus a series of life-sized animals, representing Grant's triumphal world tour, after Grant's retirement.

Much of the next ten years were spent in community-art projects. Danzig created and ran the "Wet Paint" community mural project, a publicly sponsored effort in New Jersey. Danzig was also Artistic Director of the Columbus Homes Community Art Project in Newark, New Jersey, responsible for producing a dozen mosaic-tile decorative panels.

Danzig's first "signed" mosaic tile mural project, in 1987, was granted by the Essex County Parks Commission. The theme of "The Lion" and "The Unicorn" reflects the historic English genesis of the early colonies, and was completed with the assistance of artist Sarah Lindquist Fishbone. He terms this work "stained glass mosaic tile" because, like works in stained glass, many of the larger shapes are formed from single pieces, cut to the exact, required shape. He is eager to clarify the design through such graphic devices as strong subject/background delineation; contrasts of warm colors against cool; small tiles against large and subtle rhythms of placement. He prides himself on the use of appropriate "found" materials.

During the 1990s, Danzig produced more community-minded work. Among his recent projects, Danzig completed, "A Little Light Dispels Much Darkness," depicting the traditional Jewish Shabbat table. This image, for the Chabad Center, in Rockaway, New Jersey, shows the two loaves of bread, the wine cup and the shimmering candles, symbols at the heart of the traditional Jewish observance and remembrance of the Seventh Day. This mosaic-tile work measures three feet eight inches high, by four feet eight inches wide. It was completed in 1998.

HAP SAKWA

Hap Sakwa considers his colorful, vivid, precise mosaic works Pop Art, not Folk Art. A self taught artist, he developed his own unique style by combining the ancient art of mosaic with modern American images and icons from Marilyn Monroe to John F. Kennedy to Mickey Mouse. Sakwa was inspired by the tile work he saw on a trip to "Little Havana" in Florida fifteen years before he began working in mosaic. He developed a style he calls "painted assemblage" which then grew into "mosaic collage." To incorporate the American iconographic images which are so prevalent in his work, Sakwa haunted flea markets and antique fairs to collect souvenir plates, coffee mugs, ashtrays, and theme objects. "I wanted to create an art form that was true to my time on the planet. From the time I was born (the 1950s) to the mid-nineties."

Sakwa's work ranges in size from small pieces that can be displayed on a table or console to free-standing urns up to 5 feet (1.5 meters) high. He uses black grout for strong contrast, thereby making the bright dishes and tiles extremely visible. Other found objects also play a strong role in Sakwa's work, like marbles, dice, and dominoes, and the tesserae are always placed tightly together on the project form. All of these components make Sakwa's work easily recognizable, delightfully capricious, and difficult to imitate.

Hap Sakwa is a professional photographer in northern California and no longer creates mosaics.

MARY KAY GUTH

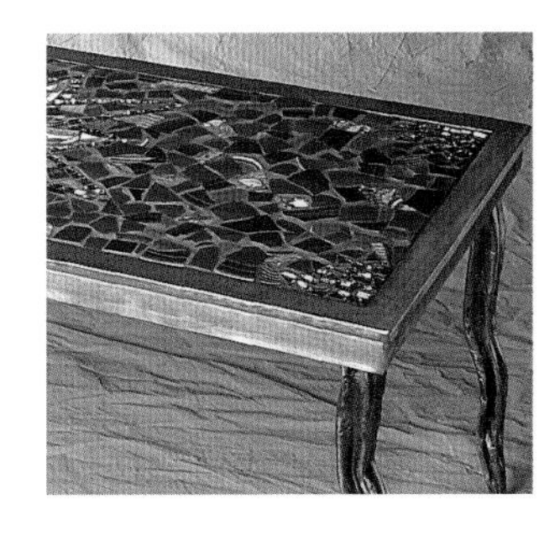

Mary Kay Guth describes her mosaic work as art with a sociological perspective. Urban anthropology. Functional materials transformed into functional art. Indeed, the ultimate recycling.

Born in central Wisconsin to a potter mother, Guth learned at an early age how to reuse the broken pieces of her mother's ceramics. Nothing was thrown away. The shards were transformed into primitive mosaics that would eventually inspire her to become an extremely prolific Folk Mosaic artist. Guth studied sociology, earning a Bachelor of Arts degree at the University of Wisconsin at Madison in 1987. Although her parents encouraged her to pursue the academic sciences, the magnetism of the fine arts proved to be too strong. After giving up a promising design and product development career in New

York, she moved to Portland, Oregon where Guth says, "life is casual and studio space is cheap."

Guth considers herself a self-taught mosaic artist. She used her own resourcefulness to learn the technical aspects of mosaic, relying on her creative visions for inspiration. Guth believes it is the responsibility of every artist to consider the audience and to force viewers to contemplate and reflect upon the art they see. In this way they become participants instead of observers. Guth consciously gives her audience information and situations that often compete with the materials she uses. This dichotomy creates an interesting depth, or second layer, to her work. It is also a possible explanation for the increasing demand for Guth's Folk Mosaics, which have been exhibited in galleries from Washington State to Texas to the Province of Quebec. Guth is currently pursuing other fine art mediums and is no longer a working mosaicist, though her work still sets an unparalleled standard for all mosaic artists.

SONIA KING

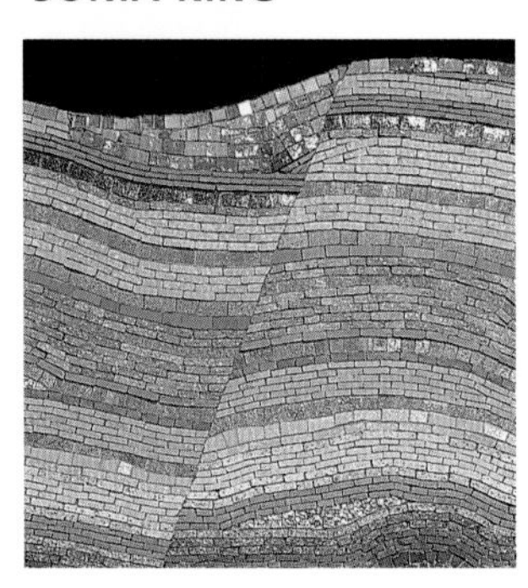

Sonia King's first contact with mosaics was as a child when her mother studied the art form. Always fascinated by the medium, her extensive travel background has taken her to visit ancient mosaic sites and to study with modern mosaic artists around the world. King earned a Bachelor of Fine Arts degree from California College of Arts and Crafts and a Master of Fine Arts degree from Southern Methodist University, but went on to a successful career in the oil business. Always attracted to the arts, she felt compelled to return to her original degree and finally gave up her day job. She now works full-time on her modern interpretation of mosaics in Dallas, Texas.

King creates mosaics to express the way she sees the world, how it is, how it could be. She combines the tangible and intangible, bits of color and texture, fragments of meaning. King says that working in a 'slow' medium forces her to fully explore the interaction between vision, design, and materials. "I discover new things about myself and my place in the world as a work is formed, piece by piece."

Through her use of traditional materials and methods, King feels a connection to ancient mosaicists. For her, mosaic is all about the essence of form—the skeletal components and elemental structures, fractured and reformed. She uses tesserae to create mosaic landscapes that are familiar and yet unreal, and her goal is for people to look at the world around them with "different eyes" after seeing her work.

King uses a variety of materials in her work ranging from traditional glass smalti, to vitreous glass, to marble and other natural materials like pebbles and stones. Her work is usually wall-mounted with dimensions under 24 x 36 inches (60 x 90 cm) and is represented in both private and corporate collections. King's exterior installations are much larger, approximately 8 x 12 feet (2.4 x 3.6 meters) and are in public spaces for all to enjoy.

ROBERT BELLAMY

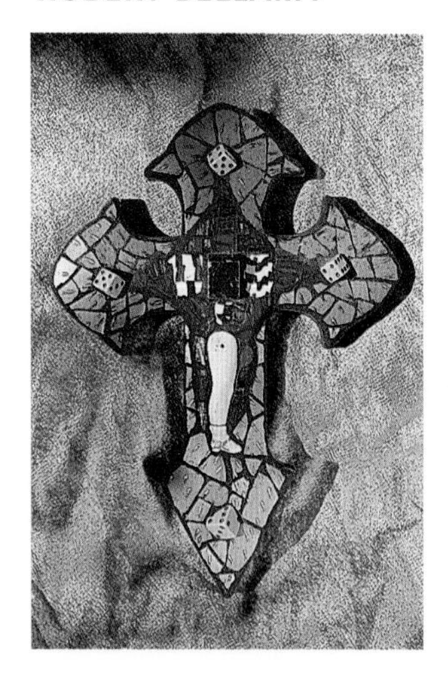

Robert Bellamy was raised in Dallas, Texas and has been a landscape designer for 25 years. Inspired by Gaudi's Sagrada Familia church in Barcelona, which is covered with shards of brightly colored ceramic and glass, he began experimenting with incorporating remnants and debris from local construction sites into his landscapes. Bellamy has transformed his own home, patio, and garden into a whimsical wonderland of broken Fiesta ware and colorful tiles. Fountains, walls, and pathways are splashed with vibrant colors and sensual textures, creating an environment of fantasy and delight. When the Texas economy crashed in the 1980s, Bellamy created "Rep-Tile" as a side venture to his landscape design business to bolster him through the lean times. His two ventures go hand-in-hand, and Bellamy's outstanding reputation in both fields precedes him.

"I am very passionate about all my work, and I have great fun creating the mosaic pieces," Bellamy says. Some of his pieces are religiously inspired, like crosses embellished with sometimes unconventional materials like fish bones and dice. Other work is quirky and fun, like a fantastical fireplace made of broken tiles and other found objects. Currently, Bellamy is focusing on designing mosaic garden furniture, some of which is inlaid with elaborate patterns of vitreous glass, the joints often filled with multiple colors of grout to enhance the geometric quality of the work.

JEANNIE LINAM

Jeannie Linam began her career as a mosaic artist in a roundabout way. She was a partial owner of a restaurant and needed an inexpensive way to finish out the lavatories. She bought a box of discontinued tile, broke it into small pieces and decorated the walls with thunderbolts, dancing skeletons, and other fanciful creatures. Even though Linam was inexperienced, her natural talent was obvious and other restaurateurs began commissioning her to mosaic their establishments. Soon Linam's career as a mosaicist took off, and she began creating custom kitchens, ceilings, stairways, tables, and fountains using traditional tesserae as well as broken ceramics, stained glass, and china. Large public artworks in hospitals, museums and city parks keep Linam's calendar full. Most recently, Linam created an enormous fountain in Helen's Park in Houston, Texas, and she will soon begin a project for a resort in Florida and then a swimming pool in California.

Linam says, "I love most when I am given the freedom to create artworks that inspire, provoke, and even teach or inform people. Most of my works have layers of meanings, and I spend a lot of time researching my designs. For example, the Helen's Park fountain has native Houston plant species and animals in it, and they correspond to the appropriate seasons and compass points on the fountain. East symbolizes spring and also dawn, and the eastern quadrant of the fountain is covered with azaleas and dogwood and irises, all in a subtle pastel palette of early morning colors."

LINDA OLDHAM & ROBIN OLDHAM

If the name Oldham sounds familiar, it should. Linda and Robin are mother and daughter to world-renowned fashion designer, Todd Oldham. But Todd isn't the only creative one in the family. Both self-taught artists dabble in many mediums, but mosaic seems to hold the most allure. Linda works with tile, china, glass, and other memorabilia. Robin uses all these materials too, but her favorite is definitely glass, either scored into squares, broken into random pieces, or shaped on her glass saw.

Linda raised four children before becoming a legal secretary and then the brains behind the business of L-7 Designs Inc., DBA "Todd Oldham" in the early 1980's. Her husband and other children are creative also: Jack carves intricate wood furniture, son Brad casts white metal and makes custom ceramic tiles, and daughter Mikell is a writer.

Robin worked as a social worker before starting a day spa business and then a wedding cake business. She then became the Director of Operations for L-7 Designs Inc. After the family sold the business to a multi-national in the spring of 1999, Robin opened *Smashing Times* with Tracy Graivier Bell. *Smashing Times* is a three-part concept: First, it is a gallery . Second, it is a working mosaic studio where the public is invited to make their own mosaics. Third, it is the headquarters and studio for the custom mosaic work Robin and Tracy do for designers, architects, and laypeople.

Robin and Linda Oldham have combined their innate creativity with hard work and tenacity to achieve success in all their undertakings. It is clear that the same holds true with their mosaic work as well.

LINDA BEAUMONT

In the early 1970s, Linda Beaumont began creating mosaics for the Public Art Program in Seattle, Washington. "Step on No Pets" was one of her first public works, made for Seattle's Animal Control Shelter in 1980. For many years since those early mosaics Beaumont has accepted private commissions and fabricated wild, eccentric entryways, courtyards, kitchens, bathrooms, and grottos, always taking great care to incorporate the client's personality into the work.

"Water for Fires" is Beaumont's personal favorite and most meaningful work. It is the entry vestibule of the Bailey Boushay AIDS Hospice in Seattle and was inspired by Simon Rodia's Watts Towers in Los Angeles. The entryway is coated with a skin of onyx and marble shards that make up a shimmering golden surface. Beaumont was attracted to the innate beauty of the stone. "'It's translucent and almost seems to breathe. I knew I didn't want to fabricate tiles, and stone is innate to the earth." Like Rodia, Beaumont also used seashells, crockery, ceramic tiles, broken glass, marbles, beads, and a host of other objects, remembrances, and mementos given to her by the people of the community to create a warm, peaceful, loving environment for the hospice residents. There are also etched images of feet walking through fire and water, which Beaumont considers a symbol of people living with AIDS. Other healing symbols, images of world culture, and meditative poetry are incorporated into the donor recognition pillar, which surrounds an actual structural support column of the building, a metaphor that Beaumont likes. The work is ultimately about giving respect to those dying of AIDS.

NANCY UNGERMAN

Thirty years ago, Nancy Ungerman encountered her first broken china mosaic piece in a roadside antique shop in Texas. It was a large flowerpot covered with bits of blue and white dishes, and the memory of it inspired her to search for more examples of the art form through the next many years. In the early 1980s on a trip to Thailand, Ungerman's search was unexpectedly fulfilled near Bangkok when she discovered the Wat Arun, the Temple of Dawn, which is completely covered in broken blue and white dishes and pottery. Inspired by this magnificent example of mosaic, as well as the increasing popularity of the art form, Ungerman could no longer ignore the urge to create mosaics herself. Longtime friend, Tracy Graivier Bell, taught her the basics, and what began as an interest became an obsession.

Ungerman refers to her mosaic work by the traditional name of Pique Assiette, named after Raymond Edouard Isadore's work. To Ungerman, it takes the serendipity of finding a smooth pebble by a trail, a glimmering coin in the street, or an iridescent seashell lying in the sand combined with the tenacity to search out interesting dishes and tiles to combine into her own unique Pique Assiette works of art. Large pieces, like murals and tables, and smaller decorative pieces, such as bowls, goblets, candlesticks, plates, and frames make up the bulk of Ungerman's work.

CLEO MUSSI

Cleo Mussi trained at Goldsmiths College, London, England, in Fine Art Textiles. On leaving college she tried to exhibit her work but found the market saturated with artists.

Inspired by pebble mosaic artist Maggie Howarth, Cleo left for a summer vacation in Normandy, France, with a sack of concrete and a wooden mold. There she collected stones from the local beaches and made a series of pebble tiles from them. On her return she brought with her a selection of French pottery, which formed the basis for a second series of tiles.

Recycled china is now most dominant in her work. Apart from its versatility and cost-effectiveness, Cleo favors broken china because she likes the idea of giving new life to something otherwise discarded and merging different elements from ceramic history into one piece of work as she feels the inherent patterns and textures tell their own story. In larger wall panels Cleo uses mass-produced tiles to give a broad range of punchy color and has recently introduced "Zillij," tesselating hand-made tiles in a traditional Moroccan technique, to her work.

Her approach to her work is wide-ranging, from functional domestic pieces to sculptural figurative work for exhibition and site-specific panels and fountains for public spaces. Being self-taught she approaches her work freely without the restraints of traditional theory and technique. Essentially, ideas are paramount and mosaic is the medium for her expression.

Cleo draws on many sources for her inspiration. Her work is pieces together from an array of cultures, crafts, ceremonies, and architecture. Her current pieces explore the imagery of Ancient Rome, Egyptian tomb effigies, African millifiori, Hopi Indian carved figures, robots, Indian miniatures, Mexican papier mache creations, and Moorish architecture. For Cleo, the word is "anything goes."

LINDA BENSWANGER

Linda Benswanger has a Bachelor of Fine Arts degree in textile design from Moore College of Art in Philadelphia. She lives in New York where she learned mosaic from a woman who was making large tables and screens using marble, slate, granite, and other natural materials. "Mosaics clicked for me because they are so much about pattern, color, and repetition … so similar to textiles, only made of harder materials." Benswanger used the basic mosaic techniques to develop her own style and then began a home furnishings company called "Mozayiks." A commitment to natural and recycled materials drives her designs in which she uses broken china, dishes, tiles, river rocks, and other found materials. Her work is generally portable: tabletops, planters, platters, picture frames, lamps, urns, and vases, and has been sold throughout the United States to retail establishments and to private clients.

PATTY GOYA

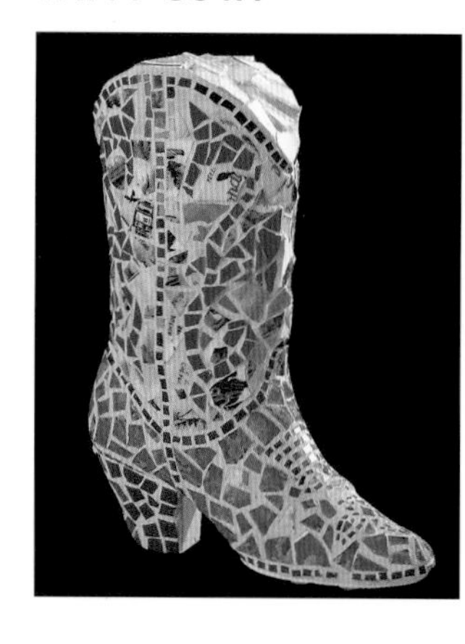

Patty Goya says she has found the perfect balance in her career as a high fashion model and a mosaic artist. She has made a name for herself in the mosaic world by covering unusual items with broken dishes and tiles like coffee percolators, toasters, baby shoes, and cowboy boots. Her work is often described as playful, yet sophisticated. It is generally brightly colored and often includes everyday images like fruit, flowers, teacups, and shoelaces of contrasting colors.

"Self-taught artisan" is a moniker Goya feels comfortable with. Her early forays into art were in leaded stained glass. The transition into mosaics was natural for Goya, as she found that both mediums allowed her to put fragments together like a puzzle to form an image; however, she finds mosaic making more fun and less serious than traditional stained glass. Goya half-jokingly says, "making mosaics is the best and cheapest form of therapy," referring to the freedom to smash and crash expensive dishes and tiles. Goya works with interior designers to create custom floors, fireplaces, signs, kitchen counters, backsplashes, and home accessories.

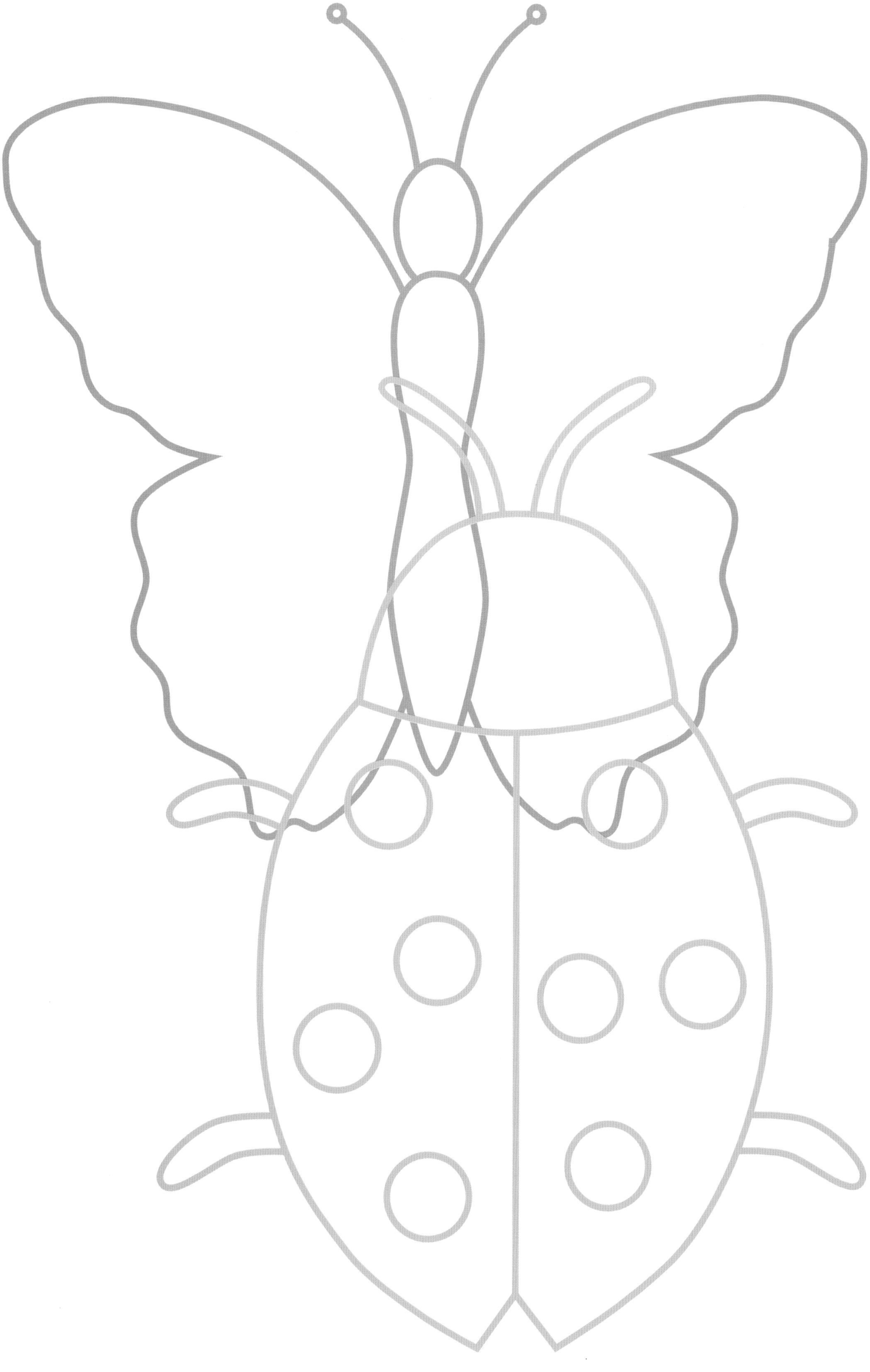

Index